Defending the Border

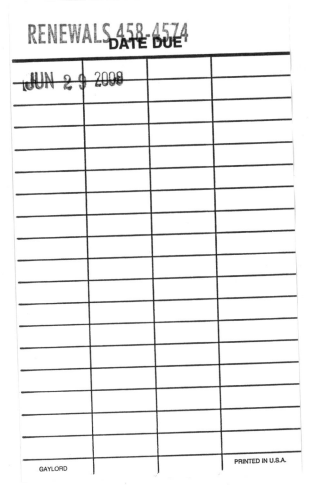

**CULTURE&SOCIETY
AFTER SOCIALISM**
A SERIES EDITED BY
BRUCE GRANT&NANCY RIES

A list of titles in this series is available at www.cornellpress.cornell.edu.

DEFENDING THE BORDER

Identity, Religion, and Modernity in the Republic of Georgia

Mathijs Pelkmans

Cornell University Press *Ithaca and London*

First published 2006 by Cornell University Press
First printing, Cornell Paperbacks, 2006

Printed in the United States of America

Library of Congress Cataloging-in-Publication Data

Pelkmans, Mathijs, 1973–
    Defending the border : identity, religion, and modernity in the Republic of Georgia \ Mathijs Pelkmans.
        p. cm. — (Culture and society after socialism)
    Includes bibliographical references and index.
    ISBN-13: 978-0-8014-4440-1 (cloth : alk. paper)
    ISBN-10: 0-8014-4440-3 (cloth : alk. paper)
    ISBN-13: 978-0-8014-7330-2 (pbk. : alk. paper)
    ISBN-10: 0-8014-7330-6 (pbk. : alk. paper)
    1. Ajaria (Georgia)—Ethnic relations.   2. Ajaria (Georgia)—Religion.   3. Ajaria (Georgia)—Boundaries—Turkey—History.   4. Turkey—Boundaries—Georgia—Ajaria—History.   5. Post-communism—Georgia—Ajaria.   I. Title.   II. Series.
    DK679.A37P45 2006
    947.58—dc22   2006007157

Cornell University Press strives to use environmentally responsible suppliers and materials to the fullest extent possible in the publishing of its books. Such materials include vegetable-based, low-VOC inks and acid-free papers that are recycled, totally chlorine-free, or partly composed of nonwood fibers. For further information, visit our website at www.cornellpress.cornell.edu.

Cloth printing   10   9   8   7   6   5   4   3   2   1
Paperback printing   10   9   8   7   6   5   4   3   2   1

To my parents,
Toon and Willy Pelkmans-Tijs

Contents

Part III

Preface

A large billboard formerly adorned the central square of the Georgian border village of Sarpi. In Russian, it read "The Entire Soviet Nation Guards the Border!" The slogan was illustrated with the figures of three serious-looking Soviet citizens who, with their united strength, ensured the defense of the border between Soviet Georgia and Turkey. This border not only secured the integrity of the Soviet state but it also protected Soviet citizens from the evils of capitalism and the alleged detrimental influence of Islam. In official rhetoric the state border was presented as a solid divide between the Georgian and Turkish nations, between communism and capitalism, between atheism (or Orthodox Christianity) and Islam, between Europe and Asia. However, this forceful rhetoric lost its cogency on the ground. The position of the billboard displayed the discrepancy between rhetoric and reality: it faced only the Soviet Georgian side and could not be read from across the border. Thus, the statement "The entire Soviet nation guards the border" was not a message to the world but rather one to be read by local residents as a reminder and warning of how they were supposed to act and think. The billboard exemplified the continuing anxieties of the Soviet state over its border, as much as fifty years after it was established. The billboard also indicated that border dwellers had not forgotten the disruptions caused by the placement of virtually impassable fences and, moreover, that they still longed to reestablish contact with their relatives, with their ethnic affiliates, and with co-Muslims across the border. Indeed, although the Soviet state was able to minimize cross-border communication and movement, it could not erase the memory of things lost, nor prevent the imagination from sustaining cross-border loyalties.

Many expected that after the iron curtain fell, and the ideology that had supported it crumbled, cross-border contacts would be revived and old loyalties and identities would be given new substance. In the early 1990s, when cross-border trade mushroomed, Muslims from across the border in Turkey established new relations with those in Georgia, while relatives who had been separated for decades met again. Many inhabitants of the border region believed that the border opening had brought them nothing but trouble, however. Such negative attitudes were not only directed at the social and economic insecurities of the post-Soviet era but also at the threat to feelings of belonging that the opening of the border came to represent. After the harsh restrictions of the iron curtain era disappeared, inhabitants of the border region began to see the iron curtain as something that had protected them and something that was still worth defending.

In this book I analyze the biography of this border and its surrounding borderlands in order to understand what happened to the cultural and ideological divides that were implicated in this iron curtain. As an ethnographic account it is based on the activities, experiences, and narratives of people I came to know during four periods of fieldwork in the Ajaria region of southwestern Georgia between 1997 and 2001. I have borrowed their voices to illustrate the numerous ironies and tragedies of their divided lives. Without their hospitality, practical help, and willingness to share their thoughts and experiences this book would never have been written. For reasons of privacy I cannot thank them by name, but I hope they will accept these impersonal words of gratitude. I am also grateful to the staff at the University of Batumi who so generously shared their knowledge about the region and its inhabitants, in particular Giorgi Masalkin, Omari Memishishi, Nugzar Mgeladze, and Teimuraz Tunadze.

In finishing the fieldwork on which this study is based I am indebted foremost to Anton Blok, Henk Driessen, and Chris Hann. They offered invaluable advice over the years. Their comments and insights have contributed greatly to the making of this book. The research for this study was made possible by grants from the Netherlands Foundation for Scientific Research and the Amsterdam School for Social Science Research. I extend my gratitude to the Max Planck Institute for Social Anthropology in Halle, Germany, for providing the support needed to complete writing this book.

A number of people read and commented on all parts of this manuscript. In particular, I thank Gerd Baumann, Matthijs van den Bos, Laurence Broers, Peter Geschiere, Melanie van der Hoorn, Willem van Schendel, Bonno Thoden van Velzen, Jojada Verrips, and Lale Yalçin-Heckmann. Thanks also to Mark Genszler, Erin Stowell, and Lois Thorpe for editorial assistance. The rigorous comments and encouragement of Cornell University Press series editors Bruce Grant and Nancy Ries, as well as external reviewer Paul Manning, have been invaluable for finalizing this project.

Chapter 8 is a revised version of "The Social Life of Empty Buildings: Imagining the Transition in Post-Soviet Ajaria," which appeared in *Focaal: European Journal of Social Anthropology* 41 (2003): 121–36.

And then there are the friends and family who have in various ways supported me in carrying out this project. I am particularly indebted to Harm van Atteveld and Christina Nichol. My parents have been an unwavering source of support and encouragement. It is to them that I dedicate this book. I also want to mention my two precious daughters, Sophie and Emma, who, unknowingly, pushed this project along and provided me with comic relief at crucial stages. Finally, I want to thank my wife, Julie, for being my most thorough critic, and, foremost, for always being there for me.

A Note on Transliteration and Translation

In transliterating Russian from the Cyrillic I have used the Library of Congress system. For Georgian I have used the National System of Romanization. I make an exception for personal or place names and religious terms that are better known in another way in English-language scholarly works. Thus, I write *Ajaria* instead of *Ach'ara*, *imam* instead of *imami*, *madrassa* instead of *madrase*, *oblast* instead of *oblast'*, and use the plural *Laz* instead of *Lazebi*. I transliterated Islamic terms that appeared in Georgian and Russian documents directly from the written sources. Where Turkish or Arabic terms appear in Georgian speech I follow Georgian spelling conventions. All translations are my own, except where noted.

Terms and Abbreviations

Language transliterated is shown in parentheses: Georgian (G); Russian (R); Turkish (T).

aghordzineba (G) revival

AMM (G) Ach'aris mkharedmtsod muzeumi (Museum of Regional Studies of Ajaria)

aspirantura (R) postgraduate study resulting in the title "candidate of science"

ASSR (R) avtonomnaia sovetskaia sotsialisticheskaia respublika (autonomous soviet socialist republic)

bey (T) provincial governor in the Ottoman Empire; formerly also used as a courtesy title for a person of high social rank

chadri (G) veil, almost totally covering the female body

CIS Commonwealth of Independent States

druzhina (R) in Soviet usage, people's patrol; semivoluntary organization of villagers assisting the military in patrolling the border zone

fez (T) brimless cone-shaped hat, made of red felt; part of the Ottoman dress code for men

GDP gross domestic product

giauri (G) infidel, nonbeliever; term of reproach used by Muslims to non-Muslims, i.e., Christians and atheists

hajj pilgrimage to Mecca

hoja (G) devout Muslim man who is respected for his knowledge of Islam

imam (Georgian *imami*) prayer leader of a mosque

KGB (R) Komitet gosudarstvennoi bezopasnosti (State Security Committee)

kolkhoz (R) *kollektivnoe khoziaistvo* (collective farm)

kolkhoznik (R) member of a collective farm

Komsomol (R) Kommunisticheskii soiuz molodezhi (Communist Union of Youth)

korenizatsiia (R) "indigenization," refers to Communist Party policies to extend its popular base among non-Russians

lari (G) Georgian monetary unit, subdivided into one hundred tetri

lira (T) Turkish monetary unit

madrassa (Georgian *madrase*) Islamic school, usually associated with a mosque

mavludi (G) the celebration of the birthday of the Prophet Muhammad

mufti (Georgian *mupti*) chairman of the Muslim council, head of a muftiate

muftiate Muslim community, in this case comprising all Muslims of Ajaria

muhajiroba (G) migration; specifically the migrations of Muslims from Georgia to the Ottoman Empire in the late nineteenth and early twentieth centuries.

mullah (Georgian *mulla*) teacher of Islam

NKVD (R) Narodnyi kommissariat vnutrennykh del (People's Commissariat of Internal Affairs); predecessor of the KGB

oblast (R) province; first administrative level below that of SSR

RaiKom (R) Raion kommitet (government of a *raion*)

raion (R) district, administrative level below oblast or ASSR

RSFSR (R) Rossiiskaia Sovetskaia Federativnaia Sotsialisticheskaia Respublika (Russian Soviet Federated Socialist Republic)

sovkhoz (R) *sovetskoe khoziaistvo* (state farm)

SSR (R) Sovetskaia sotsialisticheskaia respublika (soviet socialist republic)

supra (G) festive dinner, formal banquet, seen as an essential part of the Georgian national tradition

tamada (G) toastmaster; person responsible for raising appropriate toasts during a festive dinner

vaizi (G) sermon given by the imam preceding the actual prayers

Introduction:
Temporal Divides and Muddled Space
along the Former Iron Curtain

At midday on a July 2000 afternoon in Khulo, the district center of the eastern mountainous region of upper Ajaria, I accompanied an acquaintance as he paid his last respects to his former colleague Otari Abuladze.[1] We entered the apartment where Otari's body was on view, walked around the coffin, and expressed our condolences to family members. We left the apartment and spent a few minutes outside talking to men who had gathered in the street. At the time, I did not think the event was particularly special, but I changed my mind a few days later when Murman, an acquaintance of the deceased, dropped by to tell me and my colleague Teimuri the full story of the funeral. After Murman recounted the events, a lively discussion ensued in which it became clear that Murman and Teimuri saw the particularities of the funeral as an apt representation of the dilemmas then facing the Georgian region of Ajaria. Most importantly, the funeral revealed that the messages, experiences, and loyalties that informed Otari's life had considerably changed their meaning when social identities were redefined following the collapse of the Soviet Union.

Otari Abuladze was born in Didach'ara, a village in the mountains of upper Ajaria, which is known throughout Georgia for its "persistent" Islamic character. His parents met in his mother's native town in the north of the Georgian SSR, where Otari's father had been dispatched during World War II. They married and "returned" to Didach'ara where Otari, their first child, was born. Otari's father died when he was ten years old. He and his mother moved to the Ajarian capital of Batumi. Otari finished his education in Batumi and was sub-

---

1. In Georgia personal names are indicative of a person's ethnic, religious, and regional background. Throughout, I have used existing names that reflect the background of a person while obscuring his or her real identity. I chose Otari for this individual because it is a common name among educated middle-aged Ajarians, and Abuladze because it is a name from upper Ajaria.

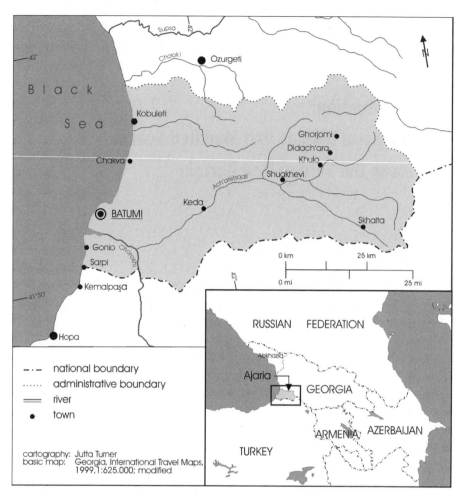

The Ajarian Autonomous Republic

sequently assigned to be a police officer in the district center of Khulo, which is located between Batumi and Didach'ara. After having completed his professional career in Khulo, Otari retired and moved back to Batumi. He lived there with his wife until he died unexpectedly at the age of fifty-three.

During the two days preceding his burial, Otari lay in a wooden coffin in the center of the living room of his apartment in Batumi. He was dressed in a black suit, his eyes were closed, and his folded hands rested on a small cross. A Bible was placed against the front end of the coffin. Floral wreaths presented by friends and colleagues surrounded the body. Female maternal relatives sat on chairs against the walls and took turns wailing.

On the day of his burial, Otari's body was brought to Khulo, where his former colleagues paid their last respects. The set-up in Khulo resembled the room in Batumi except that some items were no longer present. The most colorful floral wreaths and the maternal relatives were left behind; both Bible and cross were conspicuously absent. The ritual was sober—involving little more than a walk around the coffin and the soft whispering of condolences.

But the body had not arrived at its final destination. Otari's paternal relatives had insisted that his body be buried in the family cemetery in Didach'ara. In preparation for his final journey, Otari was undressed and wrapped in white cloth. He arrived in Didach'ara by car, where a group of village men were waiting for him. The imam led the prayers on the mud path in front of Otari's paternal home. Women were absent from these public prayers. They did not arrive until after the burial, though they remained in the cemetery until the evening verses were recited from the Qur'an.

Otari's posthumous journey reflected a life entwined in social networks formed during state atheism. Being a child of a Muslim father and a Christian mother was not uncommon in the atheist 1940s. However, such a marriage was considered sensitive even then. It was thus only logical that Otari and his mother left the Muslim village of Didach'ara after his father's death to start a new life in the cosmopolitan city of Batumi. Various threads of his biography—the different backgrounds of his paternal and maternal relatives as well as his own professional career—came together in his funeral, evoking the legacies that Soviet Communism left behind. Otari's funeral entailed a reversed tour of his life journey: from the Ajarian capital of Batumi, where he had spent the last years of his life, back to the district (*raion*) center Khulo, where he had been employed as a police officer, and finally to his place of birth in Didach'ara. The funeral also revealed the changes in the religious landscape of the region following the collapse of the socialist state. The dead body moved through an ambivalent cultural space in which religious practices overlapped and confronted each other. The corpse was initially adorned with Christian symbols, but it was subsequently unwrapped and prepared for a proper Muslim funeral. As the corpse moved through cultural spaces, it was bestowed with Christian and Muslim qualities, while the sober ritual in Khulo was to some extent reminiscent of secular Soviet funerals.

This redefinition of Otari's corpse was dramatic; it changed three times in the span of a few days. With Otari dead, his friends, relatives, and colleagues were now the ones who could isolate and prioritize one aspect of his identity while ignoring others, a feat of identity transformation not always possible with the living.[2] But the struggle of relatives and colleagues over the identity of the corpse went beyond their concern about "who Otari was." It was also a struggle for their own convictions concerning religion, nationality, and home-

---

2. As Katherine Verdery points out in her book *The Political Lives of Dead Bodies*, corpses are convenient symbols in attempts to rewrite history: they come with their own histories, while being unable to contest ambiguous interpretations of their meaning (1999, 28–29).

land. This struggle was further revealed in the disapproving way in which Teimuri and Murman discussed Otari's funeral. Whereas Murman insisted that such a funeral was disrespectful to the deceased, Teimuri held that the funeral was the result of the way Otari had led his life. "If you don't stick to *one* truth during your life," he complained, "then it is only logical that your funeral will also be a hodgepodge." But perhaps the significance of this "hodgepodge" funeral was not that Otari had wavered between "truths," as Teimuri implied. Rather, the funeral highlighted that, in this border region at least, it was deemed of utmost importance to establish clear-cut cultural markers. In Ajaria this was complicated by the fact that actual lives poorly fit the categories involved.

Otari's funeral was just one example of how in these Georgian borderlands connections between social identification and geographic location had become problematic, leaving people to struggle with the resulting dilemmas. The struggles of those involved in Otari's funeral point to the changing relations between *place* and *space*.[3] In border regions such as Ajaria, daily life is marked by signs of what does or does not belong to one's space. These signs need to be reinterpreted when the makeup of place—economic and social arrangements as well as the limits posed on movement—suddenly changes. The distinction between place and space is critical in this context as it allows us to understand how the opening of the iron curtain and changes in the political and economic environment affected cultural and social identifications.

Claims to cultural identity usually involve attempts to establish stable cores that "prove" the authenticity of specific cultural assertions and "fix" cultural difference. In Ajaria in the 1990s, such attempts were directed foremost at the pre-Soviet past. This pre-Soviet dimension was both instrumental in overcoming the Soviet past and in regaining what was "lost" during Soviet rule. The location of Ajaria along the state border complicated the imagined return to pre-Soviet identities in several important ways. During the Soviet era, inhabitants of the border region had adjusted to the existence of the iron curtain and had developed their own ideas about self and homeland in a series of routinized interactions with the state. These Soviet "legacies" made the quest for pre-Soviet identities a cumbersome one. It was problematic because the biographies of people often defied attempts to assert stable cores to particular identity referents. And it was dangerous because renewed cross-border contacts revealed unexpected differences as well as unwanted similarities. These problems and dangers meant that, paradoxically, attempts to re-create pre-Soviet identities often ended in grounding and reinforcing Soviet constructions of identity, even though they were part of a process of overcoming and

---

3. I follow Donnan and Wilson's definition of these terms: "*Space* is the general idea people have of where things should be in physical and cultural relation to each other. . . . *Place*, on the other hand, is the distinct space where people live; it encompasses both the idea and the actuality of where things are" (1999, 9).

dismissing the Soviet past. What I attempt to do in this book is to account for the complex ways in which cultural divides are created on the basis of evidence that, in fact, does not support these divides. Through exploring social life on the border, this book shows how cultural elements can accrete around existing territorial and national borders, and how such profound political divides can transform the cultures and societies they govern.

Soviet Certainties and Hidden Ambiguities in Ajaria

The Ajarian Autonomous Republic is a small triangle of land in the southwestern corner of Georgia. The region rises up from the Black Sea and shares a border with Turkey. It has an overall territory of 2,900 square kilometers and a population of approximately four hundred thousand. Apart from its capital, Batumi, with its seaport and oil refineries, Ajaria used to be highly dependent on agriculture. In the 1980s, 60 percent of the population was employed in the agricultural sector. Regional variance is reflected in the local differentiation between lower and upper Ajaria, that is, between the subtropical coastal region and the mountainous hinterland. The differences are particularly apparent when driving up the only road that connects upper Ajaria to the coast. Driving east from Batumi, one first passes through a region with large citrus and tea plantations. After some twenty kilometers the road winds through deep canyons with densely forested slopes. Above the one thousand–meter mark, the valleys widen again and allow for the cultivation of corn, potatoes, and tobacco, often in combination with animal husbandry.

Soviet encyclopedias gave the impression that Ajaria was a region firmly integrated into the Georgian Soviet Socialist Republic. Ajaria was presented as thriving economically and as being firmly embedded in the wider planned economy. Its population was classified as predominantly Georgian, and it was seen as a politically indivisible part of Soviet Georgia. Though these depictions may appear to be only political rhetoric, they reveal certain felt truths. In the 1990s people in Ajaria often remembered the Soviet period in exactly such terms. But beyond what these depictions reveal, they are equally interesting for what they attempt to hide. A reading that focuses on the silences and exaggerations in the portrayals quickly reveals that the Soviet "certainties" as presented in encyclopedias were based on ideologies that have since evaporated, on an iron curtain that has lost its physical rigidity, and on a state that has given up many of its former functions.

Economic Life along the Iron Curtain

A 1967 Soviet encyclopedia writes that Ajaria "will always be associated with citrus plantations and perfectly well-trimmed tea bushes, with the glossy fans of tropical palms rustling in the wind, and with the scenic Batumian bay . . . with its ocean steamers and oil tankers" (Davitaia 1967, 262). If we take the "tropical palms" to stand for tourism, the description covers three important pillars on which the Soviet Ajarian economy thrived. Wealth connected with oil goes back to the 1880s when Batumi developed as a transit harbor for oil from the Caspian Sea. The cultivation of subtropical cash crops first became important in the 1930s, when the collectivization of agriculture was connected to the large-scale program of draining swamps and preparing hillsides for cultivation. In the 1970s, some 60 to 65 percent of all citrus fruits in the Soviet Union were cultivated in Ajaria, and together with tea they were seen as the green and yellow gold of the region (Davitadze and Khalvashi 1986, 174). With the development of Soviet tourism, Ajaria became a popular destination. A whole series of hotels, Komsomol camps, and health resorts were erected along the Black Sea coast in the Brezhnev era. Some 230,000 tourists a year visited Ajaria, contributing significantly to the regional economy (Put'k'aradze 2001, 31).

To a large extent, these sectors thrived *because* Ajaria was, for many, the outer limit of the Soviet world as they knew it. In fact, the climate was neither optimal for citrus fruits nor tourism, but due to the protection offered by the iron curtain, tea flourished as if Ajaria was the wettest place on earth, and citrus fruits and tourism as if it was the sunniest. The opening of the border in 1988 meant that Ajaria lost this protected position and was no longer able to attract as much tourism or to sell its subtropical cash crops. In the 1990s many hotels stood empty while others were converted into homes for war refugees from Abkhazia.[4] Production levels of cash crops fell to one-fifth of their volume in the 1980s, and prices dropped far below their Soviet levels (Put'k'aradze 2001). Economic problems in the Georgian republic were further aggravated by civil war between 1992 and 1994. Although Ajaria was spared from the fighting it was nonetheless affected economically. Many businesses shifted their activities there, and cross-border trade with Turkey flourished, because trading routes to Russia were disrupted. At the same time, though, the war meant that foreign investment was postponed, bringing the oil trade practically to a standstill. In the second half of the 1990s Batumi regained some of its previous importance in the oil trade. Indicators showed that the economic decline had ended. GDP levels stabilized after 1995, but they did so at levels far below those of the Soviet period.

The opening of the border with Turkey brought new possibilities for economic gain. In the 1990s, Batumi became an important transnational hub for Turkey and the Caucasus. But although the political leadership eagerly presented the new trade as a change to a free market economy, it turned out that the "free market" became increasingly dominated by state agencies that were shaped by family, favors, and "personal" contacts. Catchwords such as "transition period," "capitalism," and "market economy" dominated official de-

---

4. During the early 1990s, 270,000 (mostly Georgian-speaking) people fled the war-torn region of Abkhazia to settle "temporarily" in various Georgian provinces (Sammut 2001). In the late 1990s an estimated five thousand refugees from Abkhazia resided in Ajaria.

scriptions of the changes and indexed the regime's vision of the future. Such neoliberalist policies and rhetoric, however, did not prevent—or may even have caused, as Mitchell asserts for a different context—a "chaotic reallocation of collective resources" (1999, 28). In Ajaria the new economic flows came to represent the growing inequality between winners and losers. For most ordinary citizens, the abrupt economic changes resulted in new uncertainties and anxieties. Although they often found ways to deal with the economic crisis, in the late 1990s they were still astonished by the unpredictable and destabilizing effects of the new economy.

The End of Socialism and the Restructuring of Power

The text of a Soviet regional handbook states that "by a decree of 16 July 1921 the Ajarian Autonomous Socialist Soviet Republic was established" (Davitadze and Khalvashi 1986, 49).[5] Significantly, such one-sentence statements were all that was usually written by Soviet authors about the origin of this political administration, the Ajarian ASSR.[6] The circumstances and reasons for Ajarian autonomy were preferably left unmentioned, certainly in popular texts. This silence is strikingly different from texts about other autonomous republics, such as Abkhazia or Tatarstan, in which the importance of autonomous status for the development of "titular categories" was expounded on extensively. Ajarian autonomy was not deliberately planned by Soviet authorities and ethnographers but rather came about as the product of a compromise reached between the new Turkish Republic and the USSR in March 1921. This compromise granted Ajaria to the Soviet Union under the condition that it would have full autonomy based on religious differences between Sunni Muslim Ajarians and Orthodox Christian Georgians. However, when the Soviet leadership in the late 1920s started to enforce its antireligious policies throughout the Soviet Union, the use of religious criteria to define the Ajarian ASSR became unacceptable. The titular category "Ajarian," which in everyday life meant "Muslim," was abolished.

While Ajarians disappeared from Soviet statistics in the 1930s, the political structure—the status of autonomy—continued to exist. In the Soviet structure the lack of a "titular category" meant the lack of any "objective" ground for political or cultural deviation from the mother republic, in this case the Georgian Soviet Socialist Republic. Thus, Ajaria was subjected to national and federal control in very much the same way as Georgian oblasts (provinces) and very much unlike other autonomous republics. Its administrative organs, ministries, educational system, state security agencies, and press continued to exist, but they were completely dependent on directives from the national cen-

5. In the 1920s the region was named the Adzharistan ASSR, The ending "-stan" was dropped in the 1930s. In Georgian the region was named Ach'aris Avt'onomiuri Sabch'ota Sotsialist'uri Resp'ublik'a.

6. For example, another textbook only mentions that "the Ajarian ASSR was formed in June 1921 within the confines of the Georgian SSR" (Zambakhidze and Mamuladze 1979, 18).

ter. However, although the existence of these institutions was not even symbolically relevant during the Soviet period, they became instrumental in post-Soviet political dynamics.

After the collapse of the Soviet Union, the new Georgian national political leaders immediately tried to abolish Ajarian autonomy (Aves 1996, 41). But in the developing power struggle between Tbilisi and Batumi, Ajaria managed to withstand these pressures and to reorganize its political coherence. The decline of overall state power in combination with the chaos that ensued from civil strife between major political factions played a crucial role. Throughout the 1990s, Georgia was depicted as "a state that no longer exists," as a country in a condition of "stable catastrophe" (Jones and Parsons 1996; Lieven 2001). The national government's impotence allowed the restructuring of power on subnational and regional levels. The "dormant" institutions that Ajaria possessed as a result of its autonomous status suddenly became of crucial importance, as they allowed the new political elite to quickly consolidate economic and political power. After 1992, with the creation of the Union of Democratic Revival (or Revival Party) headed by Aslan Abashidze, the security forces, police departments, customs and tax agencies increasingly came under control of the Ajarian government. This resulted in de facto independence from the national center. Georgian president Eduard Shevardnadze was unable (or unwilling) to challenge these newly powerful formations and allowed Abashidze to run Ajaria as his personal fiefdom (Aves 1996, 44). Abashidze's authoritarian regime remained in power until the spring of 2004, when combined national Georgian and international pressure compelled the Ajarian strongman to leave the Georgian stage and take up residence in Moscow.

These various shifts during the decade after 1991 indicate that we should be careful in using the term "postsocialism." Indeed, the direct effects of the collapse of the Soviet Union have been overtaken by newer changes. Recent suggestions to use the term "post-postsocialism" (Sampson 2002) indicate growing discomfort with the use of the term. Rather than such prefixing of existing concepts, however, I hold that the more important task is to be sensitive to the temporal and spatial dimensions of different paths from socialism. When speaking of " 'postsocialist' processes and practices one must carefully qualify the context and content in question" (Humphrey and Mandel 2002, 3). Thus, although the collapse of the Soviet system has proven to be a crucial factor in the reordering of political and economic relations in Ajaria, the initial "power vacuum" is of little help in explaining subsequent trends toward authoritarian rule. Moreover, while the appeal of capitalism was understandable in the context of the Soviet economic crisis, we need to examine the way neoliberal discourses were used by the local regime to explain the continued appeal of capitalist fantasies as well as the ways in which these fantasies have become part of very real changes.

From Soviet to Post-Soviet Nationalism

Soviet textbooks about Ajaria celebrated the diversity of Batumi's population as well as the homogeneity of its hinterland. Batumi was presented as a cosmopolitan city, a place where "Friendship of the Peoples" ensured cooperation in steady economic development. By contrast, the rural area, where more than 90 percent of the population was categorized as Georgian (Gachechiladze 1995, 76), was depicted in terms of its homogeneity. These "native inhabitants—Georgians," a 1967 encyclopedia states, "do not differ by appearance nor by language from other Georgian groups" (Davitaia 1967, 265).[7] The similarities needed to be stressed because they had been subject to much debate and popular skepticism. Well into the twentieth century, the inhabitants of Ajaria did not identify as part of the Georgian nation. Loyalties, rather, were defined in terms of local residence, family, "clan," and especially religion. The differences between Eastern Orthodox Georgians and Muslim Ajarians had long been apparent in everyday social life as well as in violent conflicts. However, as Saroyan writes about the Caucasus in general: "Traditional social identities that had been constructed around social categories such as class, clan, tribe, and local patterns of residence gave way, under Soviet policies, to a newer, overarching identity based on ethnicity" (1996, 403).

The myth of the Soviet Union as a breaker of nations has been severely criticized during the last decade (Hirsch 2000; Martin 1998; Slezkine 2000; Smith 1998; Suny 1993; Tishkov 1997). In fact, Soviet rule often facilitated the consolidation of national groups, and in some cases even created new nations out of ambiguous cultural material. Two crucial factors in this process were the ethnic categorization of inhabitants and the ethno-territorial division of Soviet space. As Hirsch has eloquently demonstrated, the construction of "ethnic nations" was neither well planned nor simply imposed from the federal center. Rather, "empire and nations 'emerged' together and were mutually supportive structures in the Soviet context" (Hirsch 2000, 213). The policies of *korenizatsiia* (indigenization)—which assured that proclaimed titular nationalities had preferential access to educational institutions, the Communist Party, and positions in the bureaucracy—meant that "ethnicity" became a crucial asset in advancing local interests.[8] The deliberate administrative division of Soviet space into ethno-geographical units and the development of educational, cultural, and academic institutions along these administrative lines provided the organizational basis for further consolidation of ethnic and national categories (see also Smith 1998).

Despite the value of the thesis of "ethnic consolidation," its applicability to local contexts is not without its difficulties. In Ajaria, because of its proximity

---

7. Another textbook stated: "Only a few minor customs differentiate Ajarians from the Georgian population of other regions" (Birina 1956, 328).

8. Korenizatsiia refers to measures aimed at increasing the popular base of the Communist Party among the nationalities of the Soviet Union.

to Turkey, Soviet ethnic policies acquired some peculiar characteristics. During the first decade of Soviet rule, there were indications that "Ajarians" would enjoy a separate ethnic status. Indeed, the very creation of an Ajarian ASSR initially seemed to allow for a degree of differentiation from the mother republic of Georgia. In the Soviet census of 1926 the population could register as Ajarian, and the different historical and religious background of these Ajarians was acknowledged in official documents. At the time, Ajarians numbered roughly seventy thousand, forming a narrow majority in their autonomous republic (Akiner 1983, 243–45).[9] But, as has been mentioned, the religious criteria soon became unacceptable to Soviet authorities. This, together with lobbying by Georgian leaders to reclassify the population as Georgians, led to the abolishment of the category of "Ajarian." From then on "Ajarian" continued to exist only as a geographical indicator.

In contrast to the Ajarians, the ethnic Laz minority (they numbered 643 in the 1926 census) of Ajaria were allowed to assert some level of difference, not least because they were seen as instrumental in reaching the Soviet goal of territorial expansion in the Laz-populated area across the border in Turkey. During the Soviet period, both Ajarians and Soviet Laz demonstrated a growing identification with Georgian nationality, a process that was greatly enhanced by the socioeconomic integration of the region into the larger Georgian SSR. But in both cases, this national integration was only partly successful. In the border village of Sarpi, people continued to cherish affiliations with their ethnic (Laz) kin across the border. Moreover, Islam retained its attraction for large portions of the population and continued to link them, at least on the conceptual level, to Muslims in Turkey and beyond.

The heightened importance of cultural identities in postsocialist countries is often presented as a return to pre-Soviet identities that were held in "cold storage" and/or as a response to the "ideological vacuum" left by the collapse of the Soviet Union. These views ignore the Soviet past and fail to understand how, often in unexpected and unintended ways, Soviet rule influenced—and continues to influence—the formation of specific patterns of identification. Instead of assuming or denying continuities between pre-Soviet and post-Soviet forms of identity as the "cold storage" and "vacuum" theories do, it is crucial to analyze how frames of reference were shaped and modified in changing social and political contexts.

The cultural, political, and economic disruptions in Ajaria have shown in a poignant and often tragic way the uncertainty of the road from socialism. The changes led to the destruction of the regional economy while simultaneously creating new economic opportunities. They brought an end to the party-state

---

9. The rest of the population consisted of Russians, Armenians, Christian Georgians, Jews, Pontian Greeks, and Laz. These minorities lived predominantly along the coast and in the port city of Batumi.

while enhancing possibilities for elite groups to strengthen their dominant position. The changes facilitated the rise of Christian Georgian nationalism, unleashing new dynamics of inclusion and exclusion. Besides these visible effects on social life, the collapse of the Soviet regime and the opening of the border also disturbed the images and perceptions Ajarians had of their region. If Soviet encyclopedias provided a distorted view of Ajaria in order to portray the region as well integrated into Soviet Georgian society, they at least delivered a flattering self-image to local communities. The border opening exposed the fragility of these depictions by rendering transparent the ideological basis on which these depictions had relied, thus simultaneously fostering a defense of "archaic" idealizations and a search for new historical and cultural reference points.

Recently, Vitebsky provocatively stated that "while the Soviet mystique has been demystified the post-Soviet mystique has only deepened" (2002, 181). Vitebsky's statement compellingly signals the elusiveness of recent changes. There is, for example, a clear need for "demystification" of the transition rhetoric that has dominated many debates about postsocialism. Likewise, more attention should be given to the discrepancies as well as connections between neoliberal visions of "transition" and the destabilizing effect of capitalism, between the collapse of the socialist state and the restructuring of power, and between nationalism and globalization. At the same time, I wonder how far the *Soviet* mystique has been demystified. The myths of "*Homo sovieticus*," of "Soviet modernization," and of the "rational atheist worldview" may have evaporated with the collapse of the Soviet Union, but, as Humphrey states, "we still have not worked out what the heritage of actually existing socialism is" (2002b, 12). Indeed, demystification of the Soviet period remains of crucial importance to assess postsocialist changes and uncertainties. This is especially true for Soviet peripheries that were largely neglected in studies of the Soviet Union (cf. Suny 1993, 293).

Anthropology in and of the Borderlands

Socialist and postsocialist borders have figured prominently in popular discourses of borders, but they have rarely been the subject of thorough empirical analysis. The Berlin wall and the iron curtain served as ultimate symbols of the two competing world systems, surfacing in many ideological statements proclaiming the superiority of either East or West. However, this discursive prominence of cold war divides was not matched by scholarly attention to the literal borders themselves, not even on the sides that were accessible to Western researchers. In this respect, it is telling that the first widely acknowledged ethnographic study of socialist borders, John Borneman's *Belonging in the Two Berlins*, appeared as late as 1992. What this void seems to indicate is that borders are capable of capturing the anthropological gaze only when they are challenged, that is, when contact across them exists or when their very existence is in dispute.

It is thus not surprising that when the socialist regimes collapsed and relations between East and West were redefined, (post)socialist borders received increasing attention. Indeed, the demise of the iron curtain has been presented as epitomizing the changing nature of borders in the contemporary world. In introductions to borderland anthropology, the changes in these East–West divides are held to signal that borders can no longer be seen as "stable, trustworthy and monolithic institutions" (Wendl and Rösler 1999, 1). Likewise, in their influential book *Borders*, Hastings Donnan and Thomas Wilson argue that anthropological interest in borders reflects global changes that have occurred since 1989, and they highlight the fall of the Berlin wall and the disintegration of the Soviet empire and state (1999, 1–4). However, the former East–West divides are conspicuously absent from the rest of both books, as if their past rigidity and their subsequent porosity are self-evident (and have self-evident consequences).[10]

This shortsighted gaze at (post)socialist borders is closely related to the academic agendas that characterized borderland anthropology in the 1980s and 1990s. Though anthropological interest in borders has early roots in studies concerning the organization of ethnicity and culture (Barth 1969; Cole and Wolf 1974), it only flourished as a critique of metanarratives in the 1980s and 1990s. An emphasis on borders proved strategic in challenging reified depictions of the nation-state as a top-down imposed entity, in critiquing views of cultures as bounded units, and in questioning the view of borders as self-evident limits of the territory of states (Kopytoff 1987; Sahlins 1989; Borneman 1992; Driessen 1992; Martínez 1994; Alvarez 1995). Also, these studies showed that the two sides of a state border often need to be seen as a single complex cultural whole. This view is perhaps most graphically worded by Hannerz in his discussion of the synergic qualities of borders, when he suggests that borders are sites characterized by "culture+culture, rather than culture/culture" (cited in Herzfeld 2001, 142). In short, if borders can be seen as constructs that simultaneously divide and connect, the focus has lately been on the latter, on how they connect rather than divide. Clearly, the rigidity of "iron curtains" was of little use in academic agendas that proclaimed the "fluid" nature of borders. Moreover, their postsocialist porosity only superficially confirms such views.[11]

Although frontiers, borders, or margins are not peripheral to the working

10. Ballinger noted a similar neglect of the Balkans and eastern Europe in the anthropology of borders and borderlands (2004, 31). Despite that, anthropologists have provided important insights into the dynamics of contact across former socialist borders (Konstantinov 1996; Veenis 1999; Hann and Bellér-Hann 1998; Svašek 1999), even if they rarely touch on their rigid socialist past. An important exception is Berdahl (1999).

11. Other students of (post)socialist borders have also been skeptical about views that celebrate the hybrid or experimental nature of borderlands. See Ballinger's (2004) analysis of "hybridity discourse" with regard to the Italian–Slovenian–Croatian borderlands and Hann and Bellér-Hann's (1998) suggestion that the opening of the Turkish–Georgian border led to "antimodern" rather than postmodern sentiments.

of the state but rather highlight crucial aspects of its everyday functioning, I believe that we should move away from the assumption that border regions are, by definition, sites where state structures are less fully articulated and where the image of the state loses its clarity.[12] Although the strategic power of citizens may be higher at the margins, and border dwellers may display more conspicuously ambiguous loyalties, these characteristics may be the precise reasons for intensified state regulation, as the history of Soviet borders amply demonstrates. Moreover, although borders may be characterized by cross-border movement and communication, such "flux" may also prompt vigorous attempts to define and solidify ideas of identity and difference, as the opening passages concerning Otari's funeral illustrated. As Berdahl has stated it in her analysis of a village located along the German iron curtain: "One of the many paradoxes of the borderland . . . is that ambiguity creates clarity" (1999, 232).[13] I believe we need to move beyond the discussion of whether borders are best described in terms of fluidity or rigidity and examine how these aspects are ultimately interconnected.

Borders and Their Things

It was almost forty years ago when Barth famously wrote that it is "the ethnic boundary that defines the group, not the cultural stuff it encloses" (1969, 15). Barth was particularly interested in demonstrating that cultural difference is a product of contact rather than a result of isolation, and that cultural differences persist "despite inter-ethnic contact and dependence" (1969, 9–10). Although these are still important insights, his emphasis on the durability and stability of boundaries is less helpful in explaining their emergence, modification, or dissolution. How, for example, should we account for the changes in—and partial dissolution of—the boundaries between Muslim Ajarians and Laz on the one hand and Orthodox Christian Georgians on the other? Moreover, how are boundaries constructed or sustained when ethnic or other differences are absent, as between the Laz on opposite sides of the border?

Berdahl notes, with regard to the creation of such boundaries between Germans on different sides of the (former) iron curtain, that in such cases "the cultural stuff" may actually prove crucial (1999, 4). Indeed, we need to pay particular attention to the ways in which state representatives as well as local actors conceptualize, mobilize, and consume cultural stuff to understand their significance in assertions of difference and commonality. In other words, we should take a more organic view of the relation between borders and "cultural stuff," looking at the ways they mutually constitute each other over time.

One useful strategy therefore is to examine the "things of boundaries," as

12. For similar concerns see Das and Poole (2004, 3).

13. More generally, Meyer and Geschiere point out that "it looks as if, in a world characterized by flows, a great deal of energy is devoted to controlling and freezing them" (1999, 5).

the historical sociologist Abbott has advocated: "It is wrong to look for boundaries between pre-existing entities. Rather, we should start with boundaries and investigate how people create entities by linking these boundaries into units. We should not look for the boundaries of things, but for the things of boundaries" (2001, 261).[14] Analogously it makes sense to start with the actual lines and boundaries drawn by distant policymakers, in order to see how they have been endowed with meaning and how they have been contested, as well as defended, by different actors in border regions.

In Georgia, the delimitation of Soviet and Turkish territory and the labeling of local inhabitants as Laz or Georgian initially did not reflect any underlying social reality. Rather, they were imposed on a region characterized by social, cultural, and economic intermingling. Although the territorial lines and ethnic classifications did not follow locally recognized distinctions, the act of delimitation made difference "official," and as such it had very real effects. Ethnic labels were inscribed in passports and other documents and formed the basis of numerous state policies. The literal border, as a "modern technique of organizing space" (Bornstein 2002, 130), could not help but become an important point of reference in response to which identities and distinctions were constructed and articulated. It is from such an interactive view of borders that we can start to analyze the dynamics of cultural mixing and unmixing. Following the biography of the border reveals the asymmetries emerging along the border, the cultural and economic flows across it, and the patterns of inclusion and exclusion that these prompt.

Borders, Frontiers, and Borderlands

Although it makes sense to start with the lines that demarcate territories, it is equally crucial to recognize that borders are created, sustained, and altered as much "from the inside out as the outside in" (Driessen 1998, 99). Though the borderline may be the most tangible point of division and contact, it is important to note that the various sociocultural dimensions of the Georgian-Turkish border do not necessarily coincide with the literal borderline. Braudel wrote about the Mediterranean world that "we should imagine a hundred frontiers, not one, some political, some economic, and some cultural" (1976, 160). Applying this metaphor to Georgia, one can say that there are not only multiple frontiers at play in one given place but that these frontiers converge into various knots throughout the region. Therefore, to grasp the relation between state borders and cultural formations we need to look at these frontiers from different angles in order to analyze how local (and more distant) actors

14. Abbott's boundaries between professions are of a different nature than the borders and boundaries discussed here, but some of his findings are nevertheless useful. Abbott documented the history of "social work," noticing that the involved professions only gained coherence after basic lines were set in a largely undifferentiated field of activities. This led him to conclude that the contents of the involved professions were, in a sense, a by-product of boundary-drawing activities (2001, 261–79).

have interpreted, and acted on, these spaces and concepts. This book is divided into three parts. It begins with the literal border between Georgia and Turkey and the divided border village of Sarpi, where I did fieldwork between October 1999 and May 2000. Then it moves to the frontier between Islam and Christianity in the mountainous hinterland of Ajaria, where I spent six months in 2000 and 2001 documenting the processes of interaction between Muslim Ajarians, Georgian nationalists, Soviet "atheizers," and Orthodox Christian clergy. Finally, I explore the links between postsocialist urban space and the politics of belonging in the provincial capital Batumi, based on several research stays between 1997 and 2001.[15]

Each of these cases represents unique configurations of more general social, political, and economic processes. By presenting alternative histories of the confrontations between local communities and the wider powers along the Georgian-Turkish border, they demonstrate the various ways and degrees to which borders impinged on local life. This approach has allowed me to suggest new ways of thinking about borders and to account for their continuing relevance in an age characterized by flows that transcend them.

15. While conducting research, I relied primarily on my knowledge of Russian. This worked well in the Ajarian capital, Batumi, where a significant part of the population (30 percent) was Russian in the late 1980s, and in the border village of Sarpi, where the Soviet and later Russian military presence ensured proficiency in Russian among most people. Only relatively late in my research was I able to conduct interviews in Georgian, though even then I had to rely partly on the translations of research assistants.

PART I

A Divided Village on the Georgian-Turkish Border

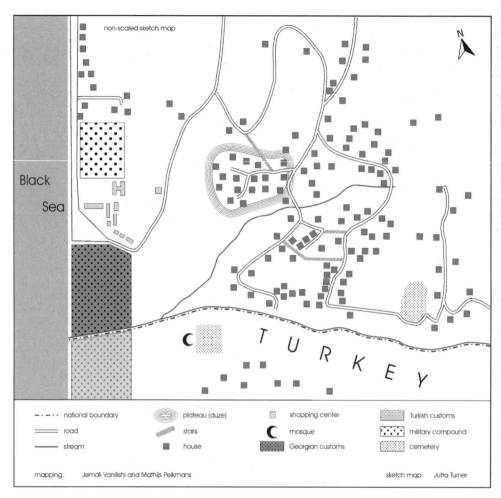

non-scaled sketch map

Black
Sea

TURKEY

N

–·–·–·– national boundary	plateau (duze)	shopping center	Turkish customs
road	stairs	mosque	military compound
stream	house	Georgian customs	cemetery

mapping: Jemali Vanilishi and Mathijs Pelkmans

sketch map: Jutta Turner

The Georgian part of Sarpi

Introduction

Divided Village

When I arrived at Aman's house in the hilly part of Sarpi, his daughter-in-law told me that he had gone to feed the cows and would be back in a minute.[1] I waited at the small table in the yard and looked out over the village beneath me. Down at the sea was the border gate connecting Georgia and Turkey. Trucks and cars entered the customs area one by one; taxis and minibuses were parked on both sides of the complex, ready to take customers to their respective destinations in one country or the other. Away from the coast, uphill, was where most villagers lived. Large white houses were scattered along the hillsides among green gardens, bushes, and citrus plantations. This part of Sarpi didn't look very different from most other villages in the region, but looks didn't tell the whole story. The state border between Turkey and Georgia divided the village in half, with 130 houses on the Georgian side and eighty on the Turkish side. During most of the Soviet period, Sarpi was part of the *zapretnaia pogranichnaia zona* (forbidden border zone), inaccessible to most nonresidents. Looking carefully, I could distinguish the barbed wire starting at the customs offices, following the small stream through the center of the village, and disappearing into the green-covered hills. Soldiers with dogs patrolled the fences, though presumably not as frequently as they used to. Strategically placed watchtowers overlooked the village. In fact, Aman's yard could be observed by both Turkish and Georgian soldiers.

When Aman arrived he noticed me looking at the fences and said, "Yes, this is where the border starts, running from here all the way to Vladivostok." His casual voice suggested that he had uttered the phrase many times and that he had grown used to the border. The fences and watchtowers had become a nat-

1. "Sarpi" is the Georgian name of the village. Across the border, in Turkey, people refer to the village as "Sarp." I use Sarp only when specifically referring to the Turkish part.

ural part of the landscape. Nevertheless, despite this visual adaptation to the divide, villagers were still plagued by the question of why the village had been cut in two. There may never have been a specific reason for its location; the officials who signed the Russo-Turkish Treaty of Friendship of March 16, 1921, simply mentioned the rivers, villages, and mountains that were to be the landmarks for the new international border.[2] These officials never needed to explain or justify the division of Sarpi, but for the villagers it was a different matter, as the imposition of the border led to numerous personal and family tragedies. Aman had his own theory about why the state border was located only a few hundred meters from his house. In his view the decision had been made almost accidentally by Lenin and Stalin who, pacing up and down in front of a map of the Soviet Union, discussed how they might bring peace to the country:

> At that moment, when negotiations started on the exact location of the boundary, the area was still occupied by the Turks. Lenin was a friend of Atatürk and eager to end all the wars. "The people in Ajaria are Muslims, so let's give the region to Atatürk," he told Stalin. "Hey, what are you doing!" Stalin interrupted. "Do you want to give away Batumi!? Our oil transport runs through that city; it is a very important harbor for us." Lenin stroked his beard and thought, "Hmm, Stalin is probably right, but I already promised Atatürk that the border will be along the Choloki River, so what should I do?"[3] Lenin got a new idea and said to Stalin, "Alright, the border will be along the Chorokhi River instead of the Choloki River; Atatürk won't know the difference." But Stalin still disagreed: "No, that is too dangerous, that is too close to Batumi. It should be a bit farther, across the first mountains. There is a small stream, which we can use as the division line," he said. This is where Sarpi happened to be, but they didn't know about that. So they decided that this stream would be the dividing line between Turkey and the Soviet Union.

The imagined discussion in the remote office in the Kremlin bespeaks the extraordinary interplay between wider political forces and the villagers. The placement of the border through the middle of Sarpi, and especially the border enforcements in subsequent decades, had a tremendous impact on all aspects of social life. Soviet Sarpi was, in some ways, distant from the empire's power centers. It did not exist on maps; it was hardly ever mentioned in the media; and for decades Sarpi was fenced off (literally) from the hinterland. But at the same time, every little change in the center was immediately felt in the village. Because of its sensitive location Sarpi attracted special attention

---

2. "The north-eastern boundary of Turkey is defined as follows [. . .] The village of Sarp (Sarpe) on the Black Sea coast—Qara Shalvar (Kara Shalvar) Dagh (5014 [height of mountain in feet]) and crossing the Chorokh to the north of the village of Mardidi." Russo-Turkish Treaty of March 16, 1921, appendix 1a, reprinted in Cornwall (1923, 446–47).

3. The Choloki is a small river that roughly follows the present administrative border between the Georgian provinces of Ajaria and Guria, located some forty kilometers north of Batumi (see map on p. 2).

from state agencies. Indeed, in this village on the border, the state was more omnipresent than in many other parts of Soviet society. Residents developed their own ways of dealing with the rigidities of the iron curtain, but, paradoxically, their actions ended up strengthening the border even further.

The exceptional geopolitical location of Sarpi proved a very fruitful site for analyzing changing patterns of belonging and nonbelonging. Prior to the establishment of the Soviet border residents had extensive relations with the people living westward along the Black Sea coast, as well as economic ties with the port city of Batumi in the east. Sarpi itself was the easternmost community of an area inhabited by the Laz, who (used to) speak their own language Lazuri (alongside Turkish) and distinguished themselves from other groups in the area, notably the Georgian-speaking Ajarians and the Christian Georgians. The almost accidental placement of the border not only limited movement but had a crucial impact on villagers' cultural horizons. Although throughout the Soviet period the Sarpians continued to identify themselves as Laz, the meaning of this category was deeply affected by seventy years of Soviet modernization and nationality politics. Thus, despite fifty years of longing for contact with ethnic kin across the border, when residents finally met they encountered unexpected differences between themselves and Laz in Turkey. The long-awaited "reunion" prompted new attempts to define patterns of belonging and nonbelonging—attempts that involved reinforcing the ideological dimensions of the iron curtain.

1 Caught between States

Whenever the weather permitted, elderly male inhabitants of Sarpi passed their leisure time in what was called the "old men's house." During my stay in the late 1990s I often sat down with the old men to ask questions, or, conversely, to be asked questions about my life in the Netherlands. On several occasions I noticed a peculiar behavior. When talking about Europe some of these men would point not to the west but to the northeast, that is, away from the border. There was some logic to this. One day a man had just started to talk about his visit to relatives in Turkey in the early 1980s and he illustrated his journey by moving his arm east and then south. Basically this mirrored the route that he had followed at the time. First, he had traveled eastward to Tbilisi, then southward to Yerevan in Armenia, then westward, crossing the Soviet-Turkish border in Leninakan, and finally northward by bus to Hopa at the Black Sea coast. All in all he had traveled fourteen hundred kilometers, over three days, to reach a place only twenty kilometers away from (and to the west of) Sarpi. Indeed, it was only logical that at the end of the world people would point to the east, the direction in which even travels to the west necessarily started.

The relevance of "east–west geography" was more dramatically displayed in another case. The house of Nazmi Koridze, a man in his seventies, was on the hillside next to the village road that connected the upper part of the village to the coast. At the back of his house, on the eastern side, citrus plantations began that were traversed by narrow paths that ran to the houses of several of his relatives. On the other side, across the road to the west, there was a splendid view over the Turkish part of the village and the hills behind it. Nazmi's house was built in the 1960s, with windows facing all directions. But in 1987, one year before the border gate at Sarpi was reopened, Nazmi took out the two windows that looked to the west, that is, in the direction of Turkey, and filled the holes with bricks. According to his daughter-in-law, the reason for this action was that whenever people passed by the house, her father-in-law would freeze, terrified that they had come to arrest him.

These anecdotes point out two features of the Soviet border. First, in Sarpi the international border was, and for some continued to be, associated with fear. Numerous stories were told about the dangers of showing interest in the border, about sanctions on antennas turned westward, and about the risk of being caught pointing or looking across the border. Second, anecdotal remarks suggested that the international border represented, in a very real sense, the outer limit of the villagers' world. Like the gestures discussed above, oral statements also indicated that, for the people living in Sarpi, the international border was fixed and unquestioned. Residents said that for fifty years, between 1937 and 1988, the border running through Sarpi was completely closed. They stressed that, except for the few who went through lengthy and risky procedures and were lucky enough to obtain official travel visas for Turkey, no one ever went to the other side. Another indication of the unquestioned rigidity was the stories told by middle-aged Sarpians about their experiences of living along the iron curtain. They often did not talk about the international border but rather about the internal ones, about the fences and checkpoints between the "border zone" and Batumi. These checkpoints had been an everyday nuisance and had limited villagers' contacts with colleagues and relatives living elsewhere in Georgia. In short, these middle-aged Sarpians had fully accommodated to the reality of the impermeability of the international border.

Clearly the border running through Sarpi was an exceptional border. It was, to use Donnan and Haller's phrase (2000, 12), a "border of fear and control," almost completely impermeable. That such impermeability is an exceptional feature when it comes to state borders can be seen from the available literature, which often argues that it is simply impossible to make borders watertight. Herzfeld, for example, writes about "the ease with which even—or especially—the most fiercely guarded borders can be penetrated" (2001, 138), and Driessen states that "no matter how clearly borders are marked on maps, how many border guards are appointed, how many fences are built, people will ignore borders whenever it suits them" (1996, 289). Indeed, evidence from the U.S.-Mexican border, the outer borders of the European Union, or the border between Israel and Palestine, all heavily guarded and patrolled borders, shows how easily the protection measures of states can be defeated. As Kearney (2004, 254–63), Driessen (1998), and Bornstein (2002) show for these respective borders, increased fortification usually pushes border crossers into a more covert and vulnerable status, but it has little influence on the occurrence of illegal cross-border movement.

So what made this border different? One obvious reason is that the Soviet Union did not depend on cross-border economic ties in the same way as "capitalist" states do, and thus it did not see its fortifications undermined by the pressure to turn a blind eye toward the influx of cheap labor.[1] The rigidity of the Soviet-Turkish border did not appear overnight, and like others it was initially a border that divided *and* connected, a border representing danger as well as opportunities. But eventually this two-sided nature was lost. This change was achieved not simply through the installation of border enforcements (including acoustic alarm systems, high-voltage fences, watchtowers, barbed wire, and patrolling guards) but took place because such enforcements were embedded in a culture of secrecy that forced villagers to test the limits of the possible and thereby aid in setting them. To understand the rigid qualities of this border, then, we need to investigate the politics of everyday life at the border: the particular interplay between state structures and local life as it developed after the establishment of Soviet power. Paradoxically, the fact that in Sarpi the border was (sometimes literally) located in people's backyards contributed to configurations that reinforced the border regime.

Of special importance in understanding the Soviet border regime was the peculiar intersection between nationality and foreign policy. Whereas, on the one hand Soviet leaders were xenophobic about potential "capitalist" infiltration from abroad, on the other hand they viewed state borders as important sites for potential expansion. During the 1920s and 1930s in particular, cross-border ethnic ties were seen as instrumental for the future expansion of the Soviet Union. Terry Martin refers to this last element as the "Piedmont principle":[2] "the Soviet attempt to exploit cross-border ethnic ties to project political influence into neighboring states" (1998, 832). This bifurcated attitude toward the border complicated actual policies. Therefore, analyzing how these policies were transferred to and implemented in local settings is essential. Following Kotkin (1995), Soviet "totalitarianism" should be seen not as a structure implanted from above but as a dialectical process that developed and was reinforced through the interactions of citizens and the state. Even on the highly politicized and fiercely guarded border in Sarpi, border dwellers were creatively exercising their limited options under extraordinary political circumstances. But by challenging the forms of control, the villagers simultaneously defined the limits of power (cf. Berdahl 1999).

Because villagers acted in ways that resulted in deeper entrenchment in the power webs spun by the state, stories about living in the border region often revealed a twofold ambiguity. On one level, this ambiguity referred to the mixture of positive memories about the certainties that socialism provided and

---

1. For example, in his discussion of the U.S.-Mexican border, Michael Kearney states that the discrepancy between the rhetoric of border containment and the de facto practice of allowing "illegal" migration stems from the fact that while cheap labor is desired, the persons in whom this labor is embodied are not (1998, 125).

2. Piedmont refers to a region in Italy, which bordered on France and Switzerland and played a crucial role in the process of Italian unification in the nineteenth century. Martin uses the term because Soviet authorities depicted Ukraine as a modern "Piedmont" that would serve to unite the scattered Ukrainian populations of Romania, Poland, and Czechoslovakia (2001, 9).

the deeply negative experiences with the severity of the border regime. Perhaps even more crucial, the ambiguity stemmed from the unexpressed awareness of villagers that they were not only victims of but also collaborators with this border regime. The stories demonstrated that people were still coping with a past that simultaneously had to be forgotten and remembered. Moreover, the convergence of victimhood and complicity also provided clues to answer the question of how, despite the hardships of deportation and the loss of close relatives, villagers continued to express nostalgic feelings for the Soviet era.

Border Regime

Sarpi was incorporated in the Russian Empire in 1878, after having been part of the Ottoman Empire for about three centuries. The new border was established at Liman, a settlement some ten kilometers west of Sarpi. With the outbreak of World War I, warfare between Russia and Turkey led most families in Sarpi to leave their homes and travel in small boats westward to towns along the Ottoman Black Sea coast. When they returned to their village in 1918 the area was briefly occupied by Turkish troops. Russia and its new Bolshevik government was left without allies and stuck in a severe civil war. To secure peace on the southern border it signed a treaty with Turkey that included the transfer of Ajaria to the Turks. At the same time, though, Georgia had declared independence and did not accept this loss of territory. But before Georgian troops arrived on the battlefields, World War I was decided in favor of the Allies. The Turkish army was replaced by British troops, which stayed in the area for a year and a half as part of a halfhearted attempt to secure their oil interests in the region. After their departure, at a moment when Turkey appeared to be advancing once again, the Bolsheviks acted quickly by instigating a Communist revolt in Tbilisi. In February 1921, the Red Army invaded Georgia and installed a new government.[3] Both Turkey and Russia were exhausted by their respective civil wars, and the two powers started peace negotiations that resulted in the drawing of the Soviet-Turkish border right through the middle of Sarpi.

Open Border: 1921–1937

After the border was delineated in 1921 the village of Sarpi officially consisted of two parts, Turkish Sarp and what became Georgian-Soviet Sarpi. Although during the first years customs posts were established and a fence was erected to mark and defend the state boundary, it was still relatively easy to cross. Many families still owned property on a narrow alluvial strip of land near Makriali (present-day Kemalpaşha) in Turkish territory where it was possible to cultivate rice. This land had either been purchased by ancestors or

---

3. Arslanian (1996) discusses the role of the British in the Caucasus in the early 1920s. For an extensive discussion of the relation between Turkey and the early Soviet state, see Gökay (1997).

Soviet soldiers pile into a truck near the border in Sarpi. The billboard text translates as: "The entire Soviet nation guards the border." Photograph by Jemali Vanilishi, approximately 1978.

obtained through marriage arrangements. Villagers received permits to travel fifteen kilometers into the bordering state, allowing them to cultivate their land. Aman Abuladze remembered how he and his mother went down to the border checkpoint when they wanted to visit relatives: "We had a document like a passport in which the soldiers wrote, for example, '[This person] is allowed to visit brother for two days.' Then we had to go through a small house where they would search us, men and women separately." Besides administrative hazards such as these, villagers had no real difficulties in crossing the border. In fact, the implementation of the border and the resulting economic differences may have *created* the reasons to cross the border.

As early as 1921 the Bolshevik leadership had begun attempting to establish a centralized distribution system that included fixed prices for most goods.[4] As a result many goods became scarce on the Soviet side of the border, while price differences between Turkey and the Soviet Union rose steeply. Smuggling was widespread, and the markets in towns near the border were especially well stocked with contraband.[5] The very existence of the border enabled

4. Between 1921 and 1929 the policies that regulated trade were often contradictory. At times private trade was allowed or even encouraged, while at other times those who engaged in it were prosecuted. From the late 1920s onward, restrictions on private trade became increasingly severe (see Ball 1987).

5. For a vivid account of Batumi's "Turkish bazaar" in the early 1920s, see Paustovksy (1969, 81–84, 136).

villagers to earn additional income by trading in goods such as silk and woolen cloth, shoes, coats, and soap.[6] The smuggling remained small scale, involving mostly European goods that could be bought in the Turkish border town of Hopa and resold in the Soviet Union at much higher prices. A report of the customs officers in 1926 states: "Smuggling is mostly unorganized, involving people without land or permanent work. The smugglers mostly carry the goods on their shoulders across the mountains south of Sarpi, an area which is almost impossible to control due to its abundant and impenetrable vegetation."[7] In those years several hundred people were caught smuggling, though only a few were from Sarpi. However, this should not lead one to conclude that the villagers' involvement was insignificant. It is more likely that their knowledge of the local geography and their extensive family networks across the border made them almost impossible to catch. As one elderly man told me, they had to be careful not to attract attention from the customs officers or soldiers, but he and his brother always managed to bring certain goods back to Sarpi without ever being caught.

Despite the existence of the border and the presence of soldiers, during the 1920s and early 1930s the two Sarpis were in several respects still an undivided village, only partially affected by the respective states. Neither the Soviet Union nor Kemalist Turkey had fully developed their state structures. The respective governments were more concerned with improving their power base than with rural life in the peripheries. Until 1924, when a new school was established, education for children in the village was provided in the madrassa on the Turkish side. The dead were still buried in the common cemetery (now located on Turkish soil), and elderly men continued to attend the Friday prayers in the mosque, which was also on the Turkish side. This situation, however, did not continue for long. From the late 1920s onward, when the Soviet ban on religion was first enforced, the number of men attending the Friday prayers declined, reportedly because they feared possible repercussions. Furthermore, although the mosque was located on Turkish soil, the imam lived in Soviet Sarpi. He was forced to turn in his passport, forbidden to speak in public, and thus could no longer perform his duties. The increasing restrictions of the early 1930s forecast to some extent what was to come. As Aman put it: "When [Atatürk] died and the authorities over here started their search for Trotskyites, these [trips to the other side] were over once and for all."

Fortifications: 1937–1956

In 1937 this period of relative freedom of movement abruptly ended. Aise Tandilava, an elderly woman who was born in Turkey but who married a young man from the Georgian side, recalled: "My husband and I were har-

---

6. Ach'aris ASSR tsent'raluri sakhelmts'ipo arkivi [Central State Archive of the Ajarian ASSR], fond 44, files 1 and 2: March 1923–February 1928.

7. Ach'aris ASSR tsent'raluri sakhelmts'ipo arkivi, fond 44, file 3: September 1925–November 1926.

vesting our plot in Turkish Sarpi. We had almost finished and planned to go back the next morning to collect the crop. But when we arrived at the gate the soldiers started laughing: 'You are not allowed to go any more,' they said. 'We just closed the border.'" But although 1937 was usually mentioned as the year in which the border became impermeable, several residents remembered that, initially, limited communication continued between the two sides of Sarpi.[8] One elderly man sang to me the same song his relatives had sung across the border when his sister had her first child:

> Listen to the happiness that has overcome us,
> Our Feride she is fine and doing well,
> It is a boy who has been born to her,
> And Omar is his name.

These lines were sung while working on the land and thus appeared to be nothing more than an innocent folk song. Since the border guards did not know Lazuri they did not understand what was being communicated. But the same people who told me about these early forms of communication also explained that singing was only possible during the first years after the closing of the border. Aman remembered: "When someone died we would cry and then they cried from the other side, so that people knew in which house there was a funeral. But afterward they even forbade that. They said, 'If you want to cry, go home and cry there.'" This ban on open-air crying was not the only measure. With the growing threat of a possible war between the Soviet Union and Turkey, new restrictions were introduced to halt cross-border communication. It was forbidden to leave the house after sunset and windows had to be covered with black cloth. Everyone vividly remembers these restrictions, and many recalled how they would sit in the dark at home, afraid that the soldiers' footsteps would halt in front of their house. Even the smallest irregularities could be interpreted as sending messages to the enemy. Villagers told me that during those years, and long after, no one even dared to look in the direction of Turkey. When I pressed an acquaintance to find out whether there were perhaps other ways of communication, he replied: "No, no, those things didn't exist. Who would ever try it? The people were simply afraid; they didn't even *try* to look in that direction."

During the 1940s and 1950s Soviet Sarpi was subdivided into several sections. A zone of restricted movement was announced, including part of the village and a five-hundred-meter-wide stretch of land along the border. This was the area where many Sarpians had their own private plots for cultivating vegetables and fruits. To work their lands they had to descend first to the seashore where they would receive written permission to work during pre-

---

8. Covert techniques of maintaining contact, such as "border-singing," are also noted in descriptions of the Turkish side of the border (Hann and Bellér-Hann 1998, 245; Pereira 1971).

cisely fixed hours. Further restrictions on movement were made in the 1950s when a fence was placed along the seashore. Whenever residents needed to enter the beach area, they first had to go to the military camp to fetch a soldier who would open a gate. A subsequent commander removed the fence again. He decided that the existence of such a fence was wholly unnecessary and actually bad propaganda, for what would people on the Turkish side think of "the good life in the Soviet Union" if the whole village was fenced off? Such erratic shifts were typical of the border regime in Sarpi, in which state representatives on each level anxiously tried to prove they had complete control over the border, but in their zealous attempts tarnished the positive image of Soviet society.

Sealed Border: 1956–1988

Commenting on the border regime in the 1960s and the decades thereafter Niaz Kakabadze explained:

> If you would have tried. . . . Well, there were eight meters up to the fences where the ground was cleared. Behind it there was a fence with an alarm system and then there was a second fence. Soldiers with dogs patrolled [the area] between those two fences. They would shoot or catch you even before reaching the fence. But no one [from Sarpi] ever even tried.

Some people remembered the impermeability even as a positive development for the village. Aman, whose house was near the border, told me the following: "After 1956 we didn't need permission anymore to work [on our plots] near the border. Simply because they had fortified the border—fences, alarm systems, and so on—so that we were free in our village again."

The situation along the international border became normalized. Village life continued in a territorially constrained environment. The strictly regulated and highly limited communication that was allowed following the late 1960s fitted within this "normalized" border condition. New regulations in 1965 made it possible to send letters to relatives across the border. The letters usually took between three to six months to arrive on the other side of the village; they were censored and contained only limited information about family affairs. After 1970 it became possible to apply for visas to visit family. The application procedures required at least five and up to ten years to be approved and involved the risk of losing one's job or ruining the career opportunities of one's children. If a visa was finally issued one could go to Turkish Sarp by traveling via Tbilisi, Yerevan, and Kars, a trip of roughly fourteen hundred kilometers. The adjustments to these forms of communication, important though they were for Sarpians, also suggest that villagers by and large had accommodated to the restrictions and the limitations imposed by the state.

As an illustration, consider a novel written about Soviet Sarpi in the 1960s. *Ne boisia mama!* (Don't Worry, Mom!) was written by the popular Georgian writer Nodari Dumbadze, who had been officially assigned to write a book about the life of border guards. For this purpose Dumbadze lived in Sarpi for some time, or rather, in the military compound located at the coast. The book follows the life of one of the border guards, soldier Jakeli. Throughout the book, Jakeli repeatedly complains that life at the border is eventless and boring (Dumbadze 1986, 455, 542, 544, 616) and that during his two-year service in Sarpi not a single person has even attempted to cross the border (this changes at the end of the novel when the soldiers arrest a Russian youth who tries to escape to Turkey). In the novel, life in Sarpi is peaceful and harmonious. The villagers assist the soldiers by forecasting the weather and supply food and drinks to them (534–35), and friendships are established between the soldiers and villagers. The rosy descriptions converge in the main message of the novel, which is to present the border as a regrettable though necessary defense, as an accepted part of everyday life. Many villagers had read Dumbadze's novel and insisted that the descriptions were not very different from reality.[9] But the timing of this novel needs to be taken into consideration. It was written thirty years after the initial closure of the border. During those thirty years many things transpired to make the border as impervious and uncontested as it was. Dumbadze was clearly not allowed to write about the events—deportations, executions, and the loss of relatives across the border—that made the "peaceful" life of the 1960s possible.

Espionage, Executions, and Deportations

The Laz of Sarpi, like all Soviet citizens, were subjected to a series of harsh and often erratic policies and regulations that were justified as a part of "the building of socialism" and "protecting Soviet society from class enemies." During the first decades of the Soviet Union, a largely rural society with a mainly uneducated population was transformed into an industrial empire. Stalinist modernization was not simply "development" but class war fought against ever reappearing "enemies" of the Soviet state. This war resulted in the elimination of private traders, the deportation of kulaks or peasant "bourgeoisie," the prosecution of Trotskyites and other internal enemies of the Communist Party, and finally the deportation of "unreliable" ethnic groups.[10] State terror took on particularly erratic characteristics in Sarpi because the border dwellers were instrumental to the Soviet state, but they were also suspected by the authorities, because of their possible loyal feelings toward relatives in Turkey. This was especially true between the 1930s and 1950s, when the region

9. One villager remarked that the novel's only shortcoming was giving too much credit to the soldiers for defending the border, while in most cases it was the druzhina (civil patrol) that spotted and captured people illegally in the border zone.

10. Conquest (1970) is an early overview of the Soviet deportations of nationalities, but see also Nekrich (1978), Bugai and Gonov (1998), and Pohl (1999).

was still a contested area: the Soviet Union made claims on a large area in Turkey, while Turkey, although comparatively much weaker, still had pretensions of including Ajaria in its territory. The intelligence services of both countries were active across the border, and the people living in the border zone were caught between both powers.

In the early 1930s, an aged villager named Omer was arrested and imprisoned in Tbilisi. The man was known in Sarpi as a hard and honest worker. He was not exceptionally rich nor was there anything extraordinary about his background. The authorities did not provide a reason for his imprisonment nor did the man ever stand trial. But several months later Omer sent a letter home in which he ordered his son to sell the gold that they had buried underneath their house. A short time later Omer was released and returned home. He refused to explain what had taken place in prison. He spent the rest of his days gardening his small plot. Never again did he go to the gathering place of the old men, preferring to stay in the safe environment of his house and associating only with his closest relatives. This episode, as little information as it contains, marks the beginning of repression in Sarpi. The case of Omer was not exceptional. Around that time, the first disastrous effects of forced collectivization in Ukraine and parts of Russia became apparent, and the authorities took desperate measures to resolve the economic crisis.

Villagers and town dwellers alike were confronted with a government decree to sell all their jewelry and gold to the state. During the preceding decades most families in Sarpi had earned quite good money through their cross-border trading activities. Of course, most villagers preferred to hide their gold rather than exchange it for what they still considered worthless Soviet paper money.[11] Even when it became possible to exchange the gold for rare consumer goods, only a few families decided to do so.[12] Trust in the new Soviet state was still low and many reckoned that sooner or later they might have to leave their village, in which case they would need their savings. Many elderly villagers had already fled Sarpi twice—during the Russo-Turkish war in the 1870s and at the outbreak of World War I in 1914. The current crisis gave them cause to anticipate still another migration. The NKVD (predecessor to the KGB) turned out to have quite precise knowledge about the amounts of gold owned by each family, and it was prepared to confiscate these hidden valuables. One day, NKVD agents entered people's houses and gave them the choice of either revealing these hiding places or of being arrested. The fact that they knew exactly what could be found implies that several local residents

---

11. During his stay in Batumi in the early 1920s, Paustovsky (1969, 86) observed that most transactions were in Turkish lira because Soviet money was scarce and unpopular.

12. Between 1930 and 1936 Torgsin (a contraction of *torgovlia s inostrantsami* or "trade with foreigners") stores sold luxury goods in exchange for gold and silver, in an attempt to increase Soviet hard currency reserves for its industrial drive (Fitzpatrick 1999, 56).

worked as informants. Sarpi was certainly not exceptional in this; the reliance on networks of informants on each level of society was a main characteristic of the repressive system of those days.

By the mid-1930s, relations between Turkey and the Soviet Union—which had been relatively friendly during the 1920s and early 1930s—started to deteriorate.[13] The position of Sarpi within the Soviet Union was distinctly affected by these changing international relations, and the Laz got caught in the middle. Sarpi was virtually the only Laz village within the boundaries of the Soviet Union; most Laz lived in Turkey.[14] Most inhabitants of Sarpi had large family networks across the border, and they maintained intensive contacts with their kin when cross-border movements were still possible. For the Soviet authorities these relationships, and the fact that the Sarpians were Muslims, made it seem very likely that their real loyalties were with Turkey instead of the USSR.

Sarpi's border status made the situation even more complicated. Because most Laz were living in Turkey, the Soviet authorities came to see Sarpi as a bridgehead for their international aspirations. The Soviet Union still had ambitions to incorporate the provinces of Kars and Ardahan, which had been part of the Russian Empire between 1878 and the 1910s. As preparation for this ultimate goal, propaganda campaigns were developed that included the introduction of a Lazuri alphabet and the publication of several booklets in Lazuri.[15] Secret agents and carriers were ordered to distribute propaganda material in Turkish Lazistan.[16] For example, young men from Soviet Sarpi were approached by NKVD agents and requested to deliver packages or collect information from contacts across the border.

Especially in the late 1930s and during World War II, when food was scarce, the rewards for performing these tasks were tempting for many Sarpians. One man said, "I remember that my mother repeatedly asked my father why he could not go to the other side [as other men did], so that we would also have white bread on the table. But father always replied with the same words: 'Wife, you better eat black bread and sleep calmly in your bed, instead of eating theirs and regretting it later on.'" The villagers were certainly aware of the dangers involved in performing these tasks. As one old man told me, "There is such a rule, that if they send a spy, they will send a second one to check what

13. The strained relationship was initially a result of Turkey's improved relations with Europe and further deteriorated when Turkey signed a nonaggression pact with Germany in 1941.

14. The Turkish census of 1945 listed 47,000 people who declared to speak Lazuri (Andrews 2002, 176).

15. For an overview of Soviet representations of Laz and Mingrelian culture during the 1930s, see Feurstein (1992).

16. Soviet propaganda addressed at Turkish Laz was not confined to the 1920s and 1930s. Even in the 1970s, a weekly radio broadcast was transmitted in Lazuri. A former radio employee told me that they never received a response from abroad and consequently the broadcast was taken off the air after a few years.

the former is doing." But refusing was not all that simple, as the following story illustrates:

> At the time my father was still single. One day he was approached by two of these *chekisty* [agents].[17] They asked him to cross the border, but he refused, firmly stressing that he wasn't a spy and would never be one. Thereupon they put a gun to his head and repeated the demand. Father replied: "I don't have a wife or children, so shoot me if you want. You can force me to go, but remember that I will only go once and never return." Then the agents gave him a pat on the back; they told him he was a good man and let him go.

This example—whether or not it happened exactly as told—displays the pressure put on people and indicates the attitude toward those who actually went. People involved in these covert activities were often suspected of working simultaneously for the Turks. One tragic case vividly illustrates the dangers involved and the atmosphere along the border in those days. Five young men were sent to Turkey. They crossed the border by boat on a dark night and awaited a signal from the coast. When they finally saw the signal and answered by flashing back, Turkish soldiers opened fire on them. Four of the men died and were anonymously buried on Turkish soil. Although villagers on the Turkish side must have recognized these men, they probably denied it, fearing the negative repercussions. Only one of the men survived the attack, and with the assistance of relatives he made it back to Soviet Sarpi. The next day he was taken away by NKVD agents and was never heard from again.

In the 1930s and 1940s the Laz community of Sarpi was living on a highly contested border, caught between the two states in multiple ways. The origin of the deportations of families from Sarpi should be understood within this context. In the aftermath of World War II, the Communist Party leadership designed a strategy to both punish those who supposedly collaborated with the Germans and purge the Soviet border regions of so-called unreliable elements.[18] The difference between these repressions and those of earlier periods was that these measures were not directed against individuals but against whole groups. But whereas many of these groups were completely deported, only part of the Laz population was exiled to Siberia and Central Asia. The ambivalent attitude of Soviet authorities toward its outer border again helps us to understand this situation. On the one hand, the inhabitants of Sarpi were distrusted because they lived right on the border. On the other hand, sending

17. The term *chekist* stems from Cheka, an early name of the state security service in the Soviet Union.

18. In 1944 and 1945 numerous groups from the Caucasus and other parts of the Soviet Union were sent into exile, ostensibly because they had collaborated with the German enemy. Deported groups from the Georgian borderlands included the Pontian Greeks and Meskhetian Turks, along with Kurds, Hemshins, and Laz (Suny 1994, 289).

all of them away was undesirable, because this would give a negative impression to the Laz living across the border in Turkey.

The first deportation that struck the village took place during World War II. These measures were directed against the Kurds and Hemshins. Approximately eight Kurdish and Hemshin[19] families resided in Sarpi and the neighboring village Kvariati. They did not live in the village proper. During the winter they kept their sheep and cattle in a compound a few kilometers up in the hills, and during the summer they traveled to grazing areas in the mountains. Their seminomadic way of life might not have been acceptable to the Communist leadership—especially in the border region—because their movements and activities were difficult to control. The Kurds and Hemshins were accused of spying for the Turkish army. Their refusal to join the collective farm (since they were unwilling to give away their cattle) likely was also a factor in the decision of the Soviet leadership. The families were sent to eastern Kazakhstan. While the victims of later deportations were allowed to return to the village, the Kurds and Hemshins were never given the opportunity to return to their place of origin. After the opening of the border and the relaxation of Soviet politics in the late 1980s, several Hemshins visited Sarpi while on their way to Turkey. They told the villagers that too much time had passed to consider returning, that they had built up new lives elsewhere.

In 1949, the next uprooting took place. This time three Laz families were deported. In all three cases the deportation involved women who had kept their Turkish passports. They were born in Turkey but had married in Georgian Sarpi in the 1920s and 1930s when it was still possible to cross the border. Although they had moved to the Soviet Union and had married Soviet citizens, they officially remained citizens of Turkey. Several villagers mentioned that these women never changed their passports because they wished to retain the possibility of easily crossing the border should the border situation improve. Others maintained however that it was not possible for these women to change their passports into Soviet ones. Whatever the case, the result was that in 1949 these women still carried Turkish passports. Two families were deported as a whole, while in one instance the family was divided. The children were sent with their mother to the province of Tomsk in Siberia, while their father stayed behind in Sarpi. Living circumstances in Tomsk were harsh, as a villager remarked about the deportation of his aunt: "There was nothing over there, just forest and forest. They did not even have potatoes. We had to send all the food supplies from here just to help them survive." Of the fifteen people deported to Tomsk, six died. After seven years in Siberia, those who survived were finally allowed to return to Sarpi.

---

19. The Hemshin are a group of people of Armenian origin who converted to Islam in the eighteenth century and by and large adopted the Turkish language. They live predominantly in the mountains of the eastern Black Sea region.

Given these previous experiences, the largest deportations, those of 1951, did not come as a complete surprise. Villagers had been living in fear for more than a decade and several had prepared for the worst. During the weeks before the deportations, the NKVD had been checking the files and documents of collective-farm workers and individual villagers. One man told me that his father had prepared a box with essentials in case they were sent away. A former deportee told me that his mother had hidden gold coins in her underwear, which later helped them to survive. In this round of deportations ten (nuclear) families were exiled (roughly 8 percent of the village population). Although the experience was traumatic for all, their living conditions during exile varied. For example, Necat, who ended up in a collective farm in Kazakhstan, said he and his family sold homemade wine to other deportees and in this way managed to provide a basic living. Most deportees were less successful and suffered from impoverishment, exhaustion, and even starvation. Niaz Kakabadze, a survivor, said:

The soldiers came to our house and told us that we had to go with them. We were only given half an hour to pack our belongings. A truck was waiting in the village center to transport us straight to the Batumi train station. I remember that the train we boarded had large banners saying "Volunteers," implying that we had volunteered to cultivate the steppes of Central Asia. They put us in a wagon that was usually used for cattle—twenty-eight people were packed in together. On New Year's Day we went beyond the Ural Mountains. It was freezing cold. They only opened the door once a day so that you could go to the toilet. I didn't see it myself, but they told me that there was even a woman who gave birth. . . . Two weeks later we arrived in Kazakhstan. . . . The land was empty—steppe and mountains; many people died on the dry steppe. Our only luck was that at the time of deportation we had stored several sacks of grain at home [which they brought along] and that our neighbors gave what they had. It is only because of this that we managed to survive.

My sister and I had to start working right away. I was only thirteen years old at the time, but there was no other choice since my father was disabled. The collective farm specialized in cotton production. The laborers had to carry bags that weighed more than fifty kilograms. I helped them, but the pay was so low and irregular that we hardly had anything to eat. My sister picked cotton. She had experience working in the tea plantations so she knew how to do it. Soon thereafter I got a new job. They were looking for volunteers who would help behind the tractors. Although the work was very heavy, I told them that I would take the job and would work night and day. At least they paid in grain and cotton oil, which we could sell or trade. The collective farm consisted of huge stretches of land, which were more than a kilometer in length. When the fields were plowed I would walk behind the machine and lift up the plow at the end of the field. The tractor would turn and then it could be set down again. In one year I earned 515 working days.[20] I was

---

20. The term "working day" applies to a centrally stipulated amount of work. Workers could try to surpass this norm in order to earn more money or goods.

such a small boy, but I worked two shifts a day—two times the official norm. Of course by the end I was little more than skin and bones. . . . We lived this way for almost two years. During that period we heard rumors that Stalin had died. Finally, in November, we were summoned to go to Tashkent. The government acknowledged that our deportation had been a mistake and we were officially repatriated. Once again we were put in wagons. It took fifteen days by train. We returned to Sarpi just before winter set in.

Between 1953 and 1957 all Laz who had been deported returned to the village. The political climate had changed after the death of Stalin in 1953 and with the rise of the new leader, Nikita Khrushchev. For once the border had a positive influence. Because Sarpi was located in the restricted border zone, the authorities did not resettle other families in Sarpi. It therefore remained the compact community it had been before the deportations. The houses left behind by the deportees were, in most cases, taken care of by relatives and could be reoccupied on their return. This does not mean that the return of the deportees was devoid of tensions, however. Emine, who at the age of thirty was deported with her only daughter to Siberia, recalls: "When we left, we had a large house near the border, but my relatives decided to tear it down. They sold the parts in order to buy goods to send to Siberia. So when we came back, we had nothing left. My son-in-law built a small house, actually more like a stable, in which we lived during the next thirty years." Nugzar, who returned as a child from exile, told me that he often felt that he was looked upon differently. The other children would make jokes about these "enemies of the state." Necat Dolidze remembered: "They didn't tell us anything—why we were sent away, what we had done wrong—nothing. Everyone thought that we were *kontrabandisty* [smugglers]." And with a laugh he added, *"Then* we didn't smuggle, but now we do." However, such tensions are minor ones in comparison to the difficulties experienced by returnees elsewhere (see Adler 1999, 10–16). The relative ease with which returnees reintegrated in Sarpi may be due to the village's small size and the density of kinship networks, which prevented people from being excluded from social life.

Evidence indicates that the border zone in which Sarpi was located was an unfortunate site where state repression met changing international relations. In hindsight, it is clear that the deportations were part of attempts to pacify the border zone by removing "unreliable elements." This "cleansing" of the border took place within a context in which information was highly constrained, where lifestyles that could not be fully controlled were perceived as dangerous by the state. The authorities on each administrative level attempted to protect themselves from accusations that could be leveled by nearly anyone about nearly everything. To counter this amorphous threat they attempted to gain full control over the situation. These characteristics of the Soviet system had often bizarre and unpredictable effects, especially along the contested border of the USSR and Turkey. The bifurcated attitude of Soviet authorities toward the border—embracing the potential for expansion and fearing possible foreign infiltration—made the outcome complicated, erratic, and at times, perilous.

Remembering and Forgetting

The Laz are hardly mentioned in the literature on the Soviet deportations.[21] The numbers of Laz deportees are small in comparison to other groups, and only part of the ethnic group was deported. Moreover, all Laz deportees from Sarpi returned shortly after Stalin's death and subsequently received official rehabilitation.[22] Nevertheless, the deportations had a strong impact on villagers' lives. Thus it is not surprising that the deportations continued to be a hotly debated topic when I visited Sarpi many years later. The ambiguities and questions that continued to trouble those who were sent to Central Asia in 1951 are exemplified in a story told by Niaz:

> Nobody really had a clue about the reasons for our deportation, and of course we immediately started writing and asking for explanations. We were certain that a mistake had been made or that there was some sort of misunderstanding. Only once did we receive an answer from Moscow. An official representing Stalin wrote that our exile had been according to the rules and that no mistake had been made. Our relatives also sent letters asking for clarification, stressing the possibility of error. We just couldn't believe it. Mother had received the award Mother Hero [awarded to women with five or more children] and my sister had a Lenin medal. My father was a very trustworthy person; he put the first pillar in the soil when the fence was constructed along the border. He worked on the collective farm and everything was built on his back. He got a medal for his work! First they gave him a medal, and then afterward. . . . There is no one who knows exactly why this has happened. I don't know, some people in the village received money and goods in exchange for certain information. . . . Perhaps they were afraid to lose this [source of] income. Maybe that is why they provided false information about us.

The issue that pervades this account is the simple question *why*? Why was it decided that ordinary villagers should be exiled to Central Asia? Why were certain people deported, while others were allowed to stay behind? The questions show the bewilderment of former deportees who could not comprehend why they were treated in such a manner. Moreover, they show the continued importance of creating meaningful and livable pasts from contradictory experiences and memories.

21. The Laz are not even mentioned in an overview of the Soviet deportations (Pohl 1999), which otherwise includes a section on Meskhetian Turks, Kurds, and Hemshins.

22. The fate of Soviet Laz elsewhere was different. Those living in Anakli (a town eighty kilometers north of Batumi) were never deported, whereas Laz from various villages in Abkhazia were sent to Siberia in 1944, where they lived for about ten years. In the 1990s, when war erupted in Abkhazia, many decided to leave their villages to settle permanently in Turkey.

Purifying the System

Everyone in Sarpi knew what tragedy had befallen which family, who had been deported to Central Asia or Siberia, and who had lost relatives as a result of state terror. When they discussed the reasons for the deportation they not only recalled the fates of specific people but also evaluated the nature of the Soviet state. The important question was the extent to which purges and deportations were understood as inherent characteristics of Soviet Communism. Perhaps they were simply unintended side effects of a basically just system? The nature of the responses and stories varied according to a person's age, as well as by the social distance between narrator and victim, between those who had lost close relatives and those who had remained relatively unaffected by the events of the period from the 1930s to the 1950s.

The remarks of middle-aged villagers—those who had not directly witnessed the tragedies of the Stalinist period—often displayed a certain detachment. My host father, born in 1938, was routinely critical of "the Communists," but at the same time he defended their behavior by saying that if you wish to build an empire you cannot expect to do it without force. He frequently fell back on the geopolitical location of Sarpi: "This was a cold war border, where the Warsaw Pact opposed NATO, so what do you expect?" He had come of age during the 1950s and 1960s and had no close relatives who had been deported, so he was able to keep a distance from the tragedies. For him it was out of the question to denounce all the benefits of socialism. He told me once: "Right now it is fashionable to criticize the Communists, but one thing I know, there *were* Trotskyites, and they *really* tried to take over the government." Like my host father, others of his generation maintained a positive view of the Soviet period and would say that life was good then. If only the border hadn't been here, it would even have been better.

Such detachment was more difficult for elderly villagers. Osman Narakidze, a retired physician, witnessed the deportation of his older sister to Siberia. He told me, right before he abruptly decided to change the subject: "All the neighbors are guilty, they simply betrayed one another, but nobody knows why." Another accused the "dictatorlike" chairman of the collective farm (a Laz from Sarpi), who was in office during the Stalinist era, of being responsible for the deportations: "Instead of protecting our village, he told them [NKVD officers] that he did not trust us—that he could not guarantee the loyalty of everyone in the village." These short statements displayed a tendency to seek the origins of the deportations on the local level, thus implying that the Communist system was inherently just.

Even former deportees tended to explain the deportations as mistakes or as the result of the evil intentions of local power holders, and only rarely as an inherent aspect of the Soviet system or as one small instance of many such deportations of ethnic groups. For an outsider, it is difficult to understand why several villagers remained devoted Communists, despite having experienced the effects of forced collectivization, the purges of the 1930s, and the deportations of their relatives.[23] This attitude is easier to understand when taking into account the diffusion of Soviet ideology and state control over information. But what may be more important is that people had to go along with the system in order to continue their lives and to establish careers for themselves and their children. As a result, the stories of elderly villagers often shuttled between positive memories about the stability offered by the Soviet system and the negative memories of deportation and execution. These shifts reveal the difficulty of creating meaningful pasts from a history that has known so many extremes.

My most vivid encounter with this deep ambivalence took place when I visited Murman Bakradze, chairman of the *kolkhoz* in the 1960s who was typified by others as a real Communist ("but a good one," some would add). What struck me immediately when I entered his house was a picture of Stalin in the prime of his life hanging opposite the doorway. We were drinking coffee at the table when the conversation turned to the deportations. Murman exclaimed: "That is the only feature of Communism I can never forgive. How could they send away those poor people? My own sister-in-law died in Siberia. She was the most honest person I knew in my whole life. What could she have done? She could barely read. She had only finished four years of school." Murman then reached for a mandarin orange, remained silent while peeling it, and then, as if he had forgotten the whole issue, started pondering the life he had lost:

> At that time [the Stalinist era] everyone worked on the collective farm. People were honest; it was unthinkable that someone would take even one kopeck as a bribe. Everyone contributed and that is why we prospered. Look at what we have now. The tea plantations have turned into forest, no one buys our fruits, and we do nothing about it. Then we lived well, we had a life. Now, we merely exist.

Besides displaying his felt ambiguity toward the Soviet past, Murman's shifts in narrative showed the cynical turn that recent history has taken. One aspect of the tragedies that befell the villagers in Sarpi was that a whole generation lived their lives under a repressive system, only to find out later that the new "freedom" implied new uncertainties including economic hardship, widespread corruption, and political chaos. As Aman remarked, "Now we don't have such a [harsh] regime anymore, but without money, where do you go? These are difficult times." The Soviet legacy left traces on all spheres of social life and engendered complex patterns of remembering and forgetting. In a way, the past gained new meanings when the frame of reference to which memories and "dis-memories" were attached—that is, the Soviet state—disappeared. Basic ambiguities about Soviet repression returned with renewed force.

23. See also Adler (1999, 16) and Nekrich (1978, 128, 142).

Purifying the Self

Why were certain people sent away while others were allowed to stay? Because most inhabitants of Sarpi were related to one another in multiple ways, people were often hesitant to speak openly about this issue. When I made inquiries about those deported, my acquaintances usually answered by reconfirming the integrity of the victims, emphasizing that they had been ordinary *kolkhozniki* (peasants), far from the life of politics.

This insistence on innocence made sense during the Soviet period. During the years after the deportations, people were required to forget about what had happened to their families. Former deportees sent endless petitions to Moscow—ritual acts of purification to regain their rights as full citizens. But even after the authorities had granted rehabilitation, denial was often the best way to avoid being stigmatized. For Sarpi residents it was usually safer to deny having relatives across the border and, if at all possible, to hide that a relative had once been classified an enemy at all. As several residents pointed out to me, the executions and deportations were never discussed in public, and even at home these topics were seldom brought up openly.

It might have been expected that the political changes of the 1990s would have replaced the need to forget with the need to remember. With the disappearance of the Soviet state there were fewer repercussions to be feared for talking about "Soviet history." But this did not imply that people could remember "freely." Indeed, the decline of shared knowledge concerning "how it used to be" provided new reasons for forgetting certain aspects even more. Claims of the "such was life" genre no longer sufficed since there were fewer people around who had experienced socialism, let alone Stalinism. Moreover, because the local media, the intelligentsia, and the political elite increasingly dismissed Communist rule as an alien, oppressive, and totalitarian implant, there was a strong need to redefine one's own positions vis-à-vis that Communist past. This resulted in new dilemmas of remembering and forgetting, especially concerning personal involvement in the socialist regime. Two stories show these dilemmas with a telling clarity.

Gulnazi and her husband Hasan lived in a house located ten meters from the fences separating Georgia from Turkey. The house had a special history of which I was unaware when I interviewed the couple for the first time. I asked them about their experiences living on the border during the Stalinist era. The discussion that ensued between husband and wife typified how the period of repression was remembered, as well as avoided, in speech.

HASAN: We led our lives, the same way as we do now. Of course then you had to conform to the rules, but that is normal when you live next to the border.

GULNAZI [in strong disagreement]: Of course it was terrible then, life is much easier now. You know, we had this window [facing Turkey] right there, where you see that wall. When Stalin was alive . . . I tell you one thing. I don't like Stalin. They may kill me for it, but I say that I despise him. I am not afraid of anything. . . . We had this window, and every night we had to nail a black piece of cloth in front of it, before we could turn on the light. If you hadn't done it correctly, they would come and knock on your door immediately, shouting "Fast! Turn off the lamp. Light is escaping!" What was the problem, I ask you? Let the light shine, what is so bad about that!

HASAN: It was war at the time.

GULNAZI [again in strong disagreement]: No! There was no war at all. Their brains didn't function. Those people weren't capable of thinking . . . pff. In Turkey people live just like me. My cousins live there. What harm would they do to me? Now that they opened the border, now that the soldiers who used to march here have gone, everything has remained quiet. Nobody ran away. So what was the problem during Stalin's era!?

In the weeks after this interview I collected more stories about the Stalinist era, and one recurring element was the windows that needed to be covered. I started to see these windows as powerful symbols of the fear that characterized the period. But it was only after I had interviewed Gulnazi's mother, Nurie, that I began to understand what the darkened windows referred to in a more literal sense.

I was nineteen years old at the time. Our [only] daughter [Gulnazi] was just one year old. She was in bad health, because there was hardly any food back then. One night she was very ill. She was crying in bed and I asked my husband [Osman] to see what the matter was. With a match he lit the lamp and he looked in the baby's bed. It turned out that she was crying in her sleep. So he let her sleep and turned the lamp on low. Not much later we suddenly heard [our baby] scream. I jumped out of bed and turned on the light. Then, maybe one minute later, soldiers rushed into the room. Without explanation they took Osman away. They thought he was signaling to the Turkish side. They took him and shot him. Only years later they discovered their mistake and they then wrote a document that said that it was very unfortunate that Osman had been shot.

This short text was an important element in Nurie's stories. On various occasions she referred to the lamp that "changed her life." The events had left her in poverty as the widowed mother of a child in difficult times. But the lamp was also a flashpoint for the community as it collected its own understandings of these years. My host father, Anzor, especially had strong doubts:

I know that story, but I don't think that the lamp had anything to do with it. You know, Osman [Gulnazi's father] used to perform activities for the KGB [actually NKVD]. I don't know exactly what he did, but in his household they always had white bread. And he had been in Turkey during the weeks before he was killed. Just to deliver a message or something. But as I told you before, the KGB never trusted its employees and always had them followed. Osman was seen with a Turkish officer in a teahouse. And you know why I especially think that the story isn't correct?

Once I overheard Nurie say to a friend of hers: "Oh! If only he hadn't gone that time, if only he had said no."

Regardless of what the exact events were that led to Osman's execution, it is clear that the stories pointed not only to a period of repression but also to the ill-fated actions that the inhabitants of Sarpi were driven to. Sarpians tried to find ways out of the situation. Whether it was by accepting small assignments from the NKVD, by keeping one's Turkish passport, or by retreating from social life, everyone tried in his or her way to deal with the larger powers. The tragedy was that many, through their attempts, ended up more deeply entrenched in the webs spun by the omnipresent state. Everyone was in his or her own way both victim *and* collaborator. As mentioned earlier, the power of the "totalitarian state" lay largely in its dialectical interplay between above and below. The webs of interdependence, indeed the daily interaction between villagers and state representatives, were crucial in the formation of the specific border regime in Sarpi (see also Berdahl 1999, 64).

It is exactly this interplay and the resulting feeling of complicity that had become impossible to express. The story of the lamp liberated those involved from the burden of "guilt." It silenced the ever returning thought, "*If only I had acted differently. . . .* " In the story people were being killed because they lit a lamp for a sick and innocent baby. The story aimed to convince the audience that the terror took random victims; it aimed to prove the arbitrariness and irrationality of Soviet state terror. But although the whimsical and unpredictable actions of the Soviet state structures cannot and should not be denied, it is important to look at the internal logic of the border regime. People were sucked into the logic of this regime, not as passive victims but through their attempts to survive. It is that two-sidedness—of border dwellers used and mistrusted, of victimhood and complicity—that is an underrepresented aspect of the tragedies of that period.

Time and the Border

At this point we may recall the large billboard in the center of Sarpi, showing the faces of a Soviet soldier, a civilian, and a child under the text "The entire Soviet nation guards the border!" In one sense the billboard referred to the practical tasks that villagers had to perform in border maintenance and defense. It referred to the activities of schoolchildren who would assist soldiers in clearing twigs and leaves from the strip of land along the fences and who helped rake the ground after rainfall so that footsteps would be visible. It also referred to the substantial number of male inhabitants of Sarpi who were members of the *druzhina*, a kind of civil guard that helped patrol the border and reportedly caught more potential refugees than the soldiers.

But the image and text on the billboard also seem to refer to another, much harsher, aspect of "united defense." Villagers defended or rather "fixed" the border through their actions. Sometimes these actions were intentional, as in the case of the man who prided himself on having caught three Russians try-ing to escape while a member of the druzhina. At other times they were per-formed unwittingly, when attempts to beat the system ended up strengthening it instead. If we look back at the deportations, it may be obvious that villagers were never a real threat to state security. Nevertheless, it is also clear that it was not simple randomness that influenced executions and deportations. As we have seen in the preceding pages, some villagers were involved in espionage activities and carried out services for the NKVD. Some were involved in smug-gling during the first seventeen years of Soviet rule, while still others decided to retain their Turkish passports to be able to cross the border at a later stage. What they did not (and could not) realize at the time was that the Soviet sys-tem was organized in such a way that each of these tacit strategies actually en-tangled them in the system even further. This made them even more vulner-able targets of the erratic decisions of Soviet authorities.

The billboard was removed shortly after the Soviet collapse. Perhaps, along with it, one type of memory was disappearing—the memory of complicity. It was gradually replaced by memories of unambiguous victimhood. Such mem-ories of victimhood were instrumental in attempts to "overcome" the Soviet past. These new memories revealed an image of the Soviet past that had been silent for decades. But although these memories opened up the potential for new imaginations, they also served to silence earlier interpretations. Merridale observes in her book about death and memory in the Soviet Union that "the rediscovery of one kind of 'real' story obscures another 'real' story, which is the process of accommodation" (2001, 175). In Sarpi, the new memories of victimhood tended to obscure the "deafening silence" of earlier memories, in-dicating how deeply residents were implicated in upholding the border re-gime.

For fifty years, Sarpi was the place where two worlds touched but did not meet. The mechanisms that created and sustained this close separation were so pervasive that they determined not only freedom of movement but also people's understanding of nation and state. This was especially true for the generations who had grown up with an impermeable border, seen as the invi-olable limits of their social world. As a middle-aged man told me, "We were born here; we didn't even feel the presence of the border." These "eternal" qualities of the physical divide encourage us to step away from the literal bor-derline and to examine how everyday life continued on the Georgian side.

2 Mobilizing Cultural Stuff with Boundaries

During a wedding celebration in Sarpi in 1999, several young men guided me into the basement of an affluent villager's house, which contained a kind of small private exhibition featuring a boat, fishing gear, and other items. As I admired this homespun museum they explained that they were all crafted in an original Laz style, preserved over many centuries. The boat owner emphasized that the Laz had once been extraordinary sailors. He traced this tradition back to the Greek legend of Jason and the Argonauts, who had traveled to the Colchis kingdom. This comment reflected local opinion that the Colchis kingdom had been located along the eastern Black Sea coast and that the Laz were among its foremost descendents. When we left the basement, one of the men, a Sarpi journalist who had recently moved to Batumi, asked what I was looking for in my research. I told him that I was interested in the recent history of the village and that I was considering extending my research by adding a comparative case study of upper Ajaria. With the affirming nods of his friends present he stressed that such a research design was bound to fail. In his view, I would completely miss the point if I did not investigate the cultural and historical roots of the very artifacts they had just shown to me. Instead of going to upper Ajaria, he continued, I should go to the Georgian capital, Tbilisi. There I could study ancient Georgian history in order to find the true origins of Laz culture: "If it is your aim to understand people, you need to understand where they come from and where their history started. Now you are only looking at the last hundred years, but a large part of our culture had already been lost by that time."

The journalist's comments revealed several notions that were common to local discussions about what it meant to be Laz. First, the journalist stressed the historical unity of Laz and Georgians, while simultaneously commenting on the unique and distinguishing features of the Laz as an ethnic group. Second, he phrased his dissatisfaction with my approach in terms of the "cultural loss" that resulted from (Soviet) modernization. At the same time, the multiple references to unique Laz artifacts and traditions suggested that their "culture" was anything but lost. The discourse of cultural loss was a central element in local constructions of ethnic identity and was tightly entwined with a view of ethnicity as deeply primordial.[1] Moreover, this understanding was based on the idea that ethnic distinctions should be measured on the basis of a strictly defined list of "cultural stuff."

Preoccupation with "the past" and with "cultural stuff" runs so deeply among the Laz of Sarpi that they have genealogies of their own. Thus, in order to understand the implications of the category "Laz" we need to explore these genealogies. In a response to Barth's famous statement that the "critical focus becomes the ethnic *boundary* that defines the group, not the cultural stuff that it encloses" (1969, 15, emphasis in original), Handelman (1977, 190) wrote that the "categorical corporate holdings of culture," far from being irrelevant, specify "a corporate history in time and space."[2] This history explains how this category has become so substantial and, in the eyes of so many, legitimate, providing group members with a social biography, connecting culture and behavior, past to present. Objectifying culture strengthens the connection between past and present even further, making cultural stuff an important tool in expressing ideas of sameness and difference in a changing world.

What makes the Sarpi case particularly interesting is that prevailing "ethnic" boundaries did not have matching historical referents. Instead, the "ethnic" boundaries between the Laz of Sarpi and its neighbors (both Turkish Laz and Ajarians) were recent products that demanded explanation. "Ethnic" and other differences emerged in response to the presence of the iron curtain and were highly dependent on the mobilization of cultural stuff, both by Soviet elites and, more important, by the residents of Sarpi themselves. It was not that the rhetoric of the Soviet state was simply accepted. On the contrary, the Soviet period was perceived as conducive to cultural loss. The most intriguing aspect is how Soviet rule "corrupted" certain cultural elements and how these "corruptions" were, in the wake of postsocialist destabilization, used for the construction of a perceived authentic Laz culture. In other words, ideas of cultural loss and cultural primordialism were intimately interwoven with the social transformation of Soviet Sarpi, developing in response to the presence of

---

1. Local primordialism tends to be dependent on ideas of cultural loss, as this "loss" allows for unambiguous projections of culture into an indefinite past (Grant 1995, 13–16).

2. Concerning the juxtaposition of cultural content versus boundary Jenkins wrote that Barth's (1969) argument might "be construed as suggesting that the cultural stuff out of which that differentiation is arbitrarily socially constructed is somehow irrelevant, and this surely cannot be true" (1997, 107). Barth wrote later that "the issue of cultural content *versus* boundary, as it was formulated, unintentionally served to mislead" and added that "to grasp what a particular ethnic identity is about, the anthropologist must attend to the *experiences* through which it is formed" (1994, 14–17, emphasis in original).

an impermeable border. My main argument, in a twist on Barth's idea, is that precisely because these boundaries were not based on long-established differences, the mobilization of cultural stuff proved crucial. Even if it is the boundary that defines the group, it is the mobilization of culture on that boundary that creates the defense.

Soviet Trajectories

When the border was established in 1921, the Soviet side of Sarpi consisted of some forty houses. At that time most inhabitants lived off fishing and cargo transport, supplemented by small-scale crop cultivation (mostly corn, beans, and rice) and limited livestock breeding.[3] Economic opportunities varied with the dynamics of the nearby port city of Batumi, with construction works initiated by the tsarist government and changes in the location of the Russo-Ottoman border.[4] The Russo-Turkish wars of the late nineteenth and early twentieth centuries caused patterns of emigration and remigration that not only uprooted local society but also deepened its interdependence with the coastal regions northeast and west.

These dynamics were radically altered with the imposition of Soviet rule. The installation and fortification of the international border, the collectivization of agriculture, and the newly introduced social and political arrangements set new frames for local life, greatly affecting the position of villagers in the wider society. To understand this, it is useful to start by outlining the histories of some of Sarpi's families. The two families described below represent distinct though overlapping ways of dealing with the Soviet state. The Abuladzes were at the lower end of Soviet society; they worked as kolkhozniki and manual laborers, while simultaneously exploiting the malfunctions of the planned economy. The Memishishis, on the other hand, were deeply involved with state institutions. Their life courses went, so to speak, through the door of the state bureaucracy.

Abduloghli/Abdulishi/Abuladze

Osman Abduloghli settled in Sarpi around 1880. He arrived from Hopa, a town across the state border. As the story goes, Ottoman authorities had demanded he fight against the Russians, but he deserted and fled his hometown because "those Russians included Georgians and Laz." He intended to return to Hopa after the war, but because he was a smith and a carpenter the old men of Sarpi didn't want him to leave. "The village needed his skills so they

---

3. Elderly villagers reported that their grandfathers regularly made trading trips to Sukhumi and Trabzon and, when economic circumstances forced them, traveled as far as Istanbul and the Danube Delta.

4. For example, between 1912 and 1915 the Russians started building a road and a railway, which were part of the expansionist dream of Tsar Nicholas to construct transport routes all around the Black Sea. Several villagers were employed in its construction and received payments in "gold rubles."

arranged for him to marry here." Osman married into a relatively well-off family, which had three daughters but no sons.

Compared to other large family groups, the Abduloghlis formed a small extended family in Sarpi. Six large houses were associated with them, four of which were in the *duze*—a small and relatively flat plateau centrally located in the village. The remaining two houses were further uphill, behind the cemetery. Members of the six houses maintained close contact; they frequently visited one another, helped with household activities, and cooperated in various economic undertakings. Until the early 1990s they exchanged yearly visits with family members who had moved to Abkhazia and Ukraine, but geopolitical changes increasingly confined them to the village.

Generation I   Osman's four sons and two daughters all married within the community, thus firmly integrating the family in local social networks. Reportedly, Osman never taught his children to be smiths and carpenters. Instead, the sea became the main source of income for the second generation. The family owned a small boat that two of Osman's sons and several of the oldest grandchildren used for transporting cargo between Hopa and Batumi, and, during the season, for catching fish, which they sold in the markets of Batumi. According to one of Osman's grandsons, the family "knew that there was no future for fishing and that soon they would confiscate all boats, so we sold ours in 1932."[5] The family members joined the collective farm, but not all at once. Following a common strategy in the village, only one member of the family entered, at least initially. This enabled them to continue their previous occupations while simultaneously obtaining access to new resources provided by the state. Moreover, "it was still considered scandalous to enter the kolkhoz and only a few did so. But within a few years people became convinced that it was the best way. Then the payments became better. Not much later everyone entered the kolkhoz."[6]

Standards of living in Sarpi worsened during World War II. Villagers did not receive payments for their work in the collective farm but were obliged to make unpaid deliveries of agricultural produce to the front instead. Whereas elsewhere in Ajaria villagers were temporarily allowed to cultivate corn and potatoes for their survival, in Sarpi the collective was forced to grow tea and citrus fruits in order to give the enemy across the border the impression that life went on as usual. Three of Osman's sons moved to the neighboring village of Gonio to work in the sovkhoz (state farm): "People were starving here, so they went to the sovkhoz where they were fed by the government." After the war two sons moved back to the parental home while the oldest son settled

5. Villagers were initially allowed to keep their boats and fishing gear and continue semi-independent activities as members of the Sarpi fishing brigade. However, in 1938 the remaining fishers were forced to sell their boats and enter the collective fishery named Krasnyi rybak (Red Fisher) in Batumi.

6. The collective farm had seventeen members in 1932, sixty-five in 1936, and two hundred in 1970 (Bakradze 1971, 33).

permanently in Gonio. The difficulties of the times prevented the remaining sons from building separate houses, so that by the late 1940s twenty-four people were crowded in the family home.

By that time Osman's third son Ali had been married for twenty years. His wife, Padime Hojaoghli, who was born in Turkish Sarpi, had received a Soviet passport. Perhaps because of that she escaped deportation to Siberia in 1949. In his youth Ali had received three years of religious education and provided basic religious services in the village during the 1930s. Padime's background and Ali's former activities were incriminating facts at the time, and understandably they tried to keep a low profile. They both worked on the cattle farm in the hills behind the village. The tending and milking of cows paid poorly, but it involved little contact with authorities. Attempts to keep a low profile were also visible in the new surname they adopted. In the late 1940s it was expected that families would reject their "Turkish" surnames, so Padime and Ali changed their name from Abduloghli to Abuladze, while Ali's brothers chose Abdulishi. The differences are significant. "Abdulishi" stayed closer to the root and has a Lazuri ending ("-shi" means "of"), while "Abuladze" drew less attention as it used the Georgian ending "-dze." As one of their children explained, "My parents were afraid of raising suspicion, and Abuladze is such a common name—no one would think anything of it."

Generation II   Ali and his family built a new house in 1954 when, for the first time, villagers were able to receive long-term credit. Not long after the family (including their two married sons with children) occupied the new house in the upper part of the village plans were made to build another house for one of the sons.[7] Ideally, the younger son, Aman, would have stayed in the parental home, but his older brother, Hasan, died in 1957, leaving behind a wife and three children. The family decided that Aman would be the one to leave the parental home while widow and children remained. They began construction of a house in the mid-1960s when the family had accumulated enough capital. Aman and his wife Ferie worked in various positions on the kolkhoz, taking jobs as tea pickers, tractor drivers, and construction workers. Most important, they took good care of their private plot of mandarin trees. "Private work" was always crucial to the family. Through his job on the kolkhoz, Aman had regular access to construction materials, enabling him to build his own house and to take up lucrative construction jobs on the homes of relatives and acquaintances.

Other important "private" endeavors were Aman's trading trips to Ukraine. Every year Aman and one of his cousins bought up their relatives' "surplus" citrus harvest, that is, the part of the harvest that exceeded the plan and did not have to be sold to the state. They sent their load by ship to Odessa

---

7. Ali and Padime's four daughters had already left the house. Two married into villages around Batumi, while the other two married Sarpians.

and then took an airplane to meet it. In Odessa they relied on the networks of a male cousin who had settled in the Ukrainian SSR. With his cousins, Aman would transport the citrus fruit further to cities in Russia or Ukraine. Such trading trips could raise as much as six thousand rubles or a third of the cost of building a house. In comparison, in the 1970s the average annual pay of collective farmers in the USSR was around twelve hundred rubles. Within twenty years Aman had moved from his grandparents' house to that of his parents and then to his own, which he also managed to furnish.[8] Aman frequently expressed favorable memories about life during the Soviet period. More than once he told me that they were much better off than their relatives across the border, and he took pride in the fact that their relatively small kolkhoz had been the first to be declared a "millionaire" in the Ajarian ASSR. "It is fashionable these days to criticize the Communists, but when you look at it we actually lived very well," he said. "Now we get a twelve ruble [actually Georgian lari] pension, and even that they won't give to us; we haven't received anything during the last months."

Generation III   The three children of Aman and Ferie grew up in the 1970s and 1980s. Jemal, the older son, moved to Batumi where he took up a job in the machine-making factory. Their other son, Kakha, briefly worked on the kolkhoz as a truck driver. Asiko, their only daughter, was still in school when the opening of the border and the breakup of the Soviet Union radically changed life in Sarpi.

Kakha, born in 1969, abandoned his work at the kolkhoz for a job at the customs office in 1990, where he made a lot of money. He remembered with some regret: "As you see, nothing of it is left. I think it was all prearranged: I mean, they encouraged us to put all our money in the bank and then they stole it." He lost his job when the Ajarian authorities reorganized the customs service. Since then he had been working as a driver of his cousin's minibus taxi service, but profits were low. He remembered the stability of old times but equally dismissed the idea that there would be a return: "You know what it is? We don't need Communists to tell us how to live. We are Laz; we have been sailors and traders throughout history. But the thing is that the Mafia is disturbing everything." The experiences of his brother and sister were not that much different. Asiko had worked in a kiosk near the border gate, selling cigarettes and drinks, since 1992. When the kiosks were replaced with a new shopping center in 1998, Asiko obtained a job in one of the stores and received a fixed wage. Within a year, however, she lost her job because the store went out of business.

Jemal, Kakha, and Asiko all lived in their parents' home in the late 1990s. Jemal earlier had settled in Batumi after he married a girl of Azeri-Russian

---

8. Due to shortages and waiting lists it was often even more difficult to furnish a house than to build one.

background. They made a good living for a while by importing and reselling goods from Turkey. Their initial success depended in part on Kakha's job at the customs office, which enabled them to circumvent some of the costs of cross-border trade. However, trading opportunities dwindled when Kakha lost his job. Jemal decided to move back to the village with his family. Although the golden days of cross-border trade had ended in Sarpi as well, there they could fall back on their social networks for additional economic support.

Memishoghli/Memishishi

When I started to gather information about the Memishishoghli family Anzor pulled out a handwritten genealogy from a drawer, illustrating the genealogical links between all male family members. The existence of this genealogy already suggested the importance of descent for notions of belonging in Sarpi. The genealogy went back to a certain Memish who was born around 1800. According to Anzor, my research would be a success if I dug deeper to trace earlier forefathers. "The tragedy is that the old men who knew about our history have died," he explained. Knowledge about family origins was also important when we discussed the various surnames of his family group. Anzor's own surname was Memishishi, the Laz equivalent of the "Turkish" name Memishoghli ("child of Memish"). "What our real name is we don't know; some of my uncles thought that the original name was Dolidze so they have adopted that name." Another branch of the family adopted the name Lazishvili, meaning "child of Laz" in Georgian, which sounded like a perfect blending of Georgian and Laz identity, though no one knew exactly why that name was chosen. According to Anzor, the origins of Memish were uncertain: "There is a rumor that the Memishishis descended from the Greeks. I can't tell you if it is true, but anyway we don't mind—at least the Greeks have an old civilization." He made this remark during a dinner with his friend Zurabi Vanilishi, jokingly adding about his friend's family: "They say that the Vanilishis descended from the Kurds; that is why they are so interested in history. They work very hard to disprove that. They don't want to be Kurds, you see."

Generation I   Anzor's father, Muhammad Memishishi, later called Mamia, was born in 1908 in one of the largest houses in Sarpi. He lived there with his parents and paternal uncles' families. After having finished school in Sarpi and in Gonio, Mamia and four other young Laz were sent to study at the Institute of Minorities in Leningrad. This institute was established to promote Communist cadres among minority groups that were underrepresented in local Communist parties. On his return in the 1930s, Mamia and his family were able to move to their own house. "It was even in the newspaper when my father built his new house," said his daughter Heva. "Everyone had to be in the picture: Mom, Dad, the children. The article said something like 'Kolkhoz workers build new houses.'" Mamia worked in the district (*raion*) administration, was subsequently appointed chairman of the village council, and later made director of the kolkhoz. Mamia was still remembered for the iron grip with which he ruled the village between 1943 and 1952. He was not thought of favorably, and some elderly inhabitants continued to blame his descendents for his purported assistance in the deportation of Sarpians, something vehemently disputed by the Memishishis. However, since the 1950s the family had not played a significant role in the kolkhoz or other village-level organizations. Instead, Mamia's children predominantly chose careers elsewhere.

Generation II   Mamia had five daughters and two sons. The two sons received higher education and both they and their oldest sister left the village for extended periods. Two of the three, Anzor and his sister Heva, had returned to the village in recent years.

Heva finished school in Sarpi and then worked in the kolkhoz as a tea picker. She remembers always being certain that she would leave the village. So she did, after having married—against her parents' wishes—an Uzbek army officer who served at the border. The couple lived for several years in a military compound in upper Ajaria. They were later transferred to Batumi, where they lived for twelve years. She recalled, "Then, without consulting me [my husband] wrote to Moscow that he wished to be transferred to Uzbekistan. I didn't want to go there, but I ended up in Tashkent anyway." Difficulties with her husband and in-laws, as well as her unwillingness to adapt to what she called "their Asian way of life," led to her divorce. "I told him that I would take my daughter with me. We divorced without many words, just like that." Heva and her daughter Natasha made their way back to Georgia and settled in Batumi, where Heva became director of a kindergarten. Natasha married not long after she entered Tbilisi University and settled, without completing her studies, in a town near the capital. Heva's son, who had already entered the university in Tashkent when she returned to Georgia, became a successful businessman.

Anzor, ten years younger than Heva, married a girl from Sarpi, Maguli. Both studied in Batumi. She became a nurse and he finished the pedagogical institute. At that time, in the 1960s, there was renewed interest in the ethnic, and especially linguistic, background of the Laz. Anzor, together with another young man from Sarpi, was invited to study at the university in Tbilisi. After graduating, Anzor worked for about fifteen years in the linguistics department at Tbilisi University and also held a part-time job at a radio station that sent weekly communiqués to the Laz living in Turkey. During these years he and his wife maintained close contacts with Sarpi. They managed to retain rights to a private plot in Sarpi and returned every summer and fall to take care of the citrus fruits. Their house in Tbilisi became a kind of center for Laz students, Maguli recalled. For many years they housed students from Sarpi who studied in the capital. Anzor was proud of the high number of "learned" people from his village. After he returned to the village he became—despite his young age of sixty-one—a valued member of the group of elders who discussed difficulties in the village, advised local authorities, and mediated conflicts when needed.

Generation III   Anzor and Maguli's children, the twins Irakli and Nino, were born in 1971 and spent most of their youth in Tbilisi. They more or less followed in their father's footsteps. Nino studied in the university's linguistics department and specialized in the Georgian language, like her father. Irakli studied Turkish history and language. When they graduated in 1993, it was not possible to start an academic career. Civil strife and deteriorating standards of living in the capital made it increasingly difficult to survive; in 1995 the family decided to move back to Sarpi.

When I first met them in 1997, both Irakli and Nino were jobless and trying to find some sort of official position. Nino had started to work on a dissertation concerning Laz poetry but had not managed to move beyond the initial stages, unconvinced that a dissertation would help her establish a career and with no funds for her endeavor. Nino regretted returning to Sarpi. She was even more despondent about the seeming impossibility of returning to Tbilisi. She regarded herself as too old to find a husband and didn't want one from the village anyway.

Her twin brother Irakli showed less regret and to some extent liked the comforts the village community provided. After failed attempts to secure a job at the customs office (for which he saw himself well positioned because of his knowledge of Turkish) he settled for a job with the electricity distribution company and was responsible for securing timely payments from villagers. He also spent time hanging around the village center with some of his friends waiting for interesting economic transactions to turn up. The money he made was sufficient for everyday purposes but not for securing some of his other dreams. He saw insufficient income as the main reason why he was rejected by the parents of an Ajarian girl from Batumi whom he wished to marry.

The family's house was one of the smaller ones in Sarpi. It was built in the 1970s as a dacha or summer house, and it certainly was not intended for occupation in winter.[9] Since 1995 the family had worked hard to make it suitable for permanent occupation. They built an outdoor toilet and improved the washing facilities. Still, living conditions compared unfavorably to their former lifestyle in Tbilisi. Heva's decision to move in with the family brought some relief of their economic troubles, because Heva's son traveled at least once a year from Tashkent to Sarpi to help his mother out financially. After his visit in 2000, they made plans to convert the basement into additional living space. Social networks ensured basic means of living, but misfortune increas-

---

9. Anzor's younger brother, Hasan, had inherited the much larger parental home.

ingly tied the family to the limits of their village. When Irakli fell seriously ill in 2001, there was no other way for the family to pay for medical treatment than to take out large loans. The last time I saw them, in summer 2001, they were seriously considering selling their apartment in Tbilisi.

The ways in which the two families dealt with the Soviet system were markedly different. The Abuladzes had focused on improving their position within Sarpi. They invested their capital in the construction of houses for all male family members and did so by exploiting the margins of the Soviet economic system—making trading trips to various parts of the Soviet Union and seeking informal jobs in addition to their work on the kolkhoz. The Memishishis had different priorities. They took up positions within the state apparatus and started careers in the city. But despite these differences the stories were also remarkably similar. Members of both families pointed out that during Communist times they all had work, that the state provided the basic necessities of life, and that they had been able to arrange for sufficient housing. Whatever the limitations of the Soviet economy or the restrictions on movement and expression, they had successfully developed ways to cope with them. During numerous informal conversations they presented "advanced socialism" as a time when things were in place, as opposed to the "chaos" of the present.

These family stories also indicated the patterns of dependency that developed between Sarpi and the Soviet Georgian hinterland. During various periods, the harshness of life at the border had pushed away residents, forcing them to seek their livelihoods elsewhere. But "the village," as in many other shortage economies, continued to play an important role in meeting everyday necessities of life. The importance of the village as a point of reference was enhanced by restrictions on settlement in Sarpi. Seen from a local male perspective, these restrictions meant that the ethnic makeup of Sarpi remained stable. As Anzor phrased it: "There was *one* good thing about the border: because of it we managed to preserve our community. In other villages there was a continuing stream of settlers from the mountains. But because Sarpi was in the restricted zone there never were resettlements. Only native people were allowed to build houses. Therefore our village is still 90 percent Laz."[10]

When economic opportunities improved in Sarpi in the late 1980s, many who had left returned to profit from the opportunities at the border. Later on the uncertainties of life in Georgian cities also caused remigrations to Sarpi. The relative homogeneity of the population made it understandable that the village continued to be seen as a bounded whole—at least by those who were born there—and illuminates why the category "Laz" continued to be important.

10. Sarpians usually only referred to the male genealogical lines and omitted that through marriage most families had mixed with Ajarians and (other) Georgians.

Marriage and Belonging

Family histories demonstrate some of the ways villagers worked the system while being simultaneously formed by it. In classic anthropological terms, Laz in Sarpi traced descent along the father's line, patrilineally, with a strong preference for residence among the husband's kin. For Sarpians, first-cousin marriages between children of same-sex siblings (parallel cousin marriage) were strictly taboo, and I came across only one case that violated this rule.[11] I collected oral reconstructions of family genealogies, to understand how ethnic belonging was defined and negotiated in Sarpi. Since marriage patterns are also influenced by factors including proximity, economic considerations, and personal preferences of the bride, groom, and their families, it should not be expected that they perfectly mirror changes in social identification.

Although the data on pre-1920 marriages are not very reliable, they show that intra-ethnic marriage was at least the general rule.[12] Before 1920, brides seem to have come mainly from present-day Turkey: from Makriali (Kemal-paşha), Hopa, and Arhavi. That a large number of brides went to, or came from, Ottoman territory indicates that the border did not present significant obstacles to marriage. Even in the period between 1921 and 1937 the new demarcation did not prevent villagers from marrying across the border.[13] During this period no less than 36 percent of the brides crossed the state border upon marriage, though from the early 1930s onward the Sarpians looked more often for potential spouses within Ajaria and the rest of Georgia. The increase in the percentage of intravillage marriages during this period testifies to the importance of marrying within the ethnic group.

After the border was closed in 1937, it became impossible to marry someone from Turkey. The marriage data covering the subsequent two decades show an increase in the number of marriages to Laz from Georgia, who lived scattered throughout settlements along the coast. Some families went to great lengths to find Laz spouses for their children. Necat recalled:

> [When] I was ready for marriage, my sister-in-law's mother introduced me to a girl from Anakli.[14] My uncle and I went there to talk with her parents, but when my uncle saw the girl he didn't want me to marry her. Instead he said, 'You are younger than me, so I will marry this girl. After that it will be your turn.' That is why my uncle's wife and my wife are both from Anakli.

11. Bellér-Hann and Hann observed that the taboo on marriages between parallel cousins is absent among the Laz in Turkey, and that it occurs relatively frequently there (2001, 144). It may be that in Sarpi the taboo stems from frequent contact with Ajarians and Georgians, who have strong traditions of marrying out.

12. One shortcoming of the pre-1920 data is that they cover only those people who continued to live in Sarpi, thus ignoring women who married outside the village.

13. The existence of the border may have encouraged such marriages because of enhanced opportunities for trading.

14. At least six brides came from Anakli—a town 120 kilometers north of Sarpi—where several Laz families lived clustered on one street.

Table 1. Marriage Patterns in Sarpi

Period	N (587)	Marriages to people of Muslim background					Marriages to people of Christian background	
		from Turkey	Laz from Georgia	from Sarpi[a]	Ajarians	Others	Georgians	Russians[b]
<1920	44	57%	—	43%	—	—	—	—
1920–1937	72	36%	7%	57%	—	—	—	—
1938–1956	113	—	11%	50%	23%	4%	3%	9%
1957–1975	124	—	5%	33%	50%	4%	6%	2%
1976–1988	149	—	4%	37%	46%	3%	5%	5%
1989–2000	85	2%	6%	27%	49%	1%	8%	7%

Note: N refers to individual Sarpians entering a marriage. Marriages involving two people from Sarpi are counted twice.

[a] Refers to whole village until 1920, but only to Soviet Sarpi for later periods.

[b] And others from the former Soviet Union.

The trend of seeking potential Laz spouses in Georgia suggests that ethnic difference was still an important element in marriage preferences. However, World War II and the subsequent deportations of Laz meant that many lived outside the village for extensive periods of time. These disruptions of the local community, in combination with changed lifestyles, meant that it became more common and partly acceptable to marry outside the ethnic group.[15] During this period, the percentage of marriages with Georgians, Russians, and others increased steeply and was even higher than during the next three decades.

The period after 1956 shows an initial increase in the percentage of marriages with the neighboring Ajarians, but no other significant proportional shifts occur up to 1988. However, this relatively stable pattern partly obscures equally important changes. After 1969 a complex system of fences, military controls, and roadblocks restricted all traffic in the borderlands, virtually shutting off Sarpi from the rest of Georgia. Because a person was only permitted to pass the roadblocks if they were registered as a resident of Sarpi, women who married outside the village, youth studying in Tbilisi, and others who had changed their place of residence were not able to easily visit their relatives in Sarpi. The villagers complained about this period, saying it became difficult to find brides who were willing to live in the village. The data partly confirm this by a slight increase in the percentage of intravillage marriages in the 1970s.

15. This freedom in choosing a spouse was true more for men than for women, as in other patrilinear societies. Of the thirteen marriages with non-Muslims documented for this period, only two involved women from Sarpi. These two women married during their exile in Siberia between 1949 and 1956.

Although potential spouses were usually reluctant to move to Sarpi, young Sarpians often decided to leave the village and start a life elsewhere. This was not only the result of the restrictions posed by the border but also because the collective farm could not absorb the growing number of inhabitants. The industrial expansion of Batumi created opportunities for starting a career in the city, something that attracted many villagers. But for most of these recent emigrants, like for the Memishishis, the links with Sarpi remained very important. A family often arranged for one member of their household to stay registered in Sarpi so that they could retain access to their private farming plots. Other emigrants returned during summer vacations and cooperated with relatives from the village to set up trade routes to other parts of the Soviet Union.

Given the expressed preference for Laz spouses it might have been expected that the border opening of 1988 would have spurred a significant number of cross-border marriages. In fact, only two marriages took place between Laz from Georgian Sarpi and Laz from Turkey between 1988 and 2000. Both marriages occurred during the first heady years after the border opening, involving young women from Georgian Sarpi. Some inhabitants had mixed feelings about these cross-border marriages. A woman in her twenties said, "I can't understand why Manana married this man. Maybe they say that they are also Laz, but they live just like other Turks. I would never marry one of them!" Manana herself, who had moved to Turkey in 1993, told me that before her marriage she "was planning to convert to Christianity. But here that is not possible, so now I am Muslim." Even in this case the differences between the Laz from opposite sides of the border were affirmed. It is even more telling that it was done by a woman who found herself partly on the other side of the boundary.

The other data for the period after 1988 are more difficult to interpret. The end of restrictions resulted in a decrease of intravillage marriages, in favor of a slightly increasing percentage of marriages to Ajarian Georgians, but especially to all Georgians of Christian background. However, the numbers themselves may underestimate the changes that have taken place, because the categories "Laz" and "Ajarian" no longer could be assumed to imply (nominal) Muslim ascription. Conversion to Orthodox Christianity went hand in hand with increased identification with the Georgian nation. Of the younger generation in Sarpi, the majority told me that they were Orthodox Christian. Sometimes this meant actual baptism and involvement in "Orthodox life," though more often it was a verbal and symbolic affiliation that did not have great implications for the everyday lives of those involved. Moreover, few elderly inhabitants stressed their Muslim background. Most of them simply stated that they had grown up in atheist times and therefore felt rather indifferent to the conversion of their younger family and community members. Although in earlier times marriage to Ajarians was considered acceptable because of their Muslim background, in the 1990s the role of religion was often reversed. Maguli Memishishi, for example, was vehemently against her children marrying

Ajarians, whom she depicted as being "still uncivilized." She explained that "in their villages people still wear veils. If my children get married it should be to a Laz or to a Georgian; it is best to stick to your tradition." This tradition was, of course, wholly different from what had been considered "tradition" in earlier decades. New ideas about tradition excluded elements perceived as Muslim or Turkish, while actively incorporating Georgian practices and ideas.

These marriage patterns closely correlate with changes in the nature of the border. Indeed, at one level they may be seen as straightforward responses to physical restraints. This was also the view of elderly male Sarpians when they explained to me why villagers increasingly had married outside their ethnic group. They stressed that their community was forced to find non-Laz spouses because of the closed border between the USSR and Turkey. There simply were not enough Laz brides and grooms not related by blood in Sarpi to go around. But this observation does not make the marriage patterns less significant as indicators of the changing social orientations. The data show a general trend toward marrying Ajarians and Christian Georgians. This trend is espe-

Men, waiting for the start of a wedding, loiter on the coastal road near the border in Sarpi. The border checkpoint (background, left) and the mosque in Turkey are visible in the distance, October 1999.

cially clear after the opening of the border, when 57 percent of all marriages involved a spouse of Ajarian or other Georgian background. The percentage of marriages to people of non-Islamic background rose to 15 percent during the 1990s.[16] These marriage patterns suggest that religious background was no longer an indisputable precondition for choosing a spouse, illustrating that boundaries between Laz, Ajarians, and Georgians had gradually loosened.

One of the most remarkable aspects of this marriage data is that, after the physical barrier between Georgia and Turkey had become permeable, only two cross-border weddings occurred. This low number was striking because popular opinion abounded in favor of the idea that marrying Laz was still preferred, and because cross-border marriages might have been economically valuable. The fact that the marriages both occurred immediately after the border opening suggests that the initial rapprochement of the two sides was only temporary and was followed by a new raising of social and conceptual borders. Ethnic unity with Laz on the other side turned out to be a chimera when the border was finally opened. To understand this situation, it is crucial to look at the way culture was mobilized in ethnic categorization and how, on the Georgian side, "cultural stuff" became such an important element for ethnic identity.

The Cultural Stuff

"Culture" was very much alive in Sarpi, so much so that I was often perplexed by the insistent desire of villagers to display *their* culture, even though the presence of an anthropologist may have seemed to call for it. Whether it was during meetings of the village choir or evenings learning to weave baskets and tie fishnets, my hosts always stressed the high cultural significance of these events. Likewise, several of my acquaintances spent their free time constructing Laz artifacts, meticulously copying the drawings in books that described Laz material culture (for example, Vanilishi and Tandilava 1964). Young men eager to prove Laz-Georgian connections once led me to a decayed storage room where old wine barrels had been found. They took me on trips to the church ruins to prove the Christian roots of the local Laz community. With similar enthusiasm, the school director showed me his collection of paintings by Hasan Helimishi, a locally famous Laz artist who had fled Turkey to settle in Soviet Georgia in the 1930s. Although the director admired the artist's representations of traditional Laz society, he also mentioned that some of the paintings were "contaminated" by Turkish elements, which he ascribed to the artist's upbringing in Turkey. In short, Sarpians were highly articulate about what was and what was not theirs. They had very clear ideas about which cultural elements were authentic and which were corruptions.

16. This does not provide precise data on interfaith marriages, since many Laz and Ajarians classified as Muslim in the table had converted to Orthodox Christianity in the 1990s.

Culture in Sarpi could not be understood as something "repressed" by Soviet rule, in the sense of something that later reemerged after the socialist "freeze." Nor could it be seen as something "covered" by layers of Soviet modernization. On the contrary, ideas of culture in Sarpi were tightly linked to Soviet ideologies and policies. The villagers' predilection for artifacts and tools paralleled the Soviet emphasis on the importance of material and labor-related values. Moreover, ideas of what constituted authentic Laz culture were (indirectly) influenced by Soviet nationality politics. Grant notes that Soviet ideas about culture and Soviet rituals are often dismissed because they are seen as "imposed from above" (1995, 8). However, far from being irrelevant, these "imposed" ideas and rituals became important elements in local cultural vocabularies. As such they are crucial elements for understanding why Soviet cultural constructions continued to be important after the collapse of socialism.

Soviet national policies had been, from the start, imbued with a deep-seated ambiguity. In theory, nationality was supposed to wither with the development of Soviet society, but it became clear with time that the government was by no means looking to erase all ethnic differences. Both official discourses and political practices left much room to the various republics to sustain local nationalisms (Slezkine 2000). The makeup of the Soviet Union itself—its division into "ethno-republics"—created the institutional space to carry out "nationalizing" policies (Smith 1998, 6). For small ethnic groups like the Laz the situation was more complex, because for them sameness and difference were measured on at least two levels, first in relation to the Communist ideal of "modern man" or *Homo sovieticus* and second in relation to the ethno-republic of which they were part.

In the 1920s and 1930s the need to root the Communist Party in local settings, coupled with the Bolshevik fear of being confronted by massive resistance, resulted in a relatively strong emphasis on ethnic difference. These policies, referred to as korenizatsiia, included preferential access to higher education and jobs in the Soviet administration, increased membership in the local Communist parties, and the creation of ethnicity-based newspapers. Soviet officials denied these privileges to Ajarians because they considered them to be ethnic Georgians. By contrast, the few thousand Laz living in the Soviet Union were classified as a distinct ethnic group, thus reaping the benefits provided by korenizatsiia. Villagers were sent to Leningrad to study at the Institute of Minorities and for a short period in the 1920s the school curriculum in Sarpi included lessons in Lazuri. During this period, newspapers and schoolbooks appeared in the native language and a Lazuri alphabet was introduced (see also Feurstein 1992).

Ethnic differentiation of the Laz vis-à-vis Georgians was initially promoted because the Soviet authorities saw Sarpi as a bridgehead for their aspirations in Turkey. The Soviet government still had ambitions to recapture the territories it had lost to Turkey, and it therefore attempted to increase the popularity of the USSR among the Turkish Laz by encouraging expressions of ethnic identity.[17] But although "difference" was to some extent institutionalized it was at the same time also dangerous. To escape persecution as well as to advance oneself in Soviet society, religious practices had to be denounced and personal ties with the Laz in Turkey needed to be kept secret or denied. Though the Laz were allowed to speak their own language, this language was increasingly purified of Turkic influences. As with the Abuladzes and Memishishis, the need for ethnic purification was also reflected in the replacement of Turkish-sounding surnames with Georgian-sounding ones. In short, the kind of "ethnic difference" that was allowed was de-Ottomanized and stripped of its "harmful traditions and customs," as religion came to be called by Soviet officials.[18]

Soviet publications, especially those written since the 1960s, tightly encased the Laz in the Georgian nation. These books stressed the similarities between Laz and Georgian culture, for example in "traditional" dress, customs, and language (for example, Vanilishi and Tandilava 1964). Studies of folklore, language, and material culture underlined the link between Laz and Georgians. An article written by a scholar from Sarpi—which discusses "the typical Laz house"—demonstrates some of the ways in which these links between Georgians and Laz were made. The author introduces the Laz as "an ancient Georgian tribe," which "up to now, preserved old economic, domestic, and familial traditions." The "unity of Georgian national culture" is clearly reflected in the Laz dialect, folklore, and material culture. And he concludes a detailed description of typical Laz dwellings by stating that "the Laz house and farming buildings have many parallels with architectural styles in other parts of Georgia, while at the same time demonstrating local variations" (Vanilishi 1978, 130–31). This text and many others like it effectively mobilized local artifacts to symbolize an "ancient" pre-Islamic Laz culture that was shared with "Mother Georgia." Through such publications, the category "Laz" was redrawn as part of the larger Georgian nation. Local material culture became integrated into the Georgian mosaic, where, rather than the differences, it was the similarities that mattered.

Far from remaining confined to scholarly domains or official rhetoric, the same ideas also thrived in local discussions about ethnicity and nationality. The relationship between Laz and Georgians was often imagined as symbiotic in the sense that both groups constituted for the other a weaker or stronger

---

17. These ambitions were formally expressed to Turkey in 1945, when the Soviet leadership demanded that Turkey return the areas of northeastern Anatolia that had been Russian between 1878 and 1918. The claim was dropped after Turkey became a full member of NATO in 1952 (Zürcher 1993, 218, 246).

18. The phrase "harmful traditions and customs" became particularly common after the Central Committee of the Communist Party of Georgia announced new antireligion measures on November 15, 1975, in its decree: "O merakh po usileniiu bor'by s vrednymi traditsiiami i obychaiami," quoted in *Sovetskaia Adzhariia*, 9 August 1978.

"brother." The idea that the Laz were an integral component of the "Georgian mosaic" was reflected in new "folk rituals" advanced by the Soviet Georgian leadership. These folk rituals poignantly illustrate the links between Soviet modernization and ethnic objectification.

"Colkhoba—An Ancient though Youthful Festival"

Folk rituals were increasingly considered important during the 1960s and 1970s, when they became central tools in the Soviet struggle against "harmful traditions." In *The Rites of Rulers* (1981), Christel Lane makes an important hypothesis concerning the link between the increasing importance of ritual and the formation of new identities. In her view, when economic development slowed down in the 1960s the discrepancies between Soviet reality and utopian Communism became more apparent, creating a problem of legitimacy for the rulers. Because the coercion and repression of the 1930s were no longer acceptable alternatives for maintaining social control and because the economic revolution already had become a distant memory, political leaders began to rely more on cultural management to induce people to accept their definitions of social reality. Moreover, Soviet scholars and ideologists were increasingly aware that *Homo sovieticus* would not automatically appear and that something had to replace the "harmful traditions and customs," as religion was generally called. Thus, old and new secular traditions were invented or given new life by Soviet authorities as a means to lead people away from other, mostly religious, holidays.

This renewed emphasis on the role of secular rituals in the atheist struggle was visible in local newspapers, with articles entitled "New Traditions Are Broadly Introduced," "Strengthening the Struggle against Harmful Traditions," "New Traditions Enter the Life of Workers," and the like.[19] Certainly, many innovations (such as socialist weddings, funerals, and political ceremonies) were opposed or resentfully accepted by citizens. However, certain rituals, especially new holidays and festivals, were effectively transformed into powerful celebrations of culture and nationality. During the 1970s, new cultural holidays were promoted throughout the Soviet Union. In Soviet Georgia cultural festivals such as Shotaoba, Iliaoba, Vazhaoba, Jakoboba, and Tbilisoba were initiated, the names of which all refer to heroic periods in the Georgian past.[20]

Sarpi had its own festival, Colkhoba, which was first celebrated on a large scale in 1979.[21] Its keystone was a play portraying the story of Jason and the Argonauts. Villagers told me that they had tried to follow as closely as possible

19. Taken from *Sovetskaia Adzhariia*; respectively 24 November 1978; 27 December 1979; 11 August 1976.

20. "Shotaoba" refers to Shota Rustaveli, author of the Georgian epic *The Knight in the Panther's Skin*. Iliaoba, Vazhaoba, and Iakoboba refer successively to Ilia Chavchavadze, Vazha Pshavela, and Iakob Gogebashvili, three revered nineteenth-century nationalist writers.

21. The heading for this section, "Colkhoba—an Ancient though Youthful Festival," is from a news report on Colkhoba in *Sovetskaia Adzhariia*, 3 November 1982.

the original story line, in which Jason and his companions sailed from central-eastern Greece to the coast of the wealthy Colchis kingdom in search of the Golden Fleece. Once they arrived in Colchis (which all villagers immediately understood to be Sarpi) Jason faced the impossible tasks set by King Aetes to hinder him from obtaining the Golden Fleece. Jason overcame these obstacles with help from the king's daughter Medea, who had fallen in love with him. His strength and her magical power also enabled them to defeat a huge, hissing dragon and retrieve the Golden Fleece from a tree on the beach.

In preparation for the play, villagers had transformed a regular modern boat into an ancient vessel and had constructed "scenes of Colchian life" on the beach. What is perhaps more interesting than the performances during that day is the way the event was portrayed in the local media. These portrayals provide insight into how the festival contributed to ideas of Laz identity as part of the broader Georgian nation. In the September 25, 1979, edition of the newspaper *Sovetskaia Adzhariia* two journalists from Batumi described the festival, quoting elaborately from the many speeches:

> Last Saturday we witnessed the rebirth of [an] ancient holiday of the inhabitants of the Georgian Black Sea region. The holiday, Colkhoba, was celebrated in the border village of Sarpi. This holiday has existed for many centuries. As a true workers' holiday, local inhabitants usually celebrated it at the end of August [or the] beginning of September, after the harvest was gathered and before the start of the fishing season. In the past it was called "Day of the Sea." Now they have named it Colkhoba in honor of the ancient inhabitants of these places—the Colchians. When we arrived in Sarpi, two Colchians, as if reappearing from bygone centuries, unexpectedly blocked the road with their lances. They wished us a pleasant stay and insisted that we first try a national delicacy. Only then did the Colchians remove their lances and let us pass. And so we entered a world of legends, full of the atmosphere of days gone by. On the rocks near the sea, a fragment of a Colchian settlement was reconstructed, the way we know it to have been. . . .
>
> At three o'clock everyone was invited to the village center. The celebrations started. Among the guests were many prominent party functionaries . . . as well as famous writers and academics. . . . R. Bakradze, chairman of the Khelvachauri rai-ispolkom [District Executive Committee] and people's deputy, opened the festivities.[22] He told the crowd that it was the first time that Colkhoba had been celebrated on such a large scale, with the intention of reviving the ancient tradition, giving it a modern socialist direction, and moreover, displaying the features of our Soviet way of life. "On such workers' holidays, comrades from all corners of the republic will meet and enrich their cultural ties. They will exchange experiences and thus contribute to the preservation of the best of national traditions. The decree of the Central Committee of the Communist Party of the Soviet Union 'about the further improvements of ideological and political educational work' . . . has stressed the importance of Communist education among workers in the struggle

22. Rezo Bakradze was born in Sarpi. At the time his brother Murman was the kolkhoz director in Sarpi.

for Communism. The inculcation of new rituals and traditions, as is well known, is an important step that facilitates the success of these struggles. Therefore, let Colkhoba be part of our life; let it be a genuine holiday of workers, of friendship, and brotherhood."

Then the podium was given to Z. Tandilava, doctoral candidate in philology and head of the folklore and dialectology department of the Batumi Scientific Research Institute of the Georgian Academy of Science.[23] He outlined the history of the holiday and its social roots: "It originated, possibly, during paganism, when this holiday existed in different forms among many ethnographic groups inhabiting the coastal region of the Black Sea. The tradition was handed down to the Laz from the Colchians. Academician N. Marr, who traveled in Turkish Lazistan, wrote that in 1909 this holiday was dying out. And indeed, it was celebrated less and less often, approximately until the 1930s and 1940s. Komsomol members and young inhabitants of Sarpi recently decided to give the holiday a new life. Today we are witnesses of the fact that their lofty plans have been successful."

The article filled an entire page in both of the eight-page regional newspapers *Sovetskaia Adzhariia* and *Sabchota Ach'ara*.[24] In a village that did not exist on maps and could not be easily visited by outsiders, the festival was bound to have an enormous impact. Suddenly Sarpi was in the news, written about in newspapers and briefly shown on television. To the delight of some inhabitants, news about Colkhoba even reached a Polish magazine, which later sent the colorfully illustrated article back to Sarpi. Even the soldiers on the Turkish side paid attention to the festival: "They became very nervous. They probably thought we were planning an attack," a villager joked.

The text explicitly displayed the double meaning of the festival. On one hand, the play stressed the ancient roots of the inhabitants of western Georgia in the Colchis kingdom. The article stated that the holiday had been given "the name Colkhoba to honor the ancient inhabitants of these places, the Colchians." In other newspaper articles, people from Sarpi confirmed these historical ties: "Village elders explain that Colkhoba probably originated as early as pagan times, when it was a cultural holiday celebrated in various forms by the ethnic groups of the Black Sea coast: Mingrelians,[25] Georgians, and Laz. Among the Laz this tradition was probably handed down from the Colchians" (*Sovetskaia Adzhariia*, 27 October 1987). In short, Colkhoba was to be seen as an authentic holiday that existed for many centuries but which unfortunately had disappeared until it was given a new life under Soviet rule.

On the other hand, Colkhoba explicitly aimed to represent "our Soviet way

23. Ali Tandilava was born in Sarpi and was the coauthor of the ethnohistorical study *Lazeti* (Vanilishi and Tandilava 1964). The 1992 Turkish translation caused much controversy in Turkey because of the book's blatant Georgian nationalist bias (for a discussion see Bellér-Hann 1995).

24. The names of both newspapers translate as *Soviet Ajaria*, from Russian and Georgian respectively.

25. The Mingrelians were considered a distinct ethnic group until the 1930s. After that they were, like the Ajarians, classified as Georgian (see also Law 1998; Broers 2001).

A colorful billboard hanging in the center of Batumi honors Georgia's three thousand years of statehood and two thousand years of Christianity, June 2000.

of life." It was described as a holiday of working people and assigned an important role in the struggle against "harmful traditions and customs." The prominence of government officials, who inaugurated the holiday with their speeches, as well as the positioning of the holiday "after harvest and before the fishing season," emphasized its socialist features. In newspaper articles these "socialist" features were further illustrated by passages (excluded from the above text) about the achievements of the Sarpi kolkhoz.

Thus, Colkhoba referred to the distant past and the unity of "Georgian" people living along the eastern Black Sea coast, while at the same time it was invested with socialist meaning. The slogan of nationality politics in general, "socialist in content, national in form," was reflected in Colkhoba. These twofold meanings of Colkhoba were not fixed: "national form" and "socialist content" were not mutually exclusive. Therefore it is interesting to look at the various meanings attributed to the festival to see how this "socialist ritual" was locally transformed into a celebration of ethnic and national identity.

The Production and "Corruptions" of Colkhoba

The elements for the celebrations of Colkhoba had been present in Soviet Georgia for several decades. In the 1960s and 1970s, the Colchis kingdom became, in Shnirelman's words, "one of the core ideas of the Georgian myth of the past" (2001, 267). Soviet historians extensively wrote about the kingdom as a federation of "Georgian" groups such as the Mingrelians, Laz, and Gurians.[26] The regional press published articles speculating about the places where Medea had lived. A village neighboring Sarpi was a popular choice, because there "more than thirty gold items were found during excavations, adding substantial proof to the veracity of the theory of the Golden Fleece" (*Sovetskaia Adzhariia*, 11 November 1977). The first page of a book titled *Soviet Sarpi* (Sabch'ota Sarpi), written by Rezo Bakradze, mentioned the following interesting speculations: "From historical sources we know that Sarpi is derived from Apsari. Sarpi stems from Psarepi, which is the plural ending of Apsari in Lazuri. According to Plavius Arianes, 'Apsarosi' is connected to Medea's brother's name Apsyrtus" (Bakradze 1971, 7). If nothing more, this wordplay and similar guesses about the past illustrate the imaginary power that ancient history had in Soviet Ajaria. At least in Soviet publications, Sarpi had already been placed in the land of the Golden Fleece.

The initiators of the festival were well acquainted with the imagined ties between the Colchis kingdom and the village. In 1973 six students from Sarpi had been accepted at Tbilisi University during a campaign to increase the level of education among the Laz population. Inspired by the cultural vibrancy they witnessed in Tbilisi, they made their first plans. One of them remembered: "You should understand the atmosphere in Tbilisi at the time. It was buzzing with cultural activity—theater, exhibitions, and festivals. So we saw the grand festivals like Tbilisoba and others in which the history of the city was celebrated. And we were thinking how great it would be if we could organize such an event in Sarpi." What they had in mind was an event that would make the link between the origins of the Laz and contemporary Sarpi explicit. At first they played with the idea of calling their event Kvamkhazoba, after the name of a rock called Kvamkhaz from which Sarpians used to take their yearly last dive in the sea. According to the initiators, this was "a kind of holiday that already existed in Sarpi," celebrated yearly around August 18. The plays that they eventually prepared stuck to the sea as the central element, modeled after the *Argonautica*: "We tried to follow the literal text of the legend, because it best symbolized the deep roots of our people and their relation to the sea." To make the link between these deep origins and Laz culture even more evident they invited the artist Hasan Helimishi to have an exposition in Sarpi of his paintings, which were all depictions of "traditional" Laz culture and celebrated the seafaring and fishing qualities of the Laz.

The timing of their plans turned out favorably. A former resident of Sarpi and uncle of one of the initiators was secretary of the Khelvachauri District Executive Committee (*raiispolkom*) at the time. With his assistance and the help of several other influential Laz, the group managed to get the funding and

---

26. An example is Vanilishi and Tandilava (1964, 5–6). For an overview of how images of an ethnically homogeneous "Georgian" Colchis kingdom were popularized in Soviet literature, see Broers (2001) and Shnirelman (1998, 54–56).

facilities necessary to put on the festival in Sarpi in 1977. The official guests must have liked this first performance, because they allowed the initiators to organize it a second time:

> They suggested that we redo it on a wider scale, not just for Sarpi but as a perfor-
> mance for western Georgia. That was why we called it Colkhoba, so that it would
> be recognizable for the whole [of the region]. It was huge. We invited Laz repre-
> sentatives from Sukhumi [the capital of Abkhazia] and many others. People came
> from as far as Tbilisi. At that time only Sarpians performed, and it was a great suc-
> cess, something new!

After Colkhoba had become a success, the district authorities decided that it was too important to have it performed in such a small place.[27] Another possible reason was that the proximity of the border presented problems for the KGB, who had difficulties monitoring so many spectators. According to one of the initiators, "The banquet especially posed a problem because it was impossible to plan beforehand who would go where." He further explained that the KGB demanded a list that showed where every single guest would spend the night, "but it was impossible to do that. People meet up with one another and they can't refuse invitations." In such an increasingly freer time, hospitality was trumping security.

In the 1980s the organizers transferred the festival to the remains of a Roman fort in the neighboring village of Gonio. "When the performance moved to Gonio, others took over. We only got a small part, and for the rest [we] functioned as advisers. It was not bad, that performance in Gonio, but it wasn't the same." After that the festival was transferred to Khelvachauri, the district center. In the eyes of many Sarpians this shift made a mockery of the event: "By that time it was already something completely different. There is no water, so instead they transported a ship to the central square, destroying the effect we had in Sarpi." Other adjustments were made as well. The festival came to include exhibitions of agricultural successes and performances by Ajarian music and dance ensembles. Moreover, to stress the socialist nature of the celebrations, the date was shifted from August to late in the fall, "after the collection of harvest," underlining the labor-ideal behind the celebrations (*Sovetskaia Adzhariia*, 27 October 1987).

My acquaintances insisted that these modifications destroyed the connec-
tion with the past that the event was meant to symbolize. According to Anzor, it was the same tragedy that befell many Soviet festivals: "They began as spon-
taneous folk celebrations, but when they started to mix politics and tradition the [celebrations] lost their appeal." For many, the significance of Colkhoba lay in Laz history, elements that disappeared with the "Soviet corruptions."

---

27. "Soon 'Colkhoba' expanded beyond the confines of a single village. It became a holiday for the entire Khelvachauri District, even of our entire autonomous republic" (*Batumskii rabochii*, 13 October 1988).

The production of Colkhoba exemplified how the famously ambiguous message of socialism—national in form, socialist in content—had been central from the start. But over the years the balance between these two dimensions changed in favor of "socialist content," causing my acquaintances to speak of corruptions of the authentic. About the possible convergence of "socialist content" and "nationalist form" Lane wrote: "Many concessions to local traditional culture have been made but such concessions, it must be stressed, have always been on the *form* and never the content" (1981, 142, emphasis in original). However, in local interpretations and memories of the festival the distinction between form and content was never clear-cut. To quote Lane again, "There still remains . . . the danger that the old forms cannot become wedded to the new content and that instead they continue to keep alive old associations of a national kind" (1981, 142–43). This is an interesting observation, although instead of sustaining established associations, I would argue that the significance of Colkhoba was in *creating* such associations anew. In stories about Colkhoba, overt Communist messages that had been present from the start were omitted and instead the "original" Colkhoba was presented as a continuation of local customs. One suspects that such perceived corruptions even reinforced the idea of authenticity.

New Celebrations

In its Soviet form Colkhoba was celebrated for the last time in 1988. It took ten years before a movement surfaced in Sarpi to revive it again. Interestingly, whereas the Communist "content" of Colkhoba disappeared from memory in the 1990s, the idea of other, more glorious pasts was more tightly embraced. It is not surprising then that a 1999 textbook on Ajaria made no reference to the Soviet origin of the festival, stating simply that its value had been to "teach our people about the roots of their long and rich history" (Komakhidze 1999, 499–501). In essence, people selected the elements of the celebration that suited them best. The "invention of tradition" as found in Colkhoba drew on other popular images of the past. Whereas the negation of the Islamic past created difference with their Turkish Laz neighbors, the notions expressed in Colkhoba stressed the Laz people's shared past with the Georgian people, and linked them to an ancestral homeland—the old Colchis kingdom—to demonstrate unity with the Georgian nation. This deep past, moreover, provided more legitimacy than could be found in recent history.[28] Both the celebrations of Colkhoba and the dismissal of Islam strengthened cohesion, by defining what and who does or doesn't belong.

One might suspect that the celebrations would have become part of a rusty nostalgia for Soviet times, fading memories that were irrelevant to those who

---

28. Lack of interest in recent history and a preoccupation with the deep past is a feature found in other postsocialist contexts as well. See Law (1998) for Georgia and Humphrey (1992) for Mongolia.

grew up in the 1980s and 1990s (especially because the festival had not been organized since 1988). This was only partly the case. For the older generation, Colkhoba spurred memories of a time in which life was still good, when political leaders enabled them to express their culture (even though they "corrupted" it as well). Nevertheless, young villagers also discussed their Colchian origins. Moreover, images of Jason and the Argonauts were appropriated in cafés and restaurants, all along the coast at Sarpi, with names such as "The Golden Fleece," "Argo," "Colchis," and "Medea." The interior of one café displayed a map of the Colchis kingdom and a painting of Jason's struggles with the dragon. For the younger generation it was less the references to a "good Soviet past" that mattered than the possibility of expressing their ideas of belonging through the festival. This was especially evident in the comments of the organizers of the new Colkhoba (among whom were three men in their thirties). They were cited in a 1998 newspaper article expressing their wish that "Colkhoba may return to a less official and more truly folk character."[29] Contacts were established with the Ajarian authorities, who promised financial assistance.

The 2001 version of Colkhoba in Sarpi was held on the newly built soccer field next to the newly renovated village school. The choice of this place (on which the sponsors had insisted) and the spatial organization of the scene revealed the prominence of the post-Soviet Ajarian political elite in "cultural" events. The general public watched the celebrations from behind the fences that enclosed the soccer field. Within the fences were the official guests, seated behind tables with fruit and drinks and protected from the sun by large parasols. The celebration started several hours later than planned because guests from Batumi were delayed, including a locally famous novelist and the Ajarian minister of culture.

The guests opened the celebrations with elaborate speeches on the importance of keeping traditions alive and on the crucial role of the government in financing the initiative. References were made to the construction of the soccer field and the renovation of the school, which, it was stressed, were made possible by the personal involvement of Aslan Abashidze, strongman of the Ajarian Autonomous Republic. An hour and a half later the actual celebration started. From behind the fences the spectacle looked somewhat odd. The dancers and actors played their roles, but it almost seemed as if they were performing for a "jury" made up of the official guests. The jury seemed hardly interested. After the performances, the privileged guests were sequestered at a private banquet to which the actors were invited. For most villagers the celebrations had ended rather disappointingly.

The comments of several Sarpians made it clear that this was not what they had hoped for. "It was embarrassing," explained one dancer. "It was as if we

---

29. The organizers also pointed out that by creating a new version of Colkhoba, they intended to teach the Laz in Turkey about Laz culture.

were auditioning for them." Anzor, whose critique of Soviet rituals I cited earlier, told me: "Festivals during the Soviet period always had an ideological flavor, but at least the celebrations were meant for us—now it is only for them." The celebration of a new Colkhoba in "a less official and more truly folk" manner, as the initiators had intended, did not happen. On the contrary, this particular celebration reinforced the increasingly popular idea that whereas during the Soviet period "the state existed for the people . . . now the people exist for the state," as Aman phrased it. Thus, the new "corruptions" seem to have reinforced the idea that the Colkhoba of the 1970s was "original" and "authentic"—a celebration of a close-knit Laz community in more stable times.

Shifting Boundaries

The limitations on movement in the border zone and the imposition of Soviet rule had effects that went beyond the disruption of communal and familial ties. They created a division that was not only physical but increasingly social and cultural. During the first decades of Soviet rule, Sarpians adapted to changing political and economic circumstances, and in doing so they became an essential part of the fabric of Soviet Georgian life. Former barriers such as religion and language were overcome not only by Soviet propaganda and education but by the proclaimed need for villagers to advance themselves in the new society. New ideas about Laz identity that developed during socialist rule can be understood as both a reaction to and a product of Soviet society. The Laz of Sarpi came to see themselves as the direct heirs of the inhabitants of Colchis and took pride in this long history. The attractiveness of this long history was that it granted them a separate position within an overarching idea of Georgianness, while simultaneously distancing them from their Turkish counterparts. In the new situation, several older identity markers were modified to fit within a Georgian frame or were rejected altogether. "Laz" was disconnected from religious affiliation with Islam and was being retied to Christianity, which—as most adherents stressed—had older roots in Lazistan than in even Georgia proper. When I asked one man whether he saw himself as Georgian or as Laz, this idea of belonging to the "oldest Christians" was probably on his mind when he replied, "I am both. Of course I am Laz, but at the same time I am Georgian—not just a Georgian, a first-class Georgian."

A subtle distinction arises when comparing the Georgian situation with what has been written about the Turkish side, as Turkish ideas of nationality are strongly connected to Islam. Several decades ago the anthropologist Meeker argued against the applicability of Western notions of ethnic identity, as these might easily lead to the conclusion that the categories "Laz" and "Turk" are mutually exclusive (Meeker 1971, 323). In contrast to Western notions, he argued that ethnic identity, as it emerged among Laz in Turkey, referred back to the millet system of the Ottoman Empire, where such categories were ascribed on the basis of religion. Meeker maintained that in Turkey "the religious criterion [is often] indispensable for determining who is and who is not a Turk" (1971, 322). Likewise, Hann cited the German scholar Rosen, who asked some Laz in 1843, "What religion did you have before you adopted Islam?" They replied, "We have been Turk for a long time." Hann encountered the same attitude in his own fieldwork when local residents were astonished that he spoke Turkish although he was not a Muslim. Hann argued that although the Laz had a language and other local traditions that differentiated them from the Anatolian Turks, this did not undermine their adherence to the Turkish nation-state. Hann concluded, "The Turkish-Islamic synthesis is as applicable here at the periphery as it is in the Anatolian heartland" (1997, 36).

How should we interpret the cross-border differences? On the Soviet side, notions of Laz identity merged with ideas about Georgianness. In this context, the meaning of "Laz" was seen as primarily a regional category, though still occupying its own unique place. The basis on which this new identity was built referred no longer to Islam, nor did it contain a clear sense of citizenship which, after seventy years of Soviet rule, was relatively weak. Laz identity on the Georgian side pointed to deep ethnic roots and an imagined ancient community in which Laz and Georgians were one. The largest difference from the Turkish side was that the category "Laz" was purified of its Muslim connotations. Religion played some role in local patterns of belonging, but predominantly for "Christian Laz" who had returned to their "lost religion."

On the Turkish side of the border, Bellér-Hann writes about the tight connection between Laz identity and Islam, that the "internalization of merged identities is the result of centuries of Islamization and Turkicization" and should not be regarded as the product of the republican propaganda during the last seventy years (1995, 502). In this regard, during the 1980s and 1990s some Laz residing in Istanbul as well as some foreigners attempted to redefine Laz culture in terms of a classical or pre-Islamic "authentic" Lazistan (Hann and Bellér-Hann 1998). However, these attempts seemed to find little resonance with most ordinary Laz living in northeast Turkey. According to Bellér-Hann, attempts to evoke the greatness of the Laz in classical times were a "romantic quest for a past that can never be revived because it has no place in the sense of identity of the people concerned" (1995, 502–4). By contrast, on the Georgian side this Laz greatness was exactly what Soviet history had evoked. The romantic quest for an ancient past had become a living reality for the Laz of Georgia—one that further distinguished them from Laz in Turkey.

3 Lost Relatives

"On August 31, 1988, perestroika finally arrived in Sarpi." So began one Russian journalist's account of the border opening. The article continued with blunt metaphor: "After three days of subtropical rain, the sky cleared, and when the border was finally opened the sun began to shine. For the first time since 1937 villagers were allowed to meet their relatives. They embraced one another, recognized one another's old surnames, and exchanged the family news of so many years" (Mdivani 1992, 13–14). The opening of the long-closed Georgian-Turkish border was a momentous occasion for many. It was a surprising one as well. Soviet and Turkish authorities had been planning to open the border for more than ten years, but for unknown reasons the event was delayed time and again. In Sarpi, on the morning of August 31, few were aware of the events to come. State representatives arrived to make an announcement. As a villager recalled, "One of the officials asked how many years it had been since we had seen our relatives. Then he told us, 'Only two more hours, then we will open the border.' The news spread like a fire through the village. Loud voices filled the valley and within an hour the field in the center was swarming with people." Once the border was opened, "the masses could no longer be controlled, and villagers ran to the other side to meet their relatives" (*Sovetskaia Adzhariia*, 1 September 1988). One man remembered: "The plan was that only government officials would cross the border, but from the Turkish side everyone started to cross. Sarpi was completely filled with Turks who were looking for relatives, asking for this or that person. There were so many people you couldn't even walk."

During the years following 1988, residents from both sides took the chance to visit their relatives and to explore (hesitantly) the nearby but unknown country. Siblings who had been out of contact for many years reminisced about times past. Elderly inhabitants of Sarpi especially cherished the moment. For them the possibility of visiting their relatives was the fulfillment of a long-held dream. "It was a heavenly period," remembered Kake, a woman in her eighties who crossed the border six times after 1988 to visit her brother and his family in Turkish Sarp. During her last visit, her brother's son proposed that she come to live with them, but she considered herself too old for such a change. She was positive about her visits and the Turkish way of life, which she remembered as being "very civilized." "They have all kinds of kitchen tools," she told me, "and they don't take anything from the field. They just buy everything in the store."

While Kake responded positively, her attitude was not uniformly shared. Almost immediately after Kake had spoken, her daughter and my host sister said that I should not take the words of an old woman seriously. In their view, this "civilized life"—if it really existed—only concerned the material aspects of life and was the result of recent economic gains connected to the border opening as well as labor migration patterns between the region and Germany. According to Nino these factors had allowed the people of Sarp to acquire some, but only the most superficial, characteristics of "European civilization." These views were widely shared by Georgian Sarpians. In many conversations the higher standards of living across the border were downplayed or trivialized by stressing the perceived backwardness, lack of culture, and poor education of Turkish citizens.

Sarpians perhaps most keenly anticipated that the border opening would enable them to reestablish kinship ties. But as it turned out their long-separated relatives had become strangers. Not only did they dress and act differently, their moral worlds had reference points that were no longer shared. As demonstrated in the previous chapter, many of these differences could be understood as a result of the economic, social, and cultural integration of villagers into Soviet Georgian society. Due to the rigid nature of the border, these differences only became visible once the border was opened in 1988. But although differences between both sides were obvious, this by itself does not explain wholly why relations between the two sides became strained.

These issues demand an examination of the role of difference and resemblance in cross-border contact. In his article "The Narcissism of Minor Differences" Blok challenges the received wisdom that holds that "the larger the (economic, social, cultural) differences, the greater the chance of violent confrontations" (2001, 115). He argues, in fact, the opposite: "The fiercest struggles often take place between individuals, groups, and communities that differ very little—or between which the differences have greatly diminished" (115). In other words, differences matter most when they are perceived as threats to identity and when they involve people with whom one already identifies to a significant degree. The value of Blok's provocative argument is, I think, that it reminds us of the need to look critically at the way difference is managed in social relations. It is particularly fruitful to explore how perceived differences relate to expectations and social distance, themes that are interestingly related to two central aspects of the border—its impermeability and the nearness of the two sides.

Bearing in mind Blok's terms, I would counter only that it is often impossible to define whether differences are "major" or "minor." The differences that seem "minor" to the outsider may be very central, indeed "major," to the people involved, and vice versa. As Harrison has recently argued, "It is those who imagine they have the most in common—or fear that they have, or fear that they may come to have, the most in common—who are most likely to categorize each other as different, as opposites or inversions of one another" (2003, 349). Therefore, instead of looking at "objective" differences, it is more fruitful to explore how perceived differences (major or minor) relate to expectations and social distance. In the case of Sarpi, disappointments concerning renewed contacts were so striking because the differences were unexpected. Furthermore, the nearness of the two halves of the village—in terms of social relations, geography, and shared history—made the unexpected differences and unwanted resemblances problematic. This context magnified and essentialized difference, thus shaping new patterns of inclusion and exclusion. Although the opening of the border at first seemed to undo the political division of Sarpi, ten years later this division appeared more deeply imprinted than ever.

Renewed and Aborted Contacts

One way of gaining further insight into why cross-border contact became problematic is to look closely at the stories of Sarpians and their experiences with people from the other side. As with all stories, these narratives are grounded in experience, addressed to particular audiences, and intended to convey specific messages. The stories presented in this chapter told why many narrators no longer cared about the border opening and how they had become disillusioned about contacts across the border. The following conversation was recorded in 2000 during an evening with Avtandil, Zurabi, and Nino. It is important to note that Avtandil and Zurabi had frequently traveled to Turkey between 1990 and 1995. But neither they, nor Nino, still held an international passport.[1] Avtandil was in his forties and had made many trading trips to Turkey in the early 1990s, but he now earned his living as a cab driver. Zurabi was in his fifties and director of the village school. He had been involved in a number of cultural exchanges with Turkey after the border opening but had not crossed the border in the previous three years. Nino, twenty-eight at the time, had visited relatives in Turkey with her parents on a few occasions. She

---

1. After initial visits to relatives most villagers continued to cross the border only for business, and even that started to wane after the mid-1990s. This decrease in cross-border movement is primarily the result of dwindling trade opportunities (see chapter 7), but it is locally also explained by negative experiences with relatives in Turkey.

was unemployed and disillusioned not only with the cross-border contacts but more generally with the possibilities that life in Sarpi could offer. Avtandil, a gifted speaker, described the first time he met some of his relatives from the Turkish side:

> I have this aunt, who, together with her son, stayed in my house for three weeks.[2] I had not known her before, but I considered [her stay] to be a normal thing. I mean, she was a close relative. A few months later I happened to travel to Turkey for business when a neighbor asked me to deliver a message to someone. Of course I agreed. Anyway, going to Turkey was still like being on a tourist trip, and for me it was interesting to visit peoples' homes. [I ended up] not far from my relatives' house, those who had visited me here. I was thinking to myself, what [bad things] will they think if I would just pass their house without visiting? What will they think of me when they find out? So I decided to stop by. My cousin opened the door, and he just stared at me: "You!?" he said, "How come? What are you doing here?" When I entered the house I saw my aunt doing some ironing. She raised her head, only to lower it immediately after. [laughter] So there I was, standing. . . . My cousin didn't even have the guts to tell me that he was busy and wasn't able to receive guests at that moment. He didn't even apologize. So I just left by myself.

The episode was briefly discussed among the three. Zurabi remarked:

> For us those things are difficult to understand, because here relatives should come first. And there is another thing. You know how much hospitality means to us in Georgia. We have our tradition of eating and drinking. When they visit us, we know how to treat them, how to receive them well. Even if a person has nothing in his home and is in a bad economic situation, he will tell his kids: "Sorry, you will have to go to bed early. We don't have food for you; we have guests tonight. And the children won't even complain because they know how important it is to have guests. As we say, "Guests are a gift from God." . . . But over there it is not like that. They are a bit like Germans, economically that is—a little bit, a little bit of everything [implied is food, alcohol, and time]. Even their psychology is different. Seventy years may be very little for history, but it did a lot to them; they are not like we are. For us, relatives are the most valuable people, while for them kinship is obviously not that important. For them, a relative is just a person.

Nino nodded: "You see, they may be Laz, but they are still Turks. They may still know our language a little bit, but they have adopted a Turkish lifestyle. They don't care about their relatives the way we do. Perhaps they cannot help it; they lived under the Turkish regime for so many years." Avtandil picked up on the issue of the state. He asked Zurabi and Nino whether he should tell me one specific story. They pressed him to go on. Avtandil's story was about the

---

2. The term used was *deida* ("mother's sister" in Georgian). Here it referred to a younger cousin of Avtandil's mother.

trading adventures of his neighbor, Zviadi. Reportedly, Zviadi had made every effort to please a cousin from Turkey who had stayed in his house for three weeks. Before returning to Turkey the cousin offered Zviadi a risky though lucrative business deal. Zviadi would smuggle Kalashnikov bullets across the border, which they would then sell under the counter in his cousin's store. Because of the risks involved Zviadi decided to be careful on his first trip and just bring a few boxes of bullets along with other merchandise:

> He hid the bullets in his jacket and crossed the border without difficulties. But when he met his cousin, I think it was in Hopa, [his cousin] proposed to trade right there on the street, and to exhibit all the goods on the car. Well, Zviadi had some doubts about what was happening, but he had never expected that when his relative reappeared he would bring four, five policemen. They checked the merchandise on his car. Obviously they didn't find what they were looking for. Zviadi, however, became nervous as soon as he noticed the police. Luckily, before they approached closer he managed to throw [the box] behind his back in the river down the road. After that the police asked him, "Alright, where did you hide the bullets?!" Zviadi, who felt relieved now that he had gotten rid of the bullets, asked them what they were talking about. Of course the police didn't believe him. They searched everywhere in his car, even checked the tires. Finally they had to admit that there were no bullets. They apologized and left. Zviadi then turned to his cousin who had betrayed him, saying: "God helped me stay out of the Turkish prison, and you are going to help me stay out of the Georgian prison." His cousin's face showed his lack of understanding, so Zviadi went on: "You will help me by never setting a single step on Georgian territory because if you do, I will cut your throat. It is not worth spending years in jail for a nonhuman like you." That was the end of the story. You know, for Turks, God and the state are on the same level, and this way [Zviadi's] cousin wanted to show the secret services that, though he had relatives in Georgia, he was willing to sacrifice them for God, for the state.

This pejorative story conveyed the opinion of many Georgian Laz that, despite common genealogical descent, their cross-border relatives were strangers and, moreover, they needed to remain strangers. The narrators intended to underline the points of divergence between Laz in Georgia and those in Turkey, choosing stories that best exemplified that message. That Avtandil selected the story of his neighbor was no accident. He was encouraged to do so by Nino and Zurabi, probably because this story, better than any other, conveyed why they had no further interest in cross-border contacts. The story of "how Zviadi was betrayed by his cousin" pointed to absolute rejection of cross-border relatives. But betrayal is only possible between people who share something. Thus the story suggests that initially the differences between cross-border neighbors were not perceived as unbridgeable. It is therefore necessary to explore how the initial hopes of renewed contact were shattered and why ideas of unbridgeable difference came to be widely shared.

Managing Difference

The negative accounts may be seen as the product of encounters between people with different modes of thought. The accounts implicitly revealed the expectations Sarpians had about their relatives across the border. They also provided a way to structure and explain their disappointments. It is important to note that often the stories did not focus on *expected* differences, such as those between Islam and atheism or Christianity, between socialism and capitalism, or opposing nationalisms. Instead, discontent focused on more subtle differences that only became obvious in face-to-face communication, through values such as trust, hospitality, and reciprocity. The stories were so negative precisely because they involved unexpected difference, unexpected because of the close proximity between the two sides.

Expectations and Disappointments

Hospitality and reciprocity, or the lack thereof, were central elements in most accounts of cross-border contact. Sarpians told me repeatedly that when the border opened they gathered as many presents as they could and bestowed them on their long-separated relatives. And, so they say, they prepared a warm welcome, including large banquets, plentiful wine, and gifts for their guests from the Turkish side. The stress on hospitality was also evident in the stories told by Avtandil about himself and his neighbor Zviadi, in which they did everything possible to be good hosts to their relatives. Other testimonies, however biased in favor of the tellers, contained similar elements:

> When my relatives came [to Sarpi] for the first time, they arrived with an empty minivan. We were so glad that they had been able to come. Together with [neighbors] I spent two whole days preparing dishes, and [my daughter and husband] went to Batumi three times to buy them appropriate gifts. Oi, oi, oi, you should have seen how we received them. When they returned to Turkey their van was bursting with all kinds of presents.

And:

> We prepared a rich table, invited neighbors and relatives so that [the guests from Turkey] would see how much we appreciated their visit. The whole guestroom was packed with people. We drank wine; we ate; we danced. They must have thought, goodness, what expenses they've incurred. Of course, at that time everything was cheap here and we had plenty of money but, even so, we did what we could for them.

Whatever was true of these accounts, the stories about presents and food, and of providing accommodation, clearly referred to the importance of displaying hospitality in Georgian Sarpi. Extensive networks of reciprocity permeated the local community, where informal visits between neighbors and relatives formed the backbone of social life. The importance of reciprocal networks related, in part, to the nature of Soviet society. Indeed, living in a "shortage economy" meant that services, goods, and positions had to be obtained through informal networks (see Mars and Altman 1983; Dragadze 1988; Ledeneva 1998). In Sarpi, formal work obligations often came second to social obligations. The value of hospitality was locally displayed by recurring comments about Georgians (and also Laz) being the most hospitable nation in the world, by the saying that "guests are sent by God," and by insisting that festive dinners (like those for guests) were the Georgian equivalent of the "academy," the place where valuable information was exchanged and participants learned from one another's speeches.

My own experience with locally displayed hospitality was not without significance. In Sarpi I was always prepared to be a guest. At least once a week I spent long evenings drinking and eating in the company of people I barely knew, and I frequently spent the night at unforeseen addresses. As a guest I had to obey the rules and accept their displays of hospitality, and as an anthropologist I was willing to do so because of the information such events produced. Moreover, my position as an outsider was a relatively easy one: at least initially I was allowed to be ignorant of the rules of hospitality and was not expected to return their favors in a balanced way. Interestingly, Julian Pitt-Rivers pointed out in his essay on "the law of hospitality" (1977) that the position of the anthropologist resembles that of the "barbarian" more than that of the "stranger." In his view, there is a significant difference between these two categories. The "barbarian" is expected to remain an outsider to the local community, and therefore his behavior is relatively unimportant to the host. The "stranger," on the other hand, poses a greater risk to the host. He is potentially dangerous; therefore his worth needs to be tested. On the basis of this, he may be accepted or rejected (Pitt-Rivers 1977, 94–112). The situation was different for the relatives from Turkey. They were in the first instance neither "barbarians" nor "strangers." They were relatives but not "normal" ones, given the long break in relationships. Still, as relatives they were expected to become part of social relations. They were expected to fit within patterns of hospitality and reciprocity and to respond properly to hospitable displays.

However, all three demands of reciprocity—the obligation to give, the obligation to receive, and the obligation to give back—turned out to be problematic with cross-border relatives. "To refuse to give, to fail to invite, just as to refuse to receive, is tantamount to declaring war; it is to reject the bond of alliance and commonality," wrote Marcel Mauss (1990, 13). As such, in Sarpi "declarations of war," so to speak, were often made unwittingly. They were the result of people trying to extend bonds of alliance on terms that were mutually incomprehensible or potentially offensive. Reshid, an elderly inhabitant of Sarpi, provides an example of how displays of hospitality were not always appropriately accepted:

> When you serve [people from Turkey] food they always first ask what kind of meat it is. But even when you say it is beef, they still won't eat it. Last year I had canned beef from China, good stuff, and I left fifteen cans with them. It was beef, but after three months they gave it back; they didn't eat it. I reassured them it was beef and even showed the picture of a cow [which was visible] on the can. But they said, "No, no, it is pork."

Reshid told the incident as a joke to cast doubt on his relatives' capacity for understanding. Implicitly, however, such misunderstandings indicated another possibility, that some of the gifts Sarpians bestowed on their relatives were, in fact, inappropriate. The festive dinners they prepared for guests from Turkey may have included pork dishes (they often did when I was a guest), and they certainly included vodka and wine, which their guests may have interpreted as improper indeed.

Understandably, Sarpians only rarely questioned their own judgment. Rather, they focused on their relatives' shortcomings in reciprocating their hospitality. Zurabi on one occasion remarked, "When they were our guests we did not give in order to receive back the same, but you expect at least something in return. But one of the first questions they asked when we arrived was, 'How long are you going to stay?'" Another villager said: "When you visit a relative he asks you, 'Why did you come, how long will you stay, and when will you go?' I say, I don't ever want to deal with you again. I'd rather sleep in a hotel." To most inhabitants of Georgian Sarpi it was clear that hospitality was poorly developed on the Turkish side and that kinship mattered very little to their relatives across the border. Most insisted that they felt unwelcome or had been given improper treatment, for example, that "they only offered me tea, cup after cup."

This sense of disillusionment was most prominent in stories that described betrayal. This was obvious in the story told about Zviadi, in which a relative exposed him to the police. Teimur Bekirishi told me a similar story. He said that he and a group of Sarpians had been in Arhavi in Turkey to participate in a cultural festival. During their stay they visited a restaurant: "We were sitting there, and I noticed the waiter trying to eavesdrop on our conversation. I took a closer look, thought I recognized him, so I asked, 'Aren't you the son of . . .' He immediately became red in his face. It turned out that he *was* my relative. Later other people confirmed that this guy worked for the secret service." Teimur then concluded, "For them the state is like God, they even consider it normal to betray relatives to advance their own position."

The frequency with which stories of treachery were told makes it difficult to ascertain their status. Were such stories so vividly remembered and so readily told because betrayal by relatives is unforgivable? Or were they invoked (perhaps invented) because they provided a legitimate reason to "reject bonds of alliance and commonality"? In either case, such stories could only be told and shared once the relatives across the border were not considered relatives anymore. The stories concerning treachery, like the narrations of less dramatic experiences, were combined with national rhetoric to reinforce and substantiate more encompassing social and cultural boundaries. Indeed, through these stories people found confirmation of the ideological dimensions of the cold war divide. By narrating these stories, the iron curtain, as a mental construct and a barrier for social relations, was partly rebuilt.

Explanations and Categorizations

The inhabitants of Georgian Sarpi commented elaborately on what they thought had changed their relatives. They pointed out that their neighbors across the border became different because they had "lived under the Turkish regime for so many years." A sixty-five-year-old woman noted:

> You know, even at home they were very afraid to speak Lazuri. In Georgia there was only one Laz village, but still they let us speak our language. There were so many minorities in the Soviet Union . . . and they all had to learn their own language as well as Russian. That's the way it should be. But in Turkey, you are only allowed to speak Turkish. Even in their passports they could only write "Turk."

The influences of "Turkish nationalism" and the "repressive state" (quite a myopic observation for someone raised during the Stalin era) were frequently employed in explaining why Laz in Turkey had "forgotten who they were." Indeed, these factors were generally adopted to explain the lack of "ethnic awareness" among their cross-border neighbors. To account for other changes, like the lack of hospitality, there were other explanations at hand. A man in his forties said: "We discovered that hospitality is not well developed among them. It is, of course, because they hardly had anything. As recently as fifteen years ago they were very poor. Now they may be living well, but they still behave as if they have to save every lira. The times have changed. Now we are the poor ones, but, as you have seen, we still do everything to treat our guests well." What was needed, in a way, was to neutralize the feeling of economic inferiority that the changes had brought about. Or, to paraphrase Žižek, this involved stereotyping as an expression of collective frustration, concealing the imperfections of one's own society (1990, 53–57).

Another alleged cause of why Laz in Turkey had changed was that they had lived in a capitalist system. A former director of the collective farm, still a devoted Communist, used his trips to reaffirm his views of capitalism:

> You know what really surprised me in Turkey? [That] a brother who gives something to his sibling should ask money for it. Once I visited an acquaintance in Hopa. We were riding in his car and saw his brother standing besides the road. We stopped and the brother entered [the car]. When, after a few kilometers, he left the car again, he handed money to his brother. I asked why this was happening. You know what he said: "The car is mine and driving costs money, therefore he pays." They have such a custom that you need to pay for everything. And they don't care

about other people. Of course, those who have enough money live very well. My cousin, for example, is rich, while his neighbor has nothing at all. . . . It was exactly what I had learned [in school]. The capitalist always wants to become richer. He only cares about himself.

Among the Sarpians there was a strong consensus when characterizing Turkish Laz. People commented that "those people" were no longer Laz; they had forgotten their language and history; even their personalities had changed. Turkish Laz purportedly had become more orthodox in their religious beliefs than all Laz had traditionally been.[3] Some went further to say that there were no Laz left in Turkey. A young woman remarked, "Pff, they have just become Turks; only the language remains, and even that is disappearing."

To an outsider it may seem that inhabitants of both sides of the border had changed in a number of ways. But this was not how inhabitants of Georgian Sarpi perceived things. They saw Turkish Laz as the ones who had changed, while they believed themselves to have remained faithful to the true path. This does not mean that inhabitants of Sarpi were not aware of the impact of the state on their own lives. For example, they did not forget that they had changed their names to appear more Georgian, or that many of their "traditions" were recent innovations. But this awareness was reconciled with positive notions of self. Sarpians insisted that the changes on the Soviet side of the border meant that they had become "more like themselves." A short discussion between two villagers—the second of Russian descent—was revealing on this point.

FIRST VILLAGER: They [Laz in Turkey] even say that they are Turks. That is already visible in their passports. It only mentions "Turk," not a word about who they really are.

SECOND VILLAGER: You say that about them, but what about yourself? *Your* passport only mentions that you are Georgian.

FIRST VILLAGER: That is different, because Georgians and Laz have always been like siblings. They have defended and assisted each other when one [or the other] was weak. In the fourth century this region was called Lazika, and probably then the Georgians were called Laz. Now it is the other way around. We are only with a few, so we write in our passports that we are Georgian. You see, we are both Laz and Georgian.

The disillusioning experiences with Laz in Turkey were instrumental in creating unambiguous cultural boundaries. These boundaries marked differences between the self-styled "remaining Laz" or "first-class Georgians" of Georgian Sarpi and Laz across the border, who were called "Turkified Laz," or simply, "Turks." The obvious message of the passage was that because Laz and Georgians were related through history, it was only logical that they had things in common. In a similar vein, when social or cultural changes in their own vil-

---

3. One villager told me about this divergence of religious affiliations: "Of course they changed. They adopted Islam. We were also Muslims, but not like they are right now."

lage were discussed, Sarpians depicted them in positive terms as a "quest for ethnic roots." These attitudes stressed a continuity that reached back to a shared Georgian past. By contrast, the changes that had occurred on the Turkish side of the border were explained by referring—with a strong negative connotation—to "the force of Islam" and "Turkish nationalism," as well as to previous poverty and, with more ambiguity, to capitalism. In short, although the two sides had physically drawn closer in the years after 1988, this softening of the physical divide was accompanied by a hardening of cultural boundaries.

Grounding Difference

The negative impressions of cross-border contact were clearest among middle-aged men and women who had grown up with high expectations concerning their cross-border relatives and whose lives had been most entwined in Soviet Georgian society. The youth of Sarpi were less insistent. For them, renewed contacts had not been all that important; they looked to Georgian cities or to Europe for their aspirations and hardly cared about their "new" (still somewhat distant) relatives. Stories of people above sixty showed less uniformity: very positive accounts alternated with extremely negative ones. Again, social distance seems to be what mattered the most. Like Kake, the elderly woman who had positive memories about her visits to Turkish Sarp, quite a few elderly villagers were still in contact with their relatives on the other side. But although sometimes these connections meant that elderly people had ambiguous, at times even positive, feelings about life in Turkey, the connections also meant that experienced differences were potentially threatening to their ideas of self and other.

Back to "Normal"

On the afternoon of February 22, 2000, my host mother, Maguli, started to prepare for the funeral of her aunt (her father's sister). She spent two hours downstairs in the bathroom, and when she emerged she was dressed in black and ready to go. The funeral was to start at four o'clock in the afternoon, so half an hour earlier Maguli walked to the backyard of her neighbors to survey the scene. In the distance across the border, some three hundred meters away, the open space in front of a white house was just filling up with people. It was too far to see much else. Around four o'clock her aunt's body was carried out of the house. After some time had passed a group of people moved away from the house, disappearing in the distance where the road curved around a hill. Maguli then returned to her house, changed her clothes again, and started preparations for dinner. She explained that she had considered attending the funeral, but her passport had expired and it was too expensive to buy a new one. Then she said: "Anyway, I don't know how I would have felt there. They do things so differently." Later, her daughter Nino told me, "I had a strange feeling when she made all these preparations and went to [neighbor] Mamuka's terrace to watch. It reminded me of the past. I remember her standing there, looking at the houses of her relatives as if she could see what they were doing." For Nino the behavior of her mother during the funeral was a reminder of the closed border. As such it was an indication that despite the opening of the border, the distance between the two village halves had not diminished.

The funeral that Maguli observed was that of her aunt Aise, who had died in Turkish Sarp at eighty-six. Aise's family biography was typical of many of the families that were divided by the borderline. Born on the Georgian side of the village, Aise married across the border before its closure in 1937 and was prohibited from contact with her relatives until the 1980s. Two of her younger siblings were still alive and living in the Georgian part of the village, along with many of her nieces and nephews. After 1988 Aise visited her brothers in Georgian Sarpi several times until she became too ill to leave the house.

Some fifteen villagers from Georgian Sarpi attended her funeral, including Aise's two brothers, and accompanied her body to the cemetery. The funeral did not, in many respects, live up to the brothers' expectations. When I spoke with them a few days after the funeral they were still upset about the event and how they had been treated. Muhammad, one of the brothers, had barely reached the funeral in time. His financial situation had been difficult for years, and he had not been able to renew his international passport. Still wishing to visit his sister, he believed that he had diplomatically asked his nephews living on the Turkish side of the village to help him out. He was sure they would do so because they had repeatedly invited him to come. Moreover, from Muhammad's perspective, money seemed not to be a problem for his nephews as they spent large amounts on "fun trips" to Batumi. Whatever the reason, the nephews never responded, leaving him without the necessary papers. Only after the intervention of relatives on the Georgian side did he manage to get across the border—without a passport—for an hour.

The other brother, Reshid, was more disappointed, despite or perhaps because he had spent two whole days on the other side.[4] Accustomed to large Georgian funerals that involved a good deal of eating, drinking, and toasting, Reshid's experience was disillusioning. He agitatedly told me that he was only given "Turkish soup" and that he was not even invited into the house of his sister. He added that after the commemoration of his sister on the fifty-second day following her death, he would never set foot on Turkish soil again.

As I was repeatedly told after the funeral, the death of Aise was a tragic one, not only because of the grief of her close relatives but because her death disrupted the last significant family bond between families in the two villages. The funeral completed the tragedy of the unhappily divided community. Although the Georgian Sarpians would not say so, the accounts also demon-

---

4. Before Reshid decided not to cross the border again, he had often told me about his visits to Turkey. Though often joking about their "strange customs," he seemed to have enjoyed these visits.

strated another point of regret—the fact that communication, even between kin, was severely strained. The practices of the Turkish Laz struck relatives across the border as strange, uncivilized, even offensive. In the case of the funeral, conflicting values were especially apparent in the way the funeral was organized.[5] The brothers returned home with the conviction that they had been denied proper treatment.

It was not only the negative content of the stories that was striking but the way in which the stories spread. Sarpians were usually very careful to uphold a good image of their (half of the) village, and the wrongdoings of covillagers were usually kept well hidden, especially to outsiders like myself. This time, however, I did not encounter any difficulty in eliciting stories. People readily told their stories and gave their judgments of the event. Moreover, a strong consensus existed among the villagers in their negative feeling about the funeral and in their condemnation of the nephews' behavior. This made it indirectly clear that despite the local discourse of "one village unhappily divided," people in fact accepted that the two villages were not only separated but also parts of two different worlds. The inhabitants of the other Sarpi were no longer part of their own group. They had become outsiders and needed to stay on the other side of the border.

Redrawing Borders and Boundaries

In one of our conversations, Maguli told me, "It used to be that everyone wanted the border to be open, but [my husband] Anzor always said: 'If they do that then the whole village will be spoiled, then you won't recognize Sarpi any longer, because there will be more strangers than Sarpians.' And look what has happened . . . nothing has remained of the old life; it is as if [we] live in a new place." Her daughter Nino added, "It is anarchy now." Nino probably implied more than just disruptions of "ethnic homogeneity." Judging from other instances in which she had used the word *anarchy*, the phrase most likely also referred to the economic and political instability of life after socialism. Within this context of instability, there were pressing needs to reestablish order. Although the physical obstructions that regulated traffic and communication had become porous, perhaps *because* of this, inhabitants of Sarpi started to fortify social and cultural boundaries of their own.

As illustrated throughout this chapter, symbolic discourse is an important element in the construction of boundaries. But the creation of boundaries in Sarpi was not limited to the discursive level. In various ways the ideas about cultural difference were translated to, and inscribed in, the territory of Sarpi, resulting in spatial and symbolic reorganizations. Several of these "inscrip-

5. Young Sarpians in particular held very negative views of funeral practices across the border. One girl exclaimed, "They do not even mourn! Within a few days the women wear their regular clothes again. Maybe over here women wear mourning dresses too long [often more than a year], but at least we pay respect to the dead."

tions" have been mentioned in previous chapters. Restaurants and bars, for example, were adorned with names such as "Colchis" and "Golden Fleece," which were taken from Greek legends but intended to connect the Laz to ancient Georgian history. Likewise, the new version of the Colkhoba festival was intended to celebrate Georgian Laz culture as well as to demonstrate difference from the Turkish side. The clearest example, however, of how Georgian Sarpians distanced themselves from their neighbors on the Turkish side concerned religion. Since the mid-1990s a growing number of young and middle-aged Sarpians had converted to Orthodox Christianity. These converts proudly told me about their baptism and often demonstrated their shift in religious allegiance by wearing Christian crosses around their neck. But it was never very clear whether their adoption of Christianity implied personal devotion; as such, it seemed that baptism was yet one more way to distance themselves from the Turkish Laz with whom they shared an Islamic past.

For the same reason, the existence of two mosques on the Turkish side, especially the one that was built on the coastline in the early 1990s, greatly disturbed many young Sarpians. The mosque was visible from afar and was the first image of Sarpi that travelers from Batumi to Sarpi saw. One middle-aged man told me, "You know why they built that mosque over there? Just so that everyone would see it. They clearly didn't build it for the villagers, because they already had one. . . . They placed it right there on that rock, just to provoke us." This "provocation" was the more painful because it also affected how inhabitants of Georgian Sarpi were perceived by visitors from other parts of Georgia. Rezo, a well-off thirty-two-year-old Sarpian, commented:

> Visitors often make jokes about it. They say that Sarpi is already in Turkey. Therefore, we want to build a church right here on the coastline, which will be visible for everyone. But unfortunately we don't have enough money. You see, the church needs to be at least as big as the mosque, otherwise . . . well, you understand, if we build only a small chapel . . . there would be no balance.

In 1997 Rezo and his friends formed a project group to investigate the possibility of building a church. They even had an audience with the bishop in Batumi, and although the bishop was highly pleased with the villagers' intention, he was not able to help them financially.

It was difficult to judge how far advanced the plans actually were, but the amount of discussion in Sarpi suggested that the issue was at least considered important. Finding a good spot for the church appeared to be problematic. Miriani, who was one of the members of the project group, explained that they had considered various options. They preferred to build the church near the border along the coast, but the customs office claimed part of that land. Another potential location was a rock that stuck out in the sea, "visible from a large distance, just like their mosque." Miriani told me that this rock was not stable enough and would eventually be washed away by the sea:

Now we think that the best place is actually the old men's house, and when we are old we want to give that place up for a church. Some people thought about constructing it in Kalendera [a neighborhood across the hill], but that doesn't have the same result. First of all, it isn't visible from the other side of the border, and second, only the staunch believers would go there—it wouldn't have any impact on those who are in the middle.

The difficulties suggested that it would be a long time before a church was built. Moreover, religious differences between the Turkish and Georgian sides were perhaps less pronounced than the younger generation liked to admit. Some residents who were in their sixties pointed out that they were unsure whether Sarpi was "ready for it." Zurabi stated, "I think that at this moment all the youth and some 50 percent of our generation is ready. But you also have to respect the wishes of the elders." My host father, Anzor, always rather ambivalent about religion, doubted that anyone would attend the church:

Here Christianity is often only a symbol. I think it is unwise to force religion on people. Of course, Sarpi will be Christian, but according to me time should bring that about, not people. . . . Let me tell you an anecdote. Once these young men [refers to the group of Miriani] told me that they would never allow the building of a mosque in Sarpi. You know how I replied? I said, "There already is a mosque in Sarpi, there are even two mosques."

Anzor was referring to the two mosques in Turkish Sarp, and although I doubt that he actually considered the Turkish side to be part of the village, his joke pointed at the differences in perception between the different generations. Elderly inhabitants still talked about Sarpi as two parts that (once) made up one whole, but the younger generation never thought of Turkish Sarp when they talked about their village. Similarly, while the younger generation considered Islam an anomaly because of its perceived incompatibility with Georgian or Laz "culture," for the older generation Islam was a valued tradition. Residents of Georgian Sarpi actively shaped their environment in attempts to define where they did or did not belong, but the new boundaries, thus constructed, were not to be uncontested.

Anthropological border studies have devoted much attention to the ambiguities that lie beneath borderlines and to the imperfections of international divides. Baud and van Schendel, for example, write that "despite attempts by central states to control their borderlanders and to impose a 'national' culture on them, a fascinating aspect of many borderlands is the development of a 'creole' or 'syncretic' border culture" (1997, 234). In the preceding chapters I have discussed patterns of identification that transgressed state borders. These involved ambiguities that were not extinguished by seventy years of Soviet rule or by the physical and ideological enforcement of the iron curtain. However, the key aspect of identity construction in Sarpi was that imposed ideas and ideologies became crucial ingredients for the renovation of imagined boundaries, long after the taboos surrounding the border itself had fallen.

Events in the late 1980s had enabled villagers to renew contacts with long-lost relatives, contacts that clearly did not live up to expectations. In the perceptions of Laz living on the Georgian side, relatives across the border not only had different lifestyles but held radically different ideas about friendship, kinship, hospitality, and trade. The most difficult message in this reunion may have been that the people involved were not simply "others" but alienated versions of themselves, covillagers who had always been visible in the distance. Whereas one expects—or at times at least accepts—deviant behavior from outsiders, it is harder to accept deviance from nearby relatives. It is difficult to define whether the differences of which Sarpians spoke were "major" or "minor" and thus whether we can speak of "narcissism of minor differences," as Blok would have it (2001). But it is clear that the differences mattered most when (a) they were least expected, (b) social distances were shortest, and (c) they endangered local ways of life. A process was started whereby "minor" differences were enlarged and "large" differences were essentialized.

In his discussion of German unification, Borneman provides an interesting hypothesis for why "unity" was so problematic there, suggesting that West Germans may have resented "the disintegration of their mirror-image, and the collapse of a moral order that always ascribed to them superiority—at least over the *Ossies* [East Germans]" (1992, 334). In Sarpi as well, the disintegration of *their* mirror-image disturbed patterns of self and other. The fact that the economic affluence of Soviet Sarpi vis-à-vis their neighbors in Turkey was reversed perhaps only intensified the need to proclaim cultural superiority. Whereas Borneman discusses a situation in which two moieties competed and were forced to merge, villagers in Sarpi not only reacted to "the other side" but also had to deal with the expectations and suspicions of their fellow countrymen. Perhaps these two factors—the reversal of economic superiority and the danger of being labeled Turkish—made the opening particularly threatening. To counter these threats, Sarpians mobilized ideas of "cultural loss" and "Soviet corruption" to create an "authentic" culture that proved their superiority over the Laz in Turkey and firmly established their Georgian roots among their fellow countrymen.

A last comparison with the iron curtain in Germany may provide insight. Borneman predicted in 1992 that German unification would not overcome, and would even generate, "'durable forms of division' in the East–West distinction" (1992, 334). Time has shown that his predictions were only partly correct. Certainly, there still are profound differences between East and West. But, as Berdahl realistically concluded in 1999, the involvement of a new generation in a single Germany, combined with the movement back and forth across a bygone border "may prevent the solidification of identities at either end" (1999, 232). In Sarpi, the literal or physical border did not disappear. Although its porosity was initially celebrated, it came to be endowed with new cultural and social markers of division. Perhaps the local discourse of "one village unhappily divided" sums it all up. After the border was closed in 1937 many inhabitants did not live to see their siblings, parents, or children ever again. But in many ways it was only after the border was opened that they truly lost their relatives, separated by seemingly unbridgeable differences.

PART II

Frontiers of Islam and Christianity in Upper Ajaria

Introduction

Christian Incursions

The start of my fieldwork in upper Ajaria in May 2000 coincided with nation-wide festivities celebrating famous moments in Georgian history. It had been approximately three millennia since the first Georgian state was established and two millennia since Christianity made its entrance into Georgian territory. The Autonomous Republic of Ajaria played a special role in these events because of its unique history. Although the inhabitants of Ajaria are (or were) predominantly Sunni Muslim, the province is believed to be the site where Christianity first took hold. The memorable year 2000, then, was an excellent occasion for the Georgian Orthodox Church to raise awareness of Ajaria's presumed deep Christian roots and, moreover, to reinforce its missionary work among the region's Muslim population. One of the celebrations was a procession to the place where the first church in Georgia was supposed to have been built. According to the story, the apostle Andrew built a church in the heart of present-day upper Ajaria in the first century AD.[1]

On May 23, a group of priests, bishops, scholars, and locally revered writers made a pilgrimage to this perceived hearth of Georgian Christianity. The appearance of the group of Christians in the small Muslim village of Didach'ara was undoubtedly an unusual sight for its inhabitants. Black-bearded priests in black cassocks carrying a colorful icon of Saint Andrew were followed by a

1. This narrative is based on the work of Mroveli, an eighth-century Georgian bishop. Although the passages referring to Saint Andrew are considered later additions to Mroveli's work, they are increasingly accepted as proof of the ancient roots of Christianity in the region. See Bibileishvili and Mgeladze (2000) and the website of the Batumi and Skhalta diocese at http://eparchy.batumi.net/. The renewed focus on Saint Andrew breaks with earlier Georgian historiography, which traced Christianization to the missionary work of Holy Nino in the fourth century AD (see Thomson 1996).

Orthodox Christian clergy and Batumi intellectuals walk in the footsteps of Saint Andrew during a pilgrimage to Didach'ara. Photo by Julie McBrien, May 2000.

group of singing youths. They made their way through the village to the top of the hill where the church had supposedly once overlooked the valley. It is hard to guess the thoughts of the village men who sat on benches in front of the mosque watching the procession pass by. Whatever they were thinking, the men kept silent, either taken by surprise or, more likely, because they had been instructed by village authorities not to make provocations.

At the top of the hill was a small natural clearing, partly surrounded by trees, overlooking the village and the green valleys running down to the Black Sea. It was a remarkably convenient spot for the supposed existence of a church. Although there was not a single remnant of any building, the participants earnestly insisted that it had been the original site, and any reason for doubt, moreover, was erased by the placement of a commemorative plaque on the hill. Then the participants gathered around the icon of Saint Andrew. On one side stood the clergy and on the other side representatives of Batumi University. Behind this first row a group of youth gathered, while a handful of local government officials watched from a short distance. Bishop Dmitri opened a case, took out the religious requisites and began the service. The songs of the priests and children floated into the air. The bishop led the group in prayer. He then walked to the icon, sprinkled holy water over the picture of Saint Andrew, and invited the attendants to receive God's blessings. After this, the attendants made their way back to the village, preceded by the icon of Andrew.

The celebrations concluded with a *supra* (festive dinner) given by the mayor, a Muslim. The banquet was in "true Georgian style," with plenty of food, wine, and vodka. The bishop was appointed *tamada* (toastmaster) and used this position to make speeches about the region's ancient history, which, he emphasized, was a Christian one. In subsequent speeches, the priests, scholars, and writers presented their version of the life of Saint Andrew. They lamented the "unfortunate" period in Ajaria—namely three centuries of Turkish oppression—and the ensuing abandonment of Christianity by the region's inhabitants. Simultaneously, however, they trivialized this period by telling stories that purportedly proved Christianity's enduring influence. When a priest remarked that until 1929 women continued to worship clandestinely in the church in Skhalta, he intimated that residents retained their Christian faith through the Muslim period. Similarly, a discussion about the local practice of making two perpendicular cuts in homemade cornbread—a "Christian" symbol—revealed Christianity's continuing influence. In the same spirit, the bishop predicted a bright future in which the local inhabitants would return to their original, native religion.

The stress on Christianity in these stories revealed the asymmetries of power between the intellectual elite and the clergy on the one hand and the Muslim villagers on the other. But, as subsequent remarks demonstrated, the power imbalance was certainly not unchallenged. When a toast was raised to the inseparable connection between the Georgian nation and Church, one of the attending villagers loudly remarked: "Well, I am Georgian, but I am also Muslim. What about that?" The comment caused a stir in the room. Several villagers dared to laugh. For the clergy and the guests from Batumi it was an unpleasant moment, though they tried their best to keep favorable facial expressions. Not long after this minor incident the bishops and priests retreated, and discussion of ancient history ceased. Those left behind debated why there had been such a one-sided focus on Christian roots. With some cynicism, one man said, "It is really nice that Christianity has such a long history in Ajaria, but we live here *now*, and we have our own life, our own religion." In other words, whereas the clergy aimed to include Ajarians and Georgians in the same category by stressing the Christian roots of the region, the villagers (although identifying with the Georgian nation) did not accept the full implication of this inclusion and differentiated between "us Muslims" and "them Christians."

The events were telling of the social context within which the Georgian Orthodox Church was expanding its influence in the region. The participants discussed the relationship between Christianity and the Georgian nation and whether it was possible for Muslims to retain their faith and still claim Georgian nationality. Because the categories involved were perceived as being so deeply rooted in the past, this struggle was also, or perhaps primarily, a struggle over history. Against this background the importance of Andrew and the references to the persistence of Christianity become clear. The story of Saint

Andrew reinforced the idea of Georgia being a Christian nation par excellence and Ajaria being an indivisible part of that history. This gave moral weight to the Church in its attempts to Christianize Ajaria. Moreover, by claiming that Ajarians had secretly visited churches and used Christian symbols, the clergy and the intelligentsia "proved" the continuing influence of Christianity. The villagers who attended the supra disagreed as to the consequences of this historical narrative. When they were among themselves, they trivialized the stories by saying that they lived not in the past but in the present. But although this response lightened villagers' moods, it did not dispute the content of the historical narrative. In fact, the villagers' response was largely toothless because they had internalized the terms by which their Christian guests had challenged them.

In part 2 of this book, I attempt to understand the religious dynamics in post-Soviet Ajaria. Why was the Muslim renewal essentially short-lived, and why did Ajarians increasingly convert to Orthodox Christianity? Clearly, in answering this question it is crucial to address the post-Soviet sociopolitical contexts in which religious change was taking place. But, as the scenes above also suggest, it is equally important to understand the historical processes that shaped the terms of the postsocialist encounters between Muslims and Christians. By tracing the complex patterns of interaction between Muslim Ajarians, Georgian nationalists, Soviet "atheizers," and Orthodox Christian clerics, we witness the formation of the dominant narrative of the unity of Georgianness and Christianity. Moreover, these processes of interaction clarify in important ways the (im)possibilities of religious renewal in independent Georgia. As such, the "extraordinary" case of the Ajarians, who on the whole did *not* return to their pre-Soviet religious traditions, highlights the limitations of commonsensical assumptions about the "revival" of religious traditions after the "long Soviet freeze."

4 The Making and Transformation
of the Frontier

The central tenet of undisrupted Christian-Georgian continuity, as propagated by the clergy and the intelligentsia since the 1980s, gives weight to the missionary activities of the Georgian Orthodox Church in Ajaria. According to this myth, Ajarians had never *really* been Muslim but rather had always, if only subconsciously, perceived themselves as Georgians and thus, implicitly, as Christians.[1] The advancement of this myth points to a tendency that has been observed in many postsocialist countries. In Verdery's words, "Throughout the postsocialist world there has been a veritable orgy of historical revisionism, of writing the communist period out of the past" (1999, 112). In assessing the historical revisionism occurring in Ajaria, one should add three considerations. First, this revisionism did not only write off the Communist period, it obliterated the three centuries preceding 1878, when Ajaria was part of the Ottoman Empire. Second, in the case of Ajaria historical revisionism was not only a post-Soviet phenomenon but a robust continuation of Soviet historiography, now modified to attend to the renewed importance of Christianity. Third, this earlier origin of historical revisionism resulted in it becoming the only existing narrative, at least in print.

The genealogy of the master narrative of Georgian-Christian continuity reveals the shifting linkages between religious, ethnic, and national categories on the frontier. An examination of the discursive shifts and their relation to historically unfolding power structures shows how and why the Georgian-Christian discourse emerged, came to dominate, and eventually enchained Muslim narratives (cf. Wolf 2001, 379). My point is not simply to expose local myths of Georgian-Christian primordiality or to demonstrate that Georgian traditions in Ajaria were often "invented." Rather, my aim is to show that the dis-

1. For an English version of this myth, see Mgeladze (1994).

cursive as well as political shifts shaped the public sphere and as such had vast consequences for postsocialist religious dynamics. Indeed, an investigation of the particular intertwining of national and religious discourses shows why, after a long period of state atheism, a further decline of Islam and increased conversion to Christianity occurred in Ajaria.

The Making of the Frontier

Written sources on everyday religious life until the Russian conquest of the region in 1878 are scarce. Informed guesses of historians suggest that although Ajaria had been part of the Ottoman Empire since the end of the sixteenth century, adoption of Islam occurred much later. Islam was adopted earlier in the coastal region than in upper Ajaria, possibly because of more intense contact with the Ottoman heartland. Likewise, the pace of religious change differed among social strata. Throughout the seventeenth century cases of conversion were reported for members of the elite, the *beys* (governors) and *aghas* (rich landowners).[2] Little is known about the conversion of the lower strata, though several authors èstimate that it was a much slower process that was not completed until the beginning of the nineteenth century.[3] This supposed late adoption of Islam, at least when compared with the neighboring Laz and Meskhetians (Bellér-Hann 1995, 489; Benninghaus 2002, 483–84; Meeker 2002, 90), might be because the region, especially upper Ajaria, was only weakly integrated into the Ottoman Empire. Up until the nineteenth century, it had been economically and strategically unimportant. For a long time, the Ottomans pursued a policy of indirect rule and did not interfere directly in local politics (Allen 1929, 135–56; Allen and Muratoff 1953, 9).

The "peripheral" status of Ajaria changed during the first half of the nineteenth century. The advance of the Russians into the Caucasus, and especially their successes in the Russo-Ottoman wars of 1828–29, increased the strategic importance of Ajaria. The changed geopolitical position of Ajaria likely strengthened the position of Islam. There are some indicators that support this claim. First, this period saw an increase in the construction of mosques, not only along the coast where Ottoman influence was greater but also increasingly in the mountain villages of upper Ajaria.[4] Moreover, the most powerful family of upper Ajaria, the Khimshiashvilis, is said to have adopted Islam

2. For example, the genealogy of the powerful Abashidze family mentions, from 1560 onward, only Muslim first names, such as Suleiman, Ahmed, and Mustafa (Abashidze 1998, 232–323).

3. This view is based on the conclusions of the Georgian publisher Zakaria Ch'ich'inadze, who collected oral testimonies of conversion during the 1890s (1915). See also Meiering Mikadze (1999, 241–61).

4. Three of the oldest and most important mosques of upper Ajaria (those of Didach'ara, Ghorjomi, and Khulo) were built between 1820 and 1830.

as late as 1829, immediately after the first incursion of the Russian army into Ajaria (Potto 1912, 129–30; Geladze 1969).

Over the following decades Ottoman and Turkish cultural forms were gradually adopted, not least because of extensive patterns of circular migration that developed between Ajaria and Istanbul.[5] In the 1870s, Georgian and Russian visitors to Ajaria noticed that villagers had adopted Turkish names and only vaguely remembered their former Georgian family names. Likewise, the *chadri* (veil) and the fez (red felt brimless hat) became part of the standard local dress. Georgian became less important in the course of the nineteenth century. In the 1870s it was spoken only at home, and the men predominantly spoke Turkish in public. Ottoman Turkish was also the literary language, suggesting that Turkish had firmly established its position as the lingua franca (Kazbeg 1875, cited in Allen 1929, 146–47; Seidlitz 1884, 441–42).

The increased importance and visibility of Islam in the public sphere coincided with the changed strategic position of the region; Ajaria found itself on the frontline between the Ottoman and Russian armies. During these Russo-Turkish wars, the population of Ajaria sided with the Ottoman forces in their struggle against the advancing *giauri* (non-Muslims)—Russians as well as Georgians. After the first aborted invasion of Ajaria in 1828 the Russians tried in vain to persuade local beys to side with them. Instead, the beys became some of the most determined opponents of the Russians and were characterized as "fanatically anti-Christian, stoutly conservative, and attached by many personal interests to the court in Istanbul" (Allen and Muratoff 1953, 40). From the late 1850s onward the Russian army was severely challenged by attacks waged by "fierce Ajarians and Laz irregulars" (Allen and Muratoff 1953, 214). The war was eventually decided far away, on the highlands near Kars. Ajaria passed to the Russians only after an agreement had been reached at the Berlin Conference of 1878.[6]

Encounters

The second half of the nineteenth century witnessed the emergence of a nationalist movement in Georgia, which saw its own interests coinciding with the Russian advance.[7] In this nationalist perspective, Ajaria was perceived as a lost region that ought to be brought back into the orbit of the Georgian na-

5. Typically, a young Ajarian would live in Istanbul for several years and on return be able to set up a business and support a family (Megrelidze 1964, 81–83). These circular migratory patterns with Istanbul existed in many Ottoman provinces (Quataert 1993, 787).

6. For an extensive discussion of the Russian acquisition of Batumi, see Jelavich (1970).

7. Suny (1996) explains the emergence of Georgian nationalism as an effect of the incorporation of Georgia (minus Ajaria) into the Russian Empire, which created the modern basis of nationality—economic stability, modes of communication, Western education—and enabled the emergence of a national elite. His analysis explicitly draws on Gellner's theoretical framework of nationalism.

tion. In the newspaper *Iveria*, the leader of the nationalist movement, Ilia Chavchavadze, wrote the following shortly after the incorporation of Ajaria into the Russian Empire: "The Berlin treaty has done one tremendous good deed for us, and because of this a highly memorable year has passed. Our brothers in blood, the nest of our heroes, the cradle of our civilization, our ancient Georgia, were united to us" (cited in Abashidze 1998, 117).

It came as a shock to members of the nationalist movement that the rhetoric of brotherhood and Georgian unity did not encounter much enthusiasm among most Ajarians. Instead, between 1878 and 1880 a large portion of the native population decided to seek refuge in the Ottoman Empire.[8] The shock that this migration, or *muhajiroba*, caused the Georgian bourgeoisie was well conveyed by a Georgian commentator (G. Tsereteli) who wrote in the newspaper *Golos* that "for a long time I could not believe that Ajarians would wish to migrate to Turkey."[9]

The reasons for this emigration were discussed extensively at the time. In a letter to the viceroy of the tsar, a Georgian official wrote: "The inhabitants of Ajaria and Kars . . . run away from us, as if they are running from the plague! Is it possible that the single explanation for this is [religious] fanaticism? Without doubt, fanaticism partly causes it, but there are other, no less important reasons."[10] The alleged "fanaticism" was blamed on the Muslim clergy who, according to the Georgian press, stressed the impossibility of living a true Muslim life under the "heathen" rule of Russians and who spread the rumor that the Russians would force the inhabitants to convert to Christianity. The other reasons mentioned in the Georgian press included economic and political motives. First, the Ajarian elite had, by and large, lost the official positions that had secured them a steady income during the Ottoman Empire. Second, the Ottomans promised Ajarian immigrants exemptions from taxes and military service. In addition they were given access to fertile land for resettling.[11]

It may be, as the journalists implied, that economic and political factors played a larger role in the emigration than religious difference. What is interesting, though, is that individual migrants flatly rejected Georgian national rhetoric. "Every man, every soldier, in one word, every non-Ajarian takes us for people whom they can treat as dogs, because we are not Christian, because we are not Russian," one Ajarian emigrant said. "And that is exactly what they do. They [the new rulers] are not even punished if they murder an Ajarian." Another emigrant expressed similar feelings concerning the political situation after the incorporation of Ajaria into the Russian Empire, saying: "We are not

8. A rough estimation is that thirty thousand Ajarians (35 percent of the population) left the region, temporarily or permanently (Seidlitz 1884, 446).

9. Newspaper *Golos*, 5 February 1879, reprinted in Megrelidze (1964, 84–87).

10. From a letter of Grigol Orbeliani, 9 November 1879, reprinted in Megrelidze (1964, 79).

11. *Golos*, 5 February 1879, reprinted in Megrelidze (1964, 84–86). See also Baramidze (1996, 107–26); Quataert (1993, 793).

used to being treated this way. The Turks respect us. . . . We go to them. . . . There, if not better, it will certainly not be worse either."[12]

The Georgian nationalist movement responded to this exodus by downplaying the religious difference between Georgians and Ajarians. As Ilia Chavchavadze wrote, "Neither unity of language, nor unity of faith and tribal affiliation links human beings together as much as unity of history" (1955, 9). Along with other Georgian intellectuals, he strongly opposed the emigration of Ajarians from the region and contributed to a campaign for the rights of Muslim citizens in Ajaria (1955, 13; Broers 2002). This campaign had some success, because in 1880, under pressure from the Georgian national movement, tsarist authorities circulated a proclamation that attempted to stop the emigration. The decree guaranteed that Islam would be inviolable and that Muslim courts would continue to deal with familial and heritage disputes according to sharia law. Furthermore, it guaranteed that taxes would remain the same as under Ottoman rule, that the local population would be exempt from service in the army, and that Ajarians would be eligible to hold higher administrative positions.[13] Perhaps because of these guarantees, between 1881 and 1882 half to two-thirds of the emigrants returned to Ajaria.

As with the texts on migration, the descriptions of Georgian scholars who traveled through "Islamic Georgia" during the 1870s and 1880s are equally interspersed with sentiments of disappointment concerning the lack of shared national identity. They had to acknowledge that the local population plainly rejected their bourgeois nationalist ideas. The disillusionment is reflected in the writings of the Georgian historian Dmitri Bakradze, who traveled through Ajaria in the 1880s and wrote about his astonishment with what he saw as prevalent religious fanaticism: "To everything that is not related to religion they look with repulsion. . . . Leading one's life according to the Qur'an is what the Muslims are drawn to, indeed, that is what they consider as the only demand of their soul and body. No matter the subject of discussion, they will invariably trace it back to a religious theme" (Bakradze 1878, cited in Chanturia 1932, 14). These personal impressions once again suggest that Ajarians did not identify with the Georgian nation and that their most important reference for identity was Islam. The absence of a sense of Georgian nationality in social identification is effectively illustrated by a passage from Akhvlediani's work (1941, 16). The conversation he recounts took place in the first decade of the twentieth century between the novelist David Kldiashvili and a student who attended a madrassa in Batumi:

"Who are you?" asked Kldiashvili.
"I am an Ajarian," the student answered.

---

12. *Golos*, 27 June 1879, reprinted in Megrelidze (1964, 88).
13. *Golos*, 21 August 1880, reprinted in Megrelidze (1964, 91–93).

"Ajarian, Ajarian! Is that all?"

"Well, Tatar."

"What do Tatars have to do with all this?" he angrily exclaimed.

"Gürcü," the student corrected himself.[14]

"Man, you don't even know who you really are."

The student clearly identified himself as *Ajarian*. However, when this answer was not accepted by the novelist, he tried to clarify who he was by using the name that Russians attributed to all Muslims, that is, *Tatar*.[15] In his last attempt to clear things up, he used the appellation *Gürcü*, the Turkish word for Georgian, locally understood as radically different from Kartveli or Christian Georgian. Even though the student seemed confused about what the stranger wanted to hear from him, the striking aspect of this conversation is the primacy of religious identity in the student's answers.

Schools, Hojas, and the Tsarist State

Georgian scholars have frequently asserted that the tsarist administration followed a deliberate policy of divide and rule, thereby strengthening the position of Islam (Sanikidze 1999; Baramidze 1996). In Ajaria, this was a popular interpretation: it explained the existence of Islam not only by pointing to Ottoman oppression but by turning it into an even more recent development. However, the available primary documents suggest that the Russian administration had only limited control over the social processes on the frontier and was forced to maneuver uncomfortably between the Georgian bourgeoisie and the Muslim population.[16] For example, a letter from the governor of Batumi to his superior shows the weak hold the Russians had over Islamic institutions. The governor complained that the madrassas were organized without consent of the tsarist administrative bodies and that the quality of education was completely dependent on the individual teachers or mullahs (Chanturia 1932, 14). Part of the reason for the weak hold on the Muslim clergy was that the clergy retained intimate relations with Islamic centers abroad.[17] In several instances when Muslim leaders faced prosecution because of antitsarist activi-

14. Direct transliteration from the Russian text would be "Gurdzhi." Because this does not reflect its pronunciation, and because it referred to the use of a Turkish word, I used the Turkish spelling.

15. During the Soviet period "Tatar" became the official name of an ethnic group living north of the Caspian Sea. In common speech, however, "Tatar" is usually used in a derogatory fashion to refer to any Muslim.

16. In a comparative essay, Mostashari shows that the Russian stance toward Islam in the Caucasus varied depending on the ethno-religious composition of specific regions. Thus, in areas where Islam was considered weak (as in Ossetia and Ingushetia) the Russian administration supported the missionary efforts of the Russian Orthodox Church. By contrast, in places where Islam was seen as "deeply entrenched," the tsarist bureaucracy aimed at co-opting local religious leaders (Mostashari 2001, 229–49).

17. Chanturia (1932, 6–7); Ach'aris ASSR tsent'raluri sakhelmts'ipo arkivi [Central State Archive of the Ajarian ASSR], fond 1–13c, file 751: 1916–1917.

ties, the involved hojas fled to Ottoman territory, thus greatly hindering the attempts of the state to control their activities (AMM 1911, 91).[18]

The influence of religious structures on local life and the compromised position of the Russian administrators are well illustrated by the problems connected with the establishment of a church in Khulo, the district center of upper Ajaria. The church was intended to serve the religious needs of Russian and Georgian (Kartveli) soldiers based in the region. The inhabitants, and especially the Muslim clergy, perceived the presence of a Christian institution as a threat to their community and suspected that it was a part of a conspiracy to spread Christianity in the region. In 1910, not long after the establishment of the church, the Russian authorities received letters of complaint in which the priest was accused of public drunkenness and of insulting Islam. Although the priest denied the accusations and claimed that the Muslim clergy had manufactured the letters out of fear of losing their influence, the Russian authorities nevertheless decided that the complaints of the Muslims were valid and dismissed the priest (AMM 1910, 61–79).

At the outbreak of World War I, both Turks and Georgians distributed pamphlets that encouraged the population of Ajaria to take part in the war. The Georgian pamphlets emphasized that, after centuries of repression, the time had come to achieve independence from both Turkey and Russia in a united Georgia. The Turkish pamphlets incited Ajarians to take up weapons against the Russian and Georgian "infidels," to liberate Ajaria from the rule of non-Muslims and thus to defend their religion (AMM 1917, 126–28). The call of Islam found much more resonance than the call for Georgian independence, at least according to the memoirs of the Georgian general G. I. Kvinitadze. Although he initially had the idea to "unite the Ajarians with us as fellow tribesmen," he was forced to accept that "those fellow tribesmen made openly clear, with weapons in their hands, that they did not want to unite with us" (Kvinitadze 1985, 213). Summarizing his impressions, he wrote that "the population of Ajaria, the vast majority, was extremely hostile" (209). This hostility, which was difficult for him to understand, he attributed to Turkish emissaries, the Muslim clergy, and the majority of Ajarian beys.[19]

These short historical descriptions give only limited insight into pre-Soviet Ajaria. What the documents of the tsarist administration and travel reports of Georgian scholars suggest is that up until the Soviet period there was no indication that Ajarians identified themselves as Georgians. This means that both the assumed continuity of Georgian Christianity and the primacy of ethnic Georgianness are problematic. If we want to understand the post-Soviet ad-

18. Ach'aris mkharedmtsod muzeumi [Museum of Regional Studies of Ajaria], Russian Series, no. 50. Hereafter I will refer to this source as "AMM," followed by year and page. The source consists of field reports of state functionaries, communication between various levels of the Russian administration, and letters from citizens to the Russian administration.

19. See also Kazemzadeh, who, on the basis of archival research, concluded that "it became painfully clear that the population of Ajaria . . . was helping the Turks" (1951, 102).

vance of Christianity in Ajaria, it would thus be a mistake to attribute any "superficiality" to Islam's influence in Ajaria. Equally problematic would be to accept the argument of Castells that people returned to the "only source of identity that was kept in the collective memory: *national identity*" (1997, 41, emphasis in original). National identity, especially Georgian national identity, was simply absent in Ajaria prior to the era of the Soviet Union.[20] To understand post-Soviet trajectories, the dynamics of social identification are very important. But we need to examine the *ways* these identities unfolded during, and in response to, Soviet rule to understand how they did so. In previous sections, we saw that the local population rejected the ideas of ethnicity and nationality advanced by the nationalist movement. The next section examines why these same notions were increasingly accepted under Soviet rule and how, despite atheist ideology, these notions became tightly connected to Christianity.

The Transformation of the Frontier

The claim that inhabitants of Ajaria had never been "really" Muslim was a very popular one. Although this theory was the dominant one in the press, several intellectuals in Batumi believed differently. Gia Masalkin, a lecturer at Batumi University, denounced this mythical portrayal of Georgian Christianity in Ajaria. In his opinion, it was not so much ethnic immutability but the Soviet period that had brought the Ajarians back into the orbit of the Georgian nation. By destroying Muslim institutions and banning religion from public life, he reasoned, Soviet rule had reduced Islam as the prime reference for identity. This had turned Muslim Ajarians into pliable "material" for subsequent casting into the mold of Georgian Christianity. The continuing decline of Islam in Ajaria and the explosion of nationalist Georgian sentiment among Ajarians after the collapse of the Soviet Union seemed to justify this theory. To explain the post-Soviet outcome, repression of Islam is an important factor. Soviet rule in fact created the groundwork for the later expansion of Christianity, yet physical repression was only one component. To make claims about the relation between Soviet rule and the decline of Islam, we need to look both at the antireligious measures and the sociopolitical environment within which these were enforced. That is, we need to look at the position of Ajaria within Soviet political structures as well as the reactions of the Muslim community, in order to understand how the peculiar intertwining of religious and national identifications became so favorable to later Christian expansion.

20. See also Tishkov (1997, 14): "The irony is that 'Georgian' as a group identity is in fact a recent construct [that was] finalized during the Soviet period when the borders of the republic configured an ethnically complex territory with a dominant Kartli culture component."

Muslim Autonomy in Atheist Georgia

The influence of Soviet administrative classifications in the formation of "ethnic cultures" has been well documented. Less attention has been paid to the impact these classifications had on religious practice and identity, as it is often implicitly assumed that state atheist policies—even though they varied in intensity—were directed equally at all religions. The limitations of such a view become clear, however, when we look at the same issue by taking into consideration "ethnic" identity politics. In other words, to appreciate the impact of atheist policies in Ajaria, it is crucial to analyze how these permeated, and were permeated by, identity movements in twentieth-century Georgian culture.

The autonomous socialist soviet republics (ASSRs) occupied a peculiar position in the wider context of Soviet administrative divisions. They were not directly subordinate to a "civic entity"—the Union of Socialist Soviet Republics (USSR)—but to individual socialist soviet republics (SSRs). These SSRs were ethnically defined and centered on a dominant titular nation. Furthermore, by providing autonomous status to minority groups (such as in an ASSR), the legitimacy of the SSRs increasingly rested on the majority ethnic group. It thus created an opposition between minority and majority rather than forcing the SSR to become more "civic" and adopt policies that better reflected existing ethnic variation (see also Cornell 2002, 248; Saroyan 1997, 125–34).[21] To further complicate the picture, although the ASSRs were subordinate to the SSRs, their political leaders could appeal to Moscow to guarantee that their rights as a titular nationality were observed. The federal structures functioned to some extent as a counterweight to integrationist tendencies. The titular nationality of a given ASSR could claim the right to fill certain (strategic) political positions at various administrative levels. Moreover, by invoking the Soviet rhetoric of the "development of nations" they could protest an SSR's assimilation efforts.

At first glance the Ajarian ASSR fit the prototype of ethno-territorial autonomy:

> Taking into account the religion and customs of the working population of Ajaria and some other specific circumstances, the Communist Party and the Soviet government recognized the necessity of granting autonomy to the workers of Ajaria. Via a decree of 16 July 1921 the Revolutionary Committee of Georgia created the Ajarian Autonomous Soviet Socialist Republic as part of the Georgian SSR. (Merkviladze 1969, 164)

21. In creating national territories the Bolshevik leadership hoped to reduce ethnic conflict by satisfying national desires, thereby facilitating the development of class-based identities. But as Martin (1998, 826) points out, the policies had the opposite effect; they fostered an "exclusive attitude towards national territories, insisting on the majority's right to dominate their own (*nash*) national region."

However, several factors contributed to the unique position of the Ajarian ASSR. First, the immediate reasons for the creation of the Ajarian ASSR were not ideas of ethnic or cultural difference but were the direct outcome of political negotiations between the Turkish and Soviet governments, laid down in the Treaty of Kars (October 1921). The Turkish government insisted on this arrangement to guarantee protection of the Muslim population, as well as to leave open the possibility of later territorial claims. Second, the status of Ajarians remained vague. As can be seen from the quotation, autonomy was said to be based on religion, customs, and "some other specific circumstances," not on officially sanctioned nationality, as was true with all other ASSRs. The issue of whether Ajarians should be considered a separate group was vigorously debated. The Georgian political elite had been vehemently against the idea of Ajarian autonomy, claiming that Ajaria was and should be an integral part of Georgia. The resistance of Georgian Communists was only broken by the personal intervention of Stalin during a visit to Tbilisi in 1921, when he forced Georgian Communist leaders to decree autonomy for Ajaria (Chavleishvili 1989).

The contested origins of Ajarian autonomy led to an even lesser degree of cultural and religious "freedom" than was the case in many other autonomous republics. As early as November 1922, a year and a half after the institution of autonomy and at a time when Soviet officials were still relatively free to express their views, K. Iust, consul of the Russian Socialist Federal Soviet Republic (RSFSR) in Batumi, summarized some of the excesses that had taken place since the installation of Soviet rule. According to him, local Soviet administrators created an unbridgeable divide between workers and farmers by excessive raids on Muslim leaders and by combating everything that was not considered truly Georgian (Iust [1922] 1998, 14). Moreover, the absence of Ajarians in the new government structures meant that a large part of the population felt alienated from Soviet rule: "The Ajarian intelligentsia has been imprisoned. They started to avoid Soviet structures and generally moved to the opposition. . . . At the helm of power remained only Georgians—many of whom were not in the least qualified for the job" (17–18).[22]

For Iust this state of affairs explained the local population's negative attitude toward Soviet rule. He even wrote that he could not blame Ajarians for wishing to return to tsarist rule, which for them had been better than living under any other regime, including Soviet power (14). He described the state of affairs as the "Georgian colonization of Ajaria," saying it had started during Menshevik rule and had worsened since the Bolsheviks came to power, despite the autonomous status of Ajaria (15). He concluded: "Regarding the autonomy, one needs in the end to make a firm decision about the future trajectory. Either one should choose for autonomy, that is, real autonomy, which means

---

22. According to Iust, the Batumi Communist Party had in its ranks only one Ajarian member, who, after a subsequent purging, was removed from the party list ([1922] 1998, 19).

liquidating the Georgian colonization of the region and advancing self-government by real Ajarians. If not, one should liquidate the factual autonomy and enforce strong centralization" (30). According to Iust, without such changes the relation between Soviet authorities and the local population would remain disinterested and hostile. Consequently, it would inhibit the modernization of Ajaria. However, the status of Ajaria was never changed. Nor were any attempts made to advance self-government by "real" Ajarians.

Iust was the last official spokesman to write about these issues. Soon after that not only did it become dangerous to deny the achievements of Soviet rule or to write about religion other than in terms of its demise, it also became impossible to write about Ajarians as a distinct group. Whereas until 1926 the local population was still registered as "Ajarian," in the 1930s the category "Ajarian" ceased to exist in official registration, leaving the population little other choice than to register as Georgian.[23] The reclassification of Ajarians was in itself nothing exceptional. Of the 191 recognized ethnic groups that "existed" in the Soviet Union in 1924, about half had "disappeared" by the late 1930s (Hirsch 2005, 329–35).[24] This reduction in the number of ethnic groups fit the framework of ethno-territorial division of the Soviet empire. But in Ajaria, although the titular group "disappeared," the administrative structures continued to exist. Ajaria was still endowed with the same governmental structures as all ASSRs—including executive, legislative, and judicial bodies, and institutions for higher education and cultural expression—but with no "Ajarians" to fill them.

Because in pre-Soviet Ajaria most education stressed literacy in Turkish and Arabic, Ajarians were in a disadvantaged position for entering government and for developing their own intellectual elite. Moreover, the rurally based Muslim Ajarians formed a minority in their capital, Batumi, which further prevented them from playing a role in the higher political circles of the autonomous republic. Instead, non-Ajarian Georgians who had migrated to Batumi because of the economic opportunities it provided, or who had been sent there by the government in Tbilisi, began to benefit from the privileges normally given to the titular ethnic group. Until the 1950s the first secretary of the Communist Party of Ajaria was never a native Ajarian, and only in the 1960s were Ajarians becoming part of the autonomous republic's political elite (Darchiashvili 1996). But by then the predominant attitude among native Ajarians who had worked their way up the hierarchy was to stress their identification with Georgia and to oppose any tendency that might challenge this ideal.

23. The other possibility was to register as Meskhetian Turk (who were deported in 1944). Few did so, probably because it was safer to belong to a category named after the republic (see also Tishkov 1997, 20).

24. These groups were reclassified under larger ethnic categories that fit within the ethno-territorial division of the Soviet Union into SSRs, ASSRs, and autonomous oblasts.

Physical Repression and Georgian Nationalism

Several authors have noted that the outcome of the Communist struggle against Islam depended largely on the attitudes of local cadres.[25] Because the political cadres in Ajaria consisted predominantly of Georgians with Christian roots who had strong anti-Turkish and anti-Islamic sentiments, the local political elite eagerly adopted Soviet policies aimed at curtailing the influence of Islam, as the writings of Iust have indicated. Many have taken this argument as an explanation for the decline of Islam in Ajaria (Derluguian 1995; Meiering Mikadze 1999; Sanikidze 1999). Derluguian pointed to the extraordinarily harsh repression of Islam in Ajaria, writing that "the Bolsheviks in Tbilisi and their local comrades in Batumi unleashed what amounted to a war against Moslem authorities and institutions of Ajaria" (1995, 33). All 172 madrassas and 158 mosques in Ajaria (save the one in Batumi) were destroyed or transformed into stables and storage depots (Sanikidze 1999, 16–17). Religious leaders fell victim to the repression, fled across the border into Turkey, or had their movements and activities strictly controlled.

The conflict between the Georgian-oriented authorities and the rural population came to a climax in 1929. The central government had decided to close all existing religious schools and, moreover, decreed that Muslim women must remove the chadri (Suny 1994, 244–45).[26] By March of that year resistance began to spread. One villager, now in his eighties, told me:

> It started after the Communists ordered the women to come to a meeting. Then [the Communists] ripped off the [women's] chadri and threw them into the fire. It was not a large conflict, only a few villages were involved. The people had no weapons, no bombs, no cars, nothing—just some hunting rifles. Of course when the army arrived it was all over. What could those farmers do against a professional army? Not a single thing!

Others told me that the resistance was short-lived, portraying it as a hopeless, easily suppressed rebellion. Oral testimonies indicate that not more than a handful of people were killed in the rebellion. Immediately thereafter when the army demanded that all weapons be collected from villagers, terrified village functionaries complied obediently. As a result of these and other measures, the institutional basis of Islam was effectively broken by the end of the 1930s.

Religious leaders, who at the time of my research were remembered for their important role in "preserving" Islam in upper Ajaria, were all character-

25. Anderson (1994, 383) explains, from this angle, the variation in the percentage of mosque closures between republics.

26. As in other antireligious campaigns, the government claimed that the measures had been demanded by the population. In this case, the banishment of the chadri was demanded at the first congress of Muslim Georgian women in February 1929 (Sanikidze 1999).

ized as men who held a moderate stance concerning the relationship between the state and religion. Reportedly, they assisted state representatives in overcoming resistance to the establishment of Georgian language schools and urged their followers to let the interests of the state prevail over those of religion. The NKVD might well have demanded this assistance in exchange for not imprisoning the leaders. Indeed, I was told of numerous instances of the strict surveillance to which Muslim leaders were subjected. They were denied passports and regularly visited by NKVD agents. Overall, the reaction of Muslim leaders, especially after the 1930s, seems to have been one of accommodation and retreat.

Although "physical repression" was an important factor in relegating Islam to the domestic sphere, this is not enough to explain why the counteraction was so weak. Several factors may have contributed to this. First, the delimitation of the international border between the Soviet Union and Turkey had isolated Muslim Ajaria from its former religious centers. Whereas even during tsarist rule many religious leaders obtained their education in Istanbul, these contacts were made impossible after the establishment of Soviet rule. Instead, the Islamic leadership became formally accountable to the newly established Muslim Religious Board for the Transcaucasus in Baku. This board was predominantly Shi'ite in orientation and considered Ajaria of only minor importance.[27] This made it nearly impossible for Ajarian Muslims to voice their interests through official bodies.

Another reason for the easiness with which Islam was relegated to the domestic sphere can be found in the nature of Islamic institutions prior to the Soviet conquest. It has been noted that a basic difference existed between areas like Ajaria, where Islam spread as a consequence of Ottoman expansion and had an overt and public role, and areas like the North Caucasus where Muslim brotherhoods were responsible for the propagation of Islam (Bennigsen and Wimbush 1985, 5). This difference is important, for as the brotherhoods easily went underground (they formed secret societies par excellence), in Ajaria Islam had a far more open role and drew much of its organizational basis from these public institutions. With public institutions now openly hostile to Islam and without the traditional flexibility of brotherhoods, the Muslim leaders of Ajaria could not effectively deal with the changed political situation and were easily controlled by the new Soviet authorities.

It is difficult to determine which factors are the most important in explaining the retreat of Islam, especially because so little information is available. What is clear, though, is that even in the most peripheral villages Islam retreated to the domestic domain and lost a large part of its institutional basis. Still, the possibility of continuing religious practices was much greater

27. The Muslim Religious Board for the Transcaucasus was one of four official Muslim boards in the Soviet Union.

in the highlands than in administrative towns. In the mountain village of Ghorjomi, for example, people were able to continue most religious practices in secret. As a hoja explained, "We knew exactly, with every neighbor, what you could and couldn't say. In this way we were able to spread information." Despite these possibilities of continued observance of religious demands, the kind of Islam that survived Soviet rule was increasingly localized. There was infrequent contact with Muslims from other republics, and the hojas had to keep their own lunar calendar to determine the proper observance of religious rituals.

Islam became isolated in yet other important ways. Throughout the Soviet period local historians and ethnographers were engaged in re-creating Ajaria's history in a way that tightly connected the region and its inhabitants to deep Georgian history, removing it from its more recent Ottoman past. Soviet historians generally held that sheer force and violence, rather than persuasion or economic pressures, were responsible for the widespread adoption of Islam during the Ottoman era (Japaridze 1973, 101–5). In Soviet historiography, the portrayal of Islam was strictly connected with a denunciation of the Ottoman legacy. A central preoccupation of local historians was to separate indigenous history from Ottoman suppression: "Ajaria is one of the oldest regions of Georgia. It went through a difficult historical process. . . . Part of the population was massacred, while the rest, in order to save their lives, adopted Islam. But despite this oppression, the inhabitants of Ajaria preserved their language and culture" (Birina 1956, 328).[28] In the same tone, Soviet authors wrote of emigration, stressing that the Turks forced the population to emigrate and sent them to "swamps full of malaria where the majority died from diseases and starvation. The few survivors tried to make their way back to their motherland" (Akhvlediani 1941, 14). In short, the Ottoman period was portrayed as one of poverty and economic decline that followed an earlier "golden age" when Georgia had been united.

Although grounded in Soviet ideology, this vilification of Turks and Islam has fit well with post-Soviet nationalist discourse that presents Georgia as a Christian island in a stormy sea of Islam. The Georgian nationalists and Christians in Ajaria, for whom the "Soviet" criticisms of Islam and Ottoman domination were useful tools to foster their own interests, adopted a similar rhetoric. For example, when, in early 1991, one of the first churches in Ajaria was reopened, a local newspaper reported: "More than once the enemy has destroyed our region, but we have risen from ashes like the phoenix. The Georgians of our region did not abandon their feelings of discontent. For decades they have dreamed about a return to their faith and of the resurrection of churches" (*Adzhariia*, 11 January 1991). The Ajarian intelligentsia became actively involved in the creation of a comprehensive Christian-Georgian Ajarian

---

28. See also Zhgenti (1956, 1), who introduced his voluminous work with these words: "The period of Turkish domination constitutes one of the bloodiest periods of the Georgian nation."

history. This image of Ajaria was not only laid down in academic works but, more important, in newspapers and television broadcasts, gradually becoming a part of the dominant—though not uncontested—discourse of the history of Ajaria.

Even though Islam was scattered and relegated to the domestic domain, it did not disappear. In the 1980s, when the restrictions of the Soviet state concerning religion were relaxed, there was an immediate increase in religious practices. By this time anti-Islamic views were no longer backed by atheist ideology but were solely motivated by nationalist views. The "reappearance" of Islam in Ajaria was seen as an attack on the Georgian nation and as a denial of Ajaria's position within Georgia. Tellingly, the harshest reactions came not from Georgia but from within Ajaria, from Ajarians who had moved up the sociopolitical ladder. In the 1980s, when it became obvious that Islam was gaining ground in the region, the newspaper spoke of self-styled mullahs who extracted large sums of money from gullible believers before being unmasked.[29] Pridon Khalvashi, a famous Ajarian writer, published an article in the newspaper, berating "these dregs of society," who try to drag the region back into "the dark ages."[30] In a novel by Khalvashi with the suggestive title *Is It Possible for a Muslim to be Georgian?* the main conclusion is that Islam is incompatible with the Georgian national character because it preaches submissiveness (1994, 14). Islam had become the historical enemy of Georgia, an enemy that undermined Georgia's sense of national identity.

Public Religion in Contested Space

The renewed visibility of religion throughout the former Soviet Union has provoked commentators to stress the strength of "pre-revolutionary religious traditions and ideological trends which had apparently been rooted out in the Soviet era" (Filatov 1998, 267).[31] However, understanding religious renewal in terms of pre-Soviet traditions hinges on the idea that Soviet rule had merely a superfluous impact, something I have tried to disprove throughout this book. The role of religion in everyday life had radically altered during the Soviet period. Moreover, concepts of religion related differently to ideas of nation and state by the late 1980s.

One crucial aspect of religion in post-Soviet Georgia was the tight connection between national and religious affiliation (see also Dragadze 1993, 154–55). These connections triggered a variety of responses on the religious

---

29. From the newspaper *Kommunist'i*, 22 April 1986, cited in Fuller (1986, 1–4).

30. From the newspaper *Sabchota Ach'ara*, 22 January 1986. Khalvashi was the long-standing chairman of the Ajarian Society of Literature. His negative view of Islam is particularly provocative because his family is from upper Ajaria. Khalvashi's baptism (in 2000) was given wide coverage by the national media.

31. Similarly, Greeley (1994, 255) wrote that "despite 70 years of socialism, God seems to be alive and well and living in all of Russia."

frontier in Ajaria, where the link between the Georgian nation and Christianity was not unequivocally accepted. The return of religion from being a space of personal refuge during socialist rule to the public sphere in postsocialist times has had consequences for local interpretations of Islam and Christianity and for the relative success with which they have been able to advance their causes.

Christianity and Islam in Post-Soviet Georgia

When the Georgian nationalist movement gained influence in the 1980s, one of its major concerns was to defend the interests of the Church along the imagined geographical, historical, and ethnic lines of the republic (Lilienfeld 1993, 224–26). The nationalist movement and the first leaders of the independent Georgian republic presented Georgian nationality and Georgian orthodoxy as an indivisible composite. Speeches by the Orthodox Christian establishment as well as the new government were permeated with expressions like "a Georgian is Orthodox by nature and way of life" and "Georgian means Orthodox" (Shatirishvili 2000). Georgia's first president, the ultranationalist Zviad Gamsakhurdia, employed a theocratic image of dominion and envisioned a future for Georgia that would be ethnically pure and closely linked to Christianity (Crego 1996, 26; Kurbanov and Kurbanov 1995, 237). Although the most radical ideas of Gamsakhurdia were not effected in political action after his death in 1993, the Church was nevertheless successful in gaining numerous privileges and significant power in local politics and issues such as public education (Nodia 2000).[32]

The close connection of religious and national identity in Georgia implied that even people without strong religious convictions had to take sides. This was true of political leaders in many post-Soviet countries, who were quick to adopt religious rhetoric in political speech. Georgia's president Eduard Shevardnadze was no exception to this trend. After this former Communist was appointed head of the new Georgian republic in 1992, not only did he become a "democrat" but he also became "a son of the Georgian Church." Whether or not his baptism was motivated by personal conviction, it was certainly a strategic move that cleverly responded to the dominant mood in the country and showed appreciation for the new role of the Georgian Orthodox Church (see also Shatirishvili 2000).

Whereas Shevardnadze's turn to Christianity paralleled religious sentiment in Georgia proper, in Ajaria the situation was more complex. Aslan Abashidze, the leader of the Ajarian Autonomous Republic from 1992 until 2004, was one of the few political leaders in the former Soviet Union who did not openly express loyalty to a singular faith and avoided answering questions

---

32. Though Orthodox Christianity did not become the official state religion, the Church was granted special status in the constitution in 2001 for its "significant role in the history of the nation" (Papuashvili 2001).

concerning his personal convictions.[33] On numerous occasions he circumvented the question, declaring instead by way of answer, "My religion is Georgia" and "I pray in that church the name of which is Georgia" (*Adzhariia*, 1 August 1998; Smirba 1999, 63). These statements contained a double message. On the one hand, they were a patriotic reply to critics in Tbilisi who accused Abashidze of separatist intentions and who had named him a "Turkish bey" and the "pasha of Aslanistan." On the other hand, the statements intended to demonstrate his neutrality in regard to the unclear and changing religious situation in Ajaria. Muslims and Christians both claimed Abashidze as a member of their religious community.[34] Muslims stressed that Abashidze was of Ajarian—meaning Muslim—descent and that he therefore took the problems of the Muslim community to heart. Christian supporters, however, pointed out that Abashidze's grandchildren were baptized and, thus, that he himself was predisposed toward Christianity.

Abashidze's rise to power was facilitated by the support of the Muslim population. Shortly after the nationalist Gamsakhurdia became Georgia's president, public unrest among Muslims in Ajaria mounted. In a large demonstration in 1991, several thousand Muslims came to Batumi to demonstrate against the proposed abolishment of Ajarian autonomy. During the demonstrations, grievances were expressed against the anticipated campaign of forced Christianization. As a conciliatory gesture, President Gamsakhurdia appointed Abashidze as the leader of Ajaria; as a descendent of a family of Ajarian nobles, he could count on support from a large portion of the population (Aves 1996, 41).[35] Although Muslim support aided Abashidze in further consolidating his power, this did not imply that the regime itself was favorable toward Islam. In hindsight, the mobilization of rural Muslim groups appears to have been a once-only strategy of the ruling elite to secure their position in Ajaria. Moreover, in Batumi, the local center of gravity for political power, Abashidze's position was dependent on alliances with other factions, most of whom were of non-Ajarian (i.e., non-Muslim) descent and who were strong supporters of the Georgian Orthodox Church. In later years, even Abashidze himself became explicit in his backing of Georgian Orthodoxy.[36] For example,

33. Among the few who avoided identification with a particular faith was President Mintimer Shamiyev of Tatarstan, another autonomous republic located on the frontier of Christianity and Islam. However, when religious tensions rose in the mid-1990s, Shamiyev had to take sides. He converted to Islam and started to promote himself as both a political and spiritual leader (Filatov 1998, 269).

34. The Russian newspaper *Izvestiia* wrote about this issue in an intentionally humorous way. When a journalist entered the mosque he was told that Aslan Abashidze, like 80 percent of the population, was Muslim. But when he asked the same question in a church, he was told that 80 percent of the population, including Abashidze, was Christian (21 December 1993).

35. It has been suggested that Abashidze orchestrated the demonstrations to consolidate his position (Hin 2000, 9).

36. Nevertheless, support for Abashidze remained high among Muslims. Most saw no alternative in other political parties, because these were even more predisposed toward Christianity.

while he ordered several of his "clients" to contribute to the building of a new church in Khulo and had this extensively covered by the local press, not a single lari was spent on the numerous newly built mosques. Abashidze did not leave much doubt about his stance toward Islam when he stated "Islam is slowly dying in Ajaria" and insisted that only some elderly people continued to carry out Muslim practices (Meiering Mikadze 1999, 255).

The backing of Christian institutions by the political establishment was filtered through coverage by the regional media. TV-Ajaria, which was closely linked to Abashidze's Revival Party, frequently broadcast special church events and invited priests to give their opinions on moral and social issues. Similarly, the local newspaper *Adzhariia* published accounts of virtually all church openings. By contrast, during the 1990s not a single article appeared on the opening of mosques. Only once did the newspaper report Abashidze's joint visit to a mosque and a church, but the same article paid more attention to Abashidze as "the tolerant leader" than to the activities of the Muslim community (*Adzhariia*, 12 January 2000). There is some irony in that newspapers controlled by the Revival Party published stories in which Church representatives expressed gratitude to Abashidze for "the enormous work he has done to unite Georgia under one religion" (*Adzhariia*, 14 September 1994).

Religious Trends in Ajaria

The increased public support for the Georgian Orthodox Church paralleled the normalization of political relations between the Ajarian Autonomous Republic and the national government in the second half of the 1990s. The demarcation of spheres of interest meant that support from the rural Muslim population was no longer crucial to the Abashidze regime. Given these shifts in the political atmosphere, it is key to look at changes in the scope of activities performed by the Muslim and Christian clergy.

Whereas during the late 1980s and early 1990s some sixty mosques had been reopened or were newly constructed, ten years later a number of them were no longer being used. In coastal settlements rumors circulated about the misuse of community funds by "fake" mullahs and the disappearance of grants from Turkish benefactors. Jokes were made about the fact that several of the newly constructed mosques remained virtually empty. During this same period the Georgian Orthodox Church increased its scope of activity. In the early 1990s churches were mainly opened in Batumi and other coastal towns, but in the second half of the 1990s churches were constructed inland as well. In 2001, some fifteen churches were functioning in the lowlands and five new churches had been constructed in upper Ajaria. A new geographical pattern between Islam and Christianity was taking shape, which roughly corresponded to the locally employed distinction between lower and upper Ajaria. The most conspicuous exceptions to this pattern were the incursions of Christian activity in the administrative centers of upper Ajaria and the continuing influence of Islam in several settlements in lower Ajaria that only became populated in the 1960s by migrant workers from the highlands.

In lower Ajaria the population had become tightly integrated into Soviet Georgian society as a result of their proximity to urban centers. Demographic processes such as intermarriage with "Christian" Georgians and a continuing influx of non-Muslim Georgians added to a gradual adoption of Soviet Georgian lifestyles, which, although atheistic in outlook, later came to be identified with Christianity. Accordingly, in lower Ajaria the process of conversion to Christianity went relatively unchallenged and the Georgian Orthodox Church rapidly expanded its influence. Besides the construction of new churches, Christian schools were opened, and a significant portion (possibly the majority) of the population was baptized during the first decade after socialism. The influence of the Georgian Orthodox Church was particularly evident in Batumi. In the 1990s, the old churches were renovated and new ones constructed, often in prominent locations: along the boulevard, in the historical center of the city, and next to the main market.[37] Priests showed up at official meetings and were invited to be on television shows; many of Batumi's youth wore Georgian crosses. But while Christianity made a rapid advance, the desire of Muslims to reconstruct the former central Sultan Mosque, which was demolished in the 1930s, was ignored by Ajarian authorities. The call to prayer from the only mosque in town was reintroduced in the early 1990s, but it was stopped by authorities shortly thereafter when residents complained about the noise.

In upper Ajaria, Islam had continued to play an important role in domestic life during socialism. In the 1980s, when Soviet policies toward religion were softened, local networks were activated to restore Islam. However, this Islamic renewal was severely handicapped because it lacked financial resources and an educated clergy. Moreover, it also lacked links to the economic and political power holders of Ajaria who could have supported its growth. When I conducted my research, Islam was influential only in small mountain communities. Here, villagers participated in the reconstruction of mosques and sent their children to local madrassas. In Ghorjomi, for example, the mosque was usually well attended and the Muslim clergy had regained their significance in social life. The imams (prayer leaders) performed important roles in weddings and funerals and negotiated conflicts between neighbors. By and large the Muslim leaders had become the de facto authorities in these villages, despite expressions of discontent from some of the youth about the prohibition on the sale of alcohol as ordered by mosque leaders. In some villages, the mosque appeared to be the only adequately functioning organizational structure. The Muslim leaders had little difficulty in gathering regular contributions from the community, whereas the state appeared unable to collect nominal fees for electricity and use of land.[38]

37. The old churches date from the city's "golden age" between 1878 and 1914, when Batumi was an important oil port inhabited by significant Christian communities (Greek, Armenian, Russian, and Kartveli) and Muslim groups (Persian, Abkhazian, Laz, Kurd, and Ajarian).

38. The overview is based on a two-week research visit to Ghorjomi, which is twenty kilometers east of Khulo and locally known for its strict Muslim life.

The situation was different in the administrative centers of the highlands. In the 1990s the Georgian Orthodox Church selected these towns as prime locations to start their missionary activity. Their activities frequently collided with the aspirations of Muslim leaders, which made the encounter between Islam and Christianity particularly visible in these towns. Take, for example, Khulo, located eighty kilometers east of Batumi at an altitude of one thousand meters. The center of town lies one hundred meters above the river Ach'arist-sqali, where the mountain slopes flatten a bit and allow for the cultivation of crops, mainly potatoes and corn, but in socialist times also tobacco. The center of town seemed a bit out of place in this predominantly rural region. Run-down apartment buildings, the large but empty post office and cinema, the closed-down shops, and the rusty workshops of the textile factory were conspicuous reminders of more prosperous times. The town of Khulo once epitomized Soviet modernization in the region, but ten years after the Soviet collapse it represented just as forcefully the demise of an economic and ideological system. Although the remains of the former prosperity could still be seen in the town center, the neighborhoods that stretched out from it into the hills lacked visual signs of the Soviet past. Life in these neighborhoods continued to be primarily focused on agriculture. During Soviet times most inhabitants worked on the kolkhozes. Their yearly cycle was mainly defined by the demands of crops and of privately owned cattle, which needed to be guided into the mountain pastures during spring and summer. Ten years after the collapse of the Soviet economy, nearly all visible traces of the seventy-year Soviet development campaigns were gone. The kolkhoz buildings had been demolished and the parts sold or reused. The land, formally part of the kolkhoz, had been reclaimed by descendents of its former owners.

Although the heyday of Khulo was past, the town retained much of its importance as the economic center, as well as transportation and communication hub, for the region. Because of its proximity to the international border (approximately twenty kilometers), the state security agency and other governmental bodies continued to be well represented. Moreover, Khulo was an important center for both Muslims and Christians. The convergence of two religious traditions in Khulo was mirrored in the close proximity of the mosque and the church. They were located a short walk uphill from the civic center, on land that both parties considered historically significant.

Mosques, Madrassas, and Suspicion

Oral sources said the first mosque in Khulo dates from 1829 when the bey of upper Ajaria, Hasan Khimshiashvili, adopted Islam. After a fire destroyed the original wooden building in the 1890s, a new mosque was constructed of stone. This mosque and the attached madrassa made up the largest Islamic complex in upper Ajaria. Soviet authorities closed the mosque in 1938 and initially used the building as the village school. The town administration planned to destroy the building, but the director of the kolkhoz reportedly convinced the local authorities to transform it into a storage building instead. This man continued to be venerated for having "saved the mosque." The historical importance of Khulo's mosque, as well as the central location of of the town, meant that reopening the mosque was a major issue not only for the town's Muslims but also for the larger Muslim community of upper Ajaria.

In 1988, after Soviet leader Mikhail Gorbachev announced that believers had "the full right to express their convictions with dignity" (Bourdeaux 1995, 8), Muslim believers throughout Ajaria reclaimed the long-abandoned mosques. The actual pace at which former religious buildings were reopened and new ones erected varied greatly. One important reason for this was that in 1988 no one was very sure about to what degree these new laws would be enforced. Many feared that they were only temporary whims of the new leadership and that the situation would later backfire on the people. If Muslim believers doubted the sincerity of the new laws, it is no surprise that the local authorities were reluctant to allow believers to perform religious services in the mosques. In Khulo, the opening of the mosque was delayed several times, until Hoja Muhammad (the son of the last imam of Khulo) and a group of believers simply occupied the building, as described by Muhammad: "On a rainy Friday morning we broke down the door and removed everything stored inside. . . . But as soon as we had completed the prayers, the police and the town administrators arrived and forced us to leave the mosque." The conflict did not proceed further, as the police commander took the leaders aside and promised to help them receive official permission to reopen the mosque. In the meantime, the Muslims could use the mosque for their Friday prayers. The town administration, according to Muhammad, kept on delaying official permission. He attributed this attitude to the fear government officials in those "hectic times" had about taking any responsibility.

In 1990, the mosque still had not been granted official permission to function. When the nationalist movement came to power in Georgia the situation grew more tense. The town administration decided to shut down the mosque completely. Thereupon, the Muslim community sent a delegation to Moscow to demand that local authorities comply with the new laws on religion. But, as one of the delegates told me, it was all for nothing, because "in Moscow we were told that they could do nothing because the [Georgian] government would interpret it differently," meaning that any interference from Moscow would be interpreted as a hostile attack on the nation by the nationalist movement. The delegation tried to obtain the needed documents in Batumi, but again this was in vain. "So then the people decided to open the mosque by force," Muhammad said. "People from the town administration and from Batumi [tried to intervene], but the people did what they wanted to do." This precarious situation ended not long after Abashidze was installed as the chairman of the Supreme Council of the Ajarian Autonomous Republic in 1991, and official permission was granted.

The coming to power of Abashidze in combination with the general weakening of state structures in the early 1990s meant that Islam could return to the public arena. For several years Islam seemed to be steadily securing ground. A crucial element in this development was the opening of the border, which provided new contacts as well as new points of reference for Muslims in Ajaria. In 1992, the leadership of the mosque in Batumi created the Muftiate of Ajaria (Muslim community of Ajaria) and ended its uncomfortable official linkage to the Muslim Religious Board in Baku. Extensive contacts were established with Sunni Muslim organizations in Turkey and the Arabic world. In 1992, the Saudi government invited a group of fifty Ajarian men to perform the hajj to Mecca. Between 1992 and 1996 three hundred men followed religious courses of varying length in Turkey. Brochures and booklets about Islam were sent from Turkey to Ajaria, first in Turkish but in later years also in special Georgian editions. Significant contributions were made to the renovation of Ajarian mosques and madrassas. Although statistical information is unavailable, Muslim leaders estimated that twenty out of sixty mosques in Ajaria were partly or completely financed by Turkish citizens and Muslim organizations. In upper Ajaria, people stressed that these benefactors offered their contributions in order to obtain *madli* (virtue) and explained that most benefactors had singled out Ajaria because they had familial roots in the region.[39] But non-Muslim residents were suspicious of this assistance. Several newly converted Christians said they suspected that Turkey was using these religious contacts to further its political interests in the region.

During the 1990s, Muslim leaders in upper Ajaria became increasingly dissatisfied with the official religious structure. In 1994, Merjivan Abashidze (not related to Aslan Abashidze), a prominent Muslim from Khulo, was appointed mufti for Ajaria, but shortly after his appointment he became involved in a corruption scandal. The popular belief was that Merjivan accepted gifts from Abashidze, including a car and an apartment, and he was subsequently forced by the secular authorities to abandon his position. Merjivan's relatives said the scandal had been a setup and that the perpetrators were attempting to restrict the potential of Islam in Ajaria. They backed up this allegation by noting that the new mufti, Mahmud Kamashidze, appointed in 1996, had no formal religious education and readily accommodated to the demands of the authorities (cf. Sanikidze 1999). After that time the call to prayer was only heard irregularly in Batumi, while close cooperation with Turkish Muslim organizations ended. People in upper Ajaria were very dissatisfied with the Muslim leadership in Batumi. The comment of one hoja that "the mufti doesn't help us with anything because he is [tied to] the government" seemed to be the prevailing opinion.

Attempts to set up organizational structures independent of the muftiate in Batumi were taken up and dropped more than once. Since 1996, Muslim lead-

---

39. In several cases the investors were descendants of Ajarians who migrated to Turkey during tsarist and early Soviet rule.

ers from upper Ajaria have cooperated with foreign Muslim organizations without the interference of the muftiate. In 1999 and 2000, religious leaders once again explored the possibilities of an independent muftiate in upper Ajaria. The goal was to be able to assist and coordinate religious education, to facilitate contacts with other Muslim countries, and to communicate the concerns of Muslims to the authorities. But before action was taken, Kamashidze appointed a special representative to "maintain contacts with the Muslims in upper Ajaria," as he explained to me during an interview. The appointed representative seemed an odd choice because, although he was a Muslim believer and regularly attended the mosque, he had no formal religious training. It seemed, at least to other Muslims, that the underlying reason for the appointment of this representative was that his son was an officer in the state security apparatus in Khulo. As a result, many Muslims saw the representative of the muftiate as a front for the intelligence services. His appointment, even according to one moderate townsman, was motivated by political concerns: "Sixty lari a month [thirty dollars] for basically doing nothing! Do you really think that such [high] wages are provided just like that? That's not how things work here."

The renewed religious connections with Turkey and the attempts of the Muslim clergy to set up organizational structures were interpreted by the dominant (Christian) group as expressions of national disloyalty.[40] Muslim activities, moreover, raised considerable suspicion in the political establishment.[41] In the press as well as in parliament, commentators speculated about the danger of Islam to the Georgian nation, and about the possible threat of the infiltration of Turkish interests through religious practices. Although it is impossible to catalog all the forms of pressure put on Muslim leaders, the fact that their activities were closely monitored suggests that the policy of trying to control religious life was carried out more vigorously against Muslim than against Christian institutions.

Christian Schools, New Churches, and Resistance

Whereas Muslim leaders were underdogs in the public arena, the Christian clergy was primed for success because they could build on their relations with the central authorities of Georgia. In 1991, President Gamsakhurdia personally transferred the authority of the *internat* (residential school) in Khulo to the Georgian Orthodox Church as part of his new nationalist-Christian policies.[42] Because the internat, renamed the Spiritual Lyceum of the Apostle Andrew, was the only institution for vocational education in the region, the pre-

---

40. Sanikidze (1999) mentions that Georgian newspapers alleged that many of the young people studying in Turkish religious schools returned as Wahhabis and maintained close contacts with Chechens.

41. See Fuller for an overview of the suspicions voiced in the Georgian press (1993, 23–26).

42. The importance of residential schooling in Soviet and post-Soviet cultural politics is well documented in Bloch's (2004) study of the Evenki.

dominantly Muslim population protested.[43] Shortly after the changes in the status of the school, several hundred Muslims from Khulo and the surrounding villages marched to the district center to demonstrate against the presence of priests in the school. The besiegers consisted mostly of farmers, manual workers, and technicians, while the defenders of the Christian clergy typically were middle-class inhabitants (teachers, medical staff, administrative personnel) of Khulo. The position of the police and local authorities was ambiguous: they were native Ajarians and a portion of them must have sympathized with the demonstrators, but taking the side of the demonstrators would have meant professional suicide. As one resident put it, "Christianity is the religion of the state, so it was out of the question that [state representatives] would *not* support the new school. That was out of the question because, because . . . you need to earn a living, don't you?"

The Christian clergy was not all that sure of the backing it would get from the local police and called for military assistance from Adigeni, a predominantly Christian region. Within a few hours all roads to and from Khulo were blocked by the military, while at the same time the situation near the lyceum grew more tense. The priest, Father Grigori, locked himself in one of the rooms on the second floor of the school. According to one witness, he almost jumped out of the window, fearing that the gathered crowd would lynch him. However, with the help of some local followers, the priest managed to escape to Batumi and was never seen again in Khulo. Negotiations were initiated by the town administration, but the resistance ended only after Aslan Abashidze sent a delegate to convince the Muslim leaders to allow the priests to remain in Khulo.[44] The Muslim demonstrators accepted the existence of a Christian lyceum on the condition that the rector would no longer be a priest but a layman. Nevertheless, within a year of the compromise the position of rector was once again given to a priest. Thus, the Christian lyceum received official recognition despite the wishes of the majority of the citizens. Moreover, because it was the only vocational school in the region, poor Muslim families who wanted their children to continue their education were left with no choice but to send their children to this Christian lyceum.[45]

The Muslims' dissatisfaction was not only about the Christian lyceum but also about the new style of "secular" education.[46] In the mid-1990s a special governmental committee had prepared a new subject that was to fill the lack of "morality" instruction in primary education in Georgia. This subject, with the sympathetic name "Culture and Religion," was added to the school cur-

43. Information is based on oral testimonies. The local media did not report on the short-lived conflict.

44. In 2000, this delegate became the official representative of the mufti for upper Ajaria.

45. Education at the lyceum, which included a nursing school and teacher training school, had a strong focus on biblical studies and related subjects (Pelkmans 2002).

46. A representative of the Ajarian ministry of education pointed out that the goal of the educational system was to teach students the Christian basis of Georgian culture (Meiering Mikadze 1999, 259–60).

riculum in 1997. But despite its name the textbooks only covered Christianity. Consequently, the introduction of the subject caused great dissatisfaction in Ajaria.[47] Muslim believers complained that by making the subject obligatory, the state turned their children away from Islam. Cases were reported in which parents refused to have their children take this subject, while in a few mountain villages the subject was still not being taught. According to the regional secretary of education, the absence of the class in those villages was caused by a lack of specialists on the subject and had nothing to do with discontent in these villages. However, several teachers who were ordered to teach the subject told me that they had refused to comply on moral grounds.

Despite such expressions of dissatisfaction, the introduction of the class on "Religion and Culture" did not lead to any organized attempts by Muslims to change the nature of education. Instead, the majority silently accepted the new policies of the state, even though they were seen as threats to Islam. This compliance was partly a result of the absence of an organizational structure through which Muslims could express their grievances. Moreover, because Muslims formed the lower echelons of society, they had very little tactical power (Wolf 2001, 384) to alter belligerent state policies. The assistant rector of the Christian lyceum explained how Muslim students dealt with Christian education: "Most students probably think, 'Well, the government has decided that this is necessary, so what can we do?' To you this attitude might seem strange, but here people have always adjusted to the requirements of the state. They don't really study, they come to the lessons and that is all." So while Muslim children (and their parents) outwardly adjusted to the new policies, just as they had during the Soviet period, they tried to remain true to their own or familial ideas. But it is questionable how effective such strategies were, and whether they should be seen as forms of "silent resistance" or rather as "reluctant accommodation."[48] Meanwhile, the Georgian Orthodox Church was expanding its influence among the population of Ajaria.

The Problems of Going Public

To describe the increased public relevance of religion in postsocialist contexts several authors have referred to José Casanova's oft-cited book *Public Religions in the Modern World* (1994), and especially to his use of the term "deprivatization" (Hann 2000; Agadjanian 2001). Casanova argues that in the contemporary Western world religions "are refusing to accept the marginal and privatized role" to which they had been assigned and increasingly claim new and significant public roles (1994, 5–6). This observation is also applicable to develop-

47. The original intention was to name the subject "Cultural History of Christianity," but this was changed to "Culture and Religion" in order not to upset Muslims (personal communication).

48. There is a long controversy about the terms *resistance* and *accommodation* in the social sciences. Weller succinctly summarized the controversy by stating: "If resistance . . . appears to be everywhere for some, it is nowhere for others, a chimerical vision that disappears under a cold stare" (1994, 13).

ments in post-Soviet Ajaria. As we have seen, both Muslim and Christian clergy expanded their range of operations. They became more active in providing religious education, started to play more open roles in life-cycle rituals, and took a more central role in discussions of morality and social conduct. Moreover, the visibility of Islam and Christianity was enhanced by the (re)construction of mosques and churches, and by the increased use of religious symbols in everyday life. Perhaps most important, religion became a central dimension in public discussions concerning the nature of the state and the nation.

There are, however, some serious difficulties in applying Casanova's idea of "deprivatization" to the Ajarian case. The central problem is that his depiction of the "public sphere" assumes the existence of a social space that is relatively independent of the state (1994, 65–66). Such a depiction of the public sphere, problematic as it is in reference to the "Western" societies discussed by Casanova, is wholly inapplicable in reference to Ajaria. What we witness in Ajaria is not only a shift of religion out of the domestic sphere but also the appropriation of religion by the state. In Ajaria, the Christian clergy drew on financial as well as political resources generated through state structures. The activities of Muslim leaders, on the other hand, were denied recognition by the media, were frowned upon by nationalist-oriented elite groups, and were subjected to state interventions.

The support that the Georgian Orthodox Church received from the state, and the obstructions Muslim leaders faced, reveal the influence politics has on religious change. Certainly, the restrictive measures of the state were partly responsible for limiting Islam to the lower echelons. Nevertheless, we can understand the docile attitude of the Muslim majority in Ajaria and the relative success of the numerically weak Christians only if we take into account the historical encounters of Muslim Ajarians with Georgian nationalism and Soviet atheism—a process that created a favorable environment for Christian expansion. Indeed, the expulsion of Islam from the public sphere during the Soviet period is less important in understanding post-Soviet religious changes than is the transformation of the public sphere itself. Important elements in this transformation were the introduction of Soviet Georgian education, the disproportionate representation of ethnic Georgians in political structures, and the economic integration of the region within the Soviet Georgian republic as a whole. Moreover, during this period a dominant discourse emerged that portrayed Ajaria as having been oppressed by "evil" Turks for centuries and represented Ajarians as fierce Georgians who relentlessly struggled against forced Islamization and Turkification, and who kept hoping for better times under a united Georgia. This historical discourse became official history, was propagated by the intelligentsia, reproduced by the media, and at least partly accepted by the local Muslim population. After atheism, this discourse was easily modified to fit nationalist and Orthodox Christian purposes, and as such, it continued to keep Islamic expression in a defensive position.

5 Defending Muslim Identities

"During Communism we had more freedom; we still had our own lives. Now, we are losing everything." This lamentation, expressed by an imam in Khulo, succinctly summarized the feelings of many elderly Muslims in upper Ajaria. It articulated frustration with the restrictions on Muslim expression in post-Soviet Ajaria and a longing for a past in which—ironically—such restrictions were usually more severe. This nostalgia for state atheism may seem odd, as it contradicts widespread ideas about religious freedom after socialism and the repression of religion during the Soviet period. Nevertheless, I argue that the imam's statement contained a sound rationale. During socialism, religious expression *in general* was restricted, whereas after socialism the restrictions applied only to Islam. This, added to the fact that in the 1990s the advancement of Christianity was aided by the state, put Muslims, and the position of Islam, in a tenuous situation. In Soviet times public manifestations of Islam were curtailed, but Muslims could retreat to more private spheres of kinship and friendship where religious values were less contested. Islam provided a valuable counter to atheist ideology and as a result became paradoxically compatible with it. In the post-Soviet era, however, Islam lost its position as a place of refuge within a widely criticized atheist system. The public sphere had become partial to the Georgian-Christian worldview, and it was against this that Islam had to define itself.

Thus, though sanctions on religious expression had become less severe, identification with Islam became more problematic. Bringa's study on Muslim identity in Bosnia is instructive. Islam attached Bosnians to several symbolic communities; it tied them to a community of Muslims worldwide in opposition to non-Muslims, but it also tied them to a community of *Bosnian* Muslims, as opposed to other social groups such as Serbians and Croatians (1995, 197). Being Muslim thus entailed a process of *religious* as well as *socio-*

cultural identification and differentiation. But whereas in Bosnia this social and cultural difference was constructed through everyday practices of eating, dressing, name-giving, and the like (see Bringa 1995, 81), in Ajaria it was highly controversial to stress social and cultural differences from Georgians. Indeed, because of the reclassification of Ajarians as Georgians and the growing identification of Ajarians with the Georgian nation, the possibilities for such differentiation were limited. Moreover, because the links between Christianity and Georgian nationality were infused with new vigor in the 1990s, it became increasingly difficult to identify simultaneously with Islam and the Georgian nation. Given these difficulties, it is pertinent to ask what the possibilities, and impediments, were for renewed proliferation of Islam in Ajaria. I begin this chapter by describing the process of Islamic decline as witnessed by Muslim leaders, and then I will discuss how individual Muslim men dealt with the conflicting Muslim and Christian Georgian discourses in their daily lives.[1] These discussions reveal how everyday assertions of religious and national discourses intersect with the larger struggle for Islamic renewal in upper Ajaria and suggest that, despite the rhetoric of "democracy," the new national governments are not necessarily less oppressive of particular religious traditions than Soviet socialism was.

The Worries of the Hojas

Hoja Muhammad was in his early seventies, but despite his age he had lost none of the willpower that had given him a prominent position in the Muslim community. His father had been the last imam of Khulo before the mosque was closed in 1938. Muhammad had considered it his duty to follow in his father's footsteps. He had been one of the initiators of the reopening of the mosque in 1989, and angry tongues claimed that he had also been the main force behind the Muslim uprising against the opening of the Christian lyceum in Khulo. Muhammad had many worries and spoke about them whenever I visited him. His worries concerned the lack of funding for Islamic institutions, pro-Christian policies, and the threat posed by Christian clergy active in the area. But he was especially concerned about the "weaknesses" of the Muslim community.

One afternoon, not long after I first arrived in Khulo, I attended Friday prayers at the mosque, which was attended by 150 men, and heard the *vaizi* (sermon) of Muhammad.[2] He started by discussing the issue of name-giving, stressing that there was no longer any excuse for giving children two first

---

1. As a male researcher I was unable to discuss these matters with women, and the important question of how women deal with the same issues awaits further investigation by someone better situated to do so.

2. Women never attended the Friday prayers, nor did the mosque have a separate place for women. Women participated in *public* religious rituals only during special celebrations and after funerals.

names, one for the local (Muslim) community and one for official use and dealings with non-Muslims, as was common practice in Soviet times. He urged his followers to give their children only one name, a Muslim name. He mentioned that he had done so even when the Communists ruled, going through thorny procedures to give his son the Muslim name Yusup. Then he proclaimed loudly: "Islam is a beautiful faith, remember that! Don't hide that you are Muslim. Also, when you leave the mosque you should be proud of it." Somewhat later he continued in his loud and authoritative way of speaking, "What kind of believers are you if you don't raise your children properly!? Many of you are weaklings. When a Christian offers you money, you take it without even thinking about his motives. A Christian man is smart and you ought to think twice before you send your children to his school." A murmur of approval resounded through the mosque, after which Muhammad recited from the Qur'an. Just before the prayers he concluded by saying, "If you wish to be a Muslim, be one, and if you don't, then don't enter this mosque anymore."

Muhammad's lecture dealt squarely with the precarious position of Islam in Ajaria. He touched on the threats posed both by the state and the growing Georgian Orthodox Church. But even though these issues resounded in Muhammad's lecture, his words were directed not at Christians or at the state but at the Muslim community. Muhammad denounced the continuing practice of giving children two names. Moreover, he stressed the danger of sending children to the Christian lyceum, something that many of the poorer Muslim families nevertheless did, as it was the only affordable possibility for higher education. In other words, he was worried about the choices Muslims were making. This worry haunted him. Once, when I happened upon him working in the field, Muhammad condensed his concern in a single frustrated exclamation. He was sweating all over and must have been thinking about the issue for some time when he grabbed my arm and said: "You know what the bitter thing is in all this? Finally we are able to freely carry out our beliefs, but now Islam is in decline. Satan is playing his own game."

Muhammad was not the only one who considered the waning influence of Islam among the youth to be a serious threat. Another elderly man complained that "these days there is no difference anymore between the village and the city." He explained: "Islam prohibits wearing short dresses, but people watch television and they copy what they see. The television tells people to kiss and hug and that is what they do." Causes of immoral behavior were easily found. The influence of TV was a popular cause, while others stressed that it was the fault of parents who neglected their duty to raise their children properly. At other times, it was seen as a moral deficiency of the younger generation who would not listen anymore and had no respect for their elders.

The improper behavior of children (especially sons) was considered highly problematic, partly because of the conviction that after death the question of whether they raised their children as proper Muslims would weigh heavily on them. During a discussion among imams who had gathered for a *mavludi* (celebration of the birthday of the Prophet Muhammad), an imam who wasn't very careful with his words expressed this concern as follows: "At the end of the day you will have to face yourself, asking whether you really were the head of your family or more like a rooster who flies in and out." Besides the religious motivation, a major fear of religious leaders was that they would lose credibility in the community if they could not make sure their children behaved properly, which would then hasten the decline of Islam. During the same gathering, the imam of a neighboring village spoke about the issue as follows: "We try to preserve what God has given us, but that is impossible if our children don't continue [the tradition]. We say that we are Muslims, but we don't act as Muslims should act. I give sermons [vaizi] in which I tell the community what is forbidden and what is allowed. But who will believe me, if even my own son does not do as I tell him?"

These and other statements corroborated the hypothesis that Islam, at least as perceived by elderly men, was declining rapidly. There was some important truth in it; empty mosques and large-scale conversion to Christianity in lower Ajaria proved the waning influence of Islam. Still, in Khulo it was not clear how fast and straightforward this process was. It is difficult to determine whether the process of decline as witnessed by the hojas was taking place as rapidly as suggested, especially since comparisons with the Soviet period allow multiple interpretations. But it was clear that the renewed importance of Islam that was witnessed in the early 1990s had ended and that elderly Muslim leaders were losing their grip on their community.

The restrictions on Muslim organization and expression may be important in explaining why the upswing of Islam was essentially short-lived. But another important factor is that Muslim leaders failed to reconcile Islam with the ideology of the nation and the imagery of modernity. The defenders of Islam stressed the importance of their faith and the need to stay true to familial traditions, but attempts to mobilize these values encountered strong opposition from the political establishment and, more important, ambivalence from Muslims who were less active in practicing their faith.

The issues raised by Hoja Muhammad and other elderly Muslims—drinking, education, and dress codes—were not just the worries of old men. They were seen as problematic by the younger generation as well, though in pondering these dilemmas they often came to different conclusions. Among those youths who called themselves Muslim (still a majority), discussions about religion unavoidably prompted discussion of the difficulty of reconciling Muslim identity and conduct with ideas of nation and state. Their careers and social lives were often tightly embedded in Georgian contexts with explicit Christian characteristics. The resulting ambiguities in self-ascription meant that it was impossible to provide a general depiction of religious identification in upper Ajaria. Instead, shifts between competing loyalties indicate the need to pay attention to the way individuals have dealt with the dilemmas involved.

Difficulties in Restoring and Maintaining Muslim Identity

We have seen that the Muslim leaders' greatest fear was that their children would abandon the path of Islam. The dangers most frequently mentioned were consumption of alcohol, improper dress, and nonobservance of religious rituals. These elements were not very different from what Muslim leaders perceived as the evils of state atheism, but they had reappeared in a new context, with renewed vigor. Given that the Muslim clergy saw its grip on the younger generation declining, it is interesting to look at how these young Muslims dealt with issues of faith in everyday life.

Particularly revealing in this respect were the discussions during a supra to which I was invited. The specific encounter had some "political" significance because Dato—a potential convert to Christianity—had urged me to come and discuss religion with his neighbors Bejan and Enver.[3] His aim, I later discovered, was to show me that they were not as Muslim as I might have thought. Bejan was formally unemployed but had inherited land that belonged to his grandparents before collectivization. This and his talent for cultivating flowers enabled him to make a modest living.[4] Enver was a traffic police officer in a somewhat better financial position than the other two, especially because of the informal supplements to his income from bribes.[5] Bejan and Enver underlined that they were Muslims, but they also said that they paid little attention to religious obligations and had not been in the mosque for several years.

When I met Bejan and Enver at the supra, they enthusiastically told me that I was about to experience true Georgian hospitality. The evening consisted of a rotating table of dishes prepared by the spouses of Enver and Dato, and large quantities of vodka. Dato was given the honor of being tamada (toastmaster). Dato used his position to start discussions on religion, its relation to the Georgian nation, and the freedom that his neighbors would give their children in deciding what religion to choose.

When Dato asked the other two if they would allow their children to adopt Christianity, Bejan answered: "Everyone is free to choose his or her religion. If my son decides to be a Christian, then he is free to do so, but if he decides to follow *my* path, then that's also fine." Enver had a different opinion, saying: "For my part, I would *not* allow my children to abandon Islam." When Dato heard this he interrupted Enver. He leaned over the table, his face expressing disagreement. A quick exchange followed.

3. Dato worked as a mathematics teacher in the village school of Dekanashvilebi. He was baptized in August 2001, a few months after that evening.

4. This flower business was quite profitable, as competition among growers was still low.

5. Enver openly commented on the necessity of bribe taking. In his view bribe taking was necessary both to supplement his insufficient salary and to keep his job. Simply put, his superiors would fire him if he refused to take bribes because they expected to receive part of these informal revenues.

DATO: What was your grandfather?

ENVER: Muslim, of course.

DATO: And your grandmother?

ENVER: The same, Muslim.

DATO: And what about your [distant] forefathers?

ENVER: Christians.

DATO: Right.

Dato fell back in his chair and relaxed, seemingly satisfied with having made a convincing point by invoking the Christian past of Ajaria. Enver, however, did not agree with the conclusions that Dato drew from his answers and continued the discussion:

> Yes, we know that they [distant forefathers] were Christians, but we also know that at a certain point they adopted Islam. How and why they became Muslim we don't know, nor do we know whether it was voluntarily or by the sword. But we *do* know that since then they have been living as Muslims, [so] they must have considered it the true faith. I live the same way as they did and want my children to continue in the same direction.

Dato remained silent, while Bejan joined the discussion. He placed a pencil on top of a dish, looked in my direction and said:

> Do you see this? This [pencil] is God, and these [imaginary lines from the edge of the plate to the pencil] are ways that lead to God. Perhaps there are forty different religions. Do we know for sure what the shortest way to God is? No, we don't! But my grandparents have concluded that their religion, Islam, is the shortest way to God. . . . My grandparents were intelligent people. They taught me everything, so how could I dare abandon that path?

In this discussion, the ideal of keeping the familial tradition intact was a central theme. As for the continuation of tradition it seemed of little importance whether one fulfilled religious obligations, as long as one did not reject the path of Islam. Enver conveyed this when he ended a speech that he had started earlier: "Perhaps I am not actively observing the demands of my religion, but I observe the most important commandments: I don't kill people, I don't steal, and I don't sleep with other women. That is, I don't undermine my family." Bejan explained that he did not fulfill the religious demands because he had grown up in an atheist period and anyway did not have time for it. "But," he stressed, "I gave my father and brother a Muslim funeral and I would have considered it a sin if I had decided otherwise." The idea behind this is that as long as one did not abandon Islam altogether a continuation of the familial tradition was still possible. As such, it was also an implicit critique of Dato who was about to decide otherwise and convert to Christianity.

That evening Dato did not raise the issue again. The next morning, though, when we had breakfast, Dato returned to the subject: "You know, Enver's statements really surprised me. He tells you that he is a Muslim and that he won't allow his children to adopt Christianity. [laughs] But what kind of Muslim is he anyway? He doesn't go to the mosque, he drinks vodka and—I wanted to tell him then, but I didn't—he even eats pork!"[6] Despite the fact that nominal Muslims like Bejan and Enver presented their stance as a continuation of familial traditions, this perspective was not unequivocally accepted. Dato did not engage in a direct confrontation, perhaps because Bejan and Enver were united on the matter. Nevertheless, the comments Dato made behind their backs showed that it was not only converts who had to explain the reasons for their conversion but that those who defined themselves as Muslim needed to explain and defend their stance. The difference was that whereas new Christians talked openly and even self-confidently about their choices, young Muslims spoke about their religious convictions—at least to outsiders—in more cautious and modest terms. Perhaps they did so because they were aware of the gap between their religious orientation and the expectations of the wider society they were living in.

With reference to these expectations, it is possible to identify several domains in which regaining or retaining Muslim identity was problematic. I discuss three of them here, but by no means am I suggesting that this is an exhaustive list. The first is that of Georgian "culture," understood here from a local perspective as those customs that were seen as characteristic of Georgians. Especially crucial, in this respect, were the codes of social behavior around alcohol consumption. The next domain is that of Georgian "nationality" and its assumed ties to Christianity. For Muslims, this meant that they had to position themselves in relation to a national discourse that stressed the Christian roots of the Georgian nation. The last domain concerns ideas of the "future," specifically the aspirations that people held for themselves and their children.

"Culture"—Alcohol Tests

When I asked a man in his sixties what he thought the reasons were for the decline of Islam in his community, and especially for the waning interest of the younger generation in it, he provided me with the following explanation: "You know, Islam is a demanding religion, and people are simply not always strong enough to cope with that. You have to pray five times a day and you are not allowed to drink [alcohol] or to eat pork." Although the man was pointing at insufficient levels of self-control, the statement also referred to opposing codes of behavior for Christians and Muslims. The issues of consuming pork and alcohol were of course also problematic during the Soviet period, but there is reason to suspect that they gained new importance after socialism. The account of Jemali, a man who until recently had not given his religious affiliation serious thought, sheds light on the subject. "During Soviet times," Jemali said,

6. Among nominal Muslims in Ajaria eating pork was usually considered a larger sin than consuming alcohol.

"we were Muslims, of course, but we could only pray inside our homes. We didn't think badly of anyone who drank at work or offered wine to guests, as those things were simply unavoidable. Of course we knew that for Muslims it was a sin to drink [alcohol] or eat pork, but what could you do?" However, the new possibilities for religious observation after socialism changed expectations as to how one should behave as a Muslim. This was true for Jemali. In 1989, when the mosque was opened, he was twenty-six years old. He started attending the local madrassa, making it to the position of teacher there in the mid-1990s. He abandoned drinking and for several years observed all the religious obligations. However, changes in his life challenged his stance toward Islam. He received a promotion at work that made him responsible for the telephone lines running to his neighborhood. Because his position involved attending meetings and receiving guests from the district center, he started drinking again. According to Jemali, it would simply be impossible not to drink:

> It is fairly simple. You know our customs, whenever a guest arrives you have to provide him a meal, and since we have a long tradition of wine drinking, you have to serve wine and drink together. People would think badly of you if you said that alcohol was prohibited in your house. It would be the same as saying that you are not a Georgian.

Hospitality and drinking are crucial issues in the Georgian context. Mars and Altman argued that in Georgia, beyond the family, a male has "continually to prove himself as *catso*—a man. He is, in this respect, perpetually 'on show' and has constantly to demonstrate his worthiness to public opinion in general and to his colleagues and peers in particular. These require the extravagant use of display and consumption, as well as exhibitions of 'manliness'" (Mars and Altman 1987, 271). In other words, the extensive rituals of drinking and toasting were an integral part of everyday politics, of defining who is who, and of expressing gratitude and respect. Without participation in these activities, it seemed hardly possible to advance one's position in professional life. Even for Jemali, a low-level state employee, abstaining from alcohol consumption was practically impossible as it would foreclose any future job opportunities.

Mars and Altman offer valuable insights into the role of drinking in Georgia as a whole, but the issue had an extra dimension on the frontier. In Ajaria, it was not only important to prove one's manliness through alcohol consumption but also to prove that one was truly Georgian.[7] Several baptized acquaintances could not imagine that in some mountain villages in upper Ajaria there was no alcohol available at all. People would ask, "Then what did you do, you

---

7. Whenever I was invited for dinner, either in the homes of nominal Muslims or new Christians, the level of alcohol consumption struck me as significantly higher than in Christian villages. By demonstrating their ability to consume large amounts of alcohol, Ajarian men may have marked their Georgianness.

just sat there and ate?" They were amazed at the possibility and showed their disapproval about what they considered a lack of hospitality. In Ajaria, drinking had become a very powerful symbol of Georgianness. Abstaining from it not only placed you in a difficult social position but was also interpreted as a rejection of the nation.

Again we encounter the same problem noticed earlier. During the Soviet period Ajarians could be Muslim in their homes while being Georgian in public. Obviously, even then there were people who continued to observe most or all religious obligations. To do that, they had to maintain a low profile, take jobs as tractor drivers or shepherds, and refrain from membership in the Communist Party. For anyone employed in a public function, continued religious observance was not a possibility, and this was accepted even by Muslim leaders. For men with such jobs as school teacher, kolkhoz director, or police officer it was taken for granted that they could not comply with certain religious demands. Whereas then it was accepted behavior for Muslim men to drink alcohol or eat pork or fail to observe Ramadan, in postsocialist Ajaria it was more complicated to abstain from such demands and still maintain Muslim identity. Instead, social behavior needed explanation and was more easily subject to criticism from other Muslims—"You are no real Muslim"—or cynicism from new Christians—"You say that you are Muslim but actually you are not."

"Nationality"—Forced to Take a Position

The way the terms Ajarian (Ach'areli) and Georgian (Kartveli) were used locally revealed the issues at stake in discussions of nationality. Once, after Teimuri and I had been talking with some men sitting in front of the mosque, we ran into an old man whom we had not met before. The following short conversation between the two unfolded:

OLD MAN: Are you a Georgian or an Ajarian?

TEIMURI: I am a Georgian *and* an Ajarian.

OLD MAN: That is impossible! You are either one or the other.

TEIMURI: Isn't Ajaria then part of Georgia?

OLD MAN: Ajaria is Ajaria.

Here the conversation ended. When Teimuri and I were alone again he shook his head and said: "He is an old man. It is no use explaining to him that he is confusing religion with nationality. . . . Anyway, such opinions you will only encounter among the older generation; they never received any education, you know." Teimuri was right in saying that it had become fairly uncommon for Ajarians to present themselves as radically different from Georgians. Most people made it clear that they saw themselves as Georgians, sometimes specifying that they were Muslim Georgians. But although Teimuri claimed that it was a matter of understanding the difference between religion and nationality, distinguishing between the two in Ajaria often proved difficult if not impossible.

Most young Muslims I spoke with told me of painful encounters concerning their religious affiliation. These happened most frequently while traveling to places outside Ajaria—to Tbilisi or to any of the other provinces of Georgia. One villager told me about an incident that occurred while he was on a bus from Tbilisi to Batumi. When the bus crossed the administrative border from Guria into Ajaria, a passenger remarked: "I see we have arrived in Tatarstan." The Ajarian passengers were highly insulted and forced the driver to stop and kick the man off the bus. Other respondents had similar experiences. They had been called "Tatar" or "Turk," or their refusal to drink wine had provoked comments that they were not "real" Georgians.

Although these experiences were generally unpleasant, for some it offered an opportunity to talk about religious difference and to stress the possibility of reconciling Muslim and Georgian identities. In front of the mosque I overheard the following monologue in which Imam Kemal told some bystanders about an encounter he had on a trip to Guria—the oblast north of Ajaria:

> This [Gurian] man asked me about my family name, and then [after hearing the answer] replied: "That is a real Gurian name."... I asked him: "Why a Gurian name, why not Ajarian?" Then the man made some statement about Islam undermining our nation and that Georgians should be Christian. So I asked him: "Christianity came here in the first century; what religion did people have *before* that period?" Animism was his reply. So I asked him, "Were those animists Georgians?" Yes, of course they were Georgians. And he also agreed with me that they stayed Georgian when they adopted Christianity. So then I told him that if Georgians stayed Georgian despite having changed their religion, they also stayed Georgian after having adopted Islam. Then the man gave in, saying: "I'll have to think about that."

The bystanders laughed and nodded in agreement. "That is how it is," one remarked. "Kemal knows how to say it." Within the Muslim community these and other stories "proved" that there was no real problem in combining Muslim and Georgian identity and that claims to the contrary were those of people who lacked intelligence. Still, the issue troubled many. Even the monologue presented above had limited impact, despite the fact that it skillfully used the contradictions in nationalist rhetoric. It was a response to a dominant discourse, but as a reaction it was ineffective because part of the Georgian message—its historical "truth"—was nevertheless accepted. Moreover, because it claimed rights as a religious minority it still placed Ajarians in a position of difference, something that was often inconvenient to members of the younger generation.

Negative experiences in expressing religious difference might have contributed to the fact that (especially in public) many Muslims displayed an accommodating attitude. Muslims stressed the importance of believing in one God and emphasized that differences between religions were of only secondary importance. They said they respected Christianity but it happened that they were Muslim. Furthermore, they stressed that Islam was the tradition of their parents and grandparents, which in some cases almost sounded like an apology. This was also true of Muslim teenagers who attended the Christian lyceum in Khulo. One female student noted in an essay: "We know that our ancestors were Christians who were Islamized by the Turks during the three-hundred-year domination. Christianity is probably our true religion, but thereafter we became Muslims. [Islam] was handed down from generation to generation, and therefore we believe in Islam." Although she wrote that she was Muslim, in the same sentence she mentioned that Christianity was probably her "true religion." The quotation not only demonstrates the clash between national and local traditions but also suggests that this student had internalized the nationalist rhetoric about religion—a rhetoric that made it very difficult to reconcile being Muslim and Georgian.

Conflicting Ideas about the Future

Despite their stated religious affiliation, many Muslims faced difficulties in making a place for Islam in the aspirations they had for themselves and for their children. More broadly, it was often difficult for them to imagine an Islamic future for a "Georgian" Ajaria. One reason was that the elderly Muslims who had dominated religious life in the 1990s stuck to interpretations of Islam that were difficult to align with the aspirations of the younger generation.

Young Muslims openly distanced themselves from what they saw as an attempt by Muslim leaders to restore a kind of pre-Soviet Islam. Amiran, a thirty-seven-year- old judge in Khulo, made it clear what he thought the basic problem was: "I am not saying that Islam is backward. You only have to go to Turkey to see that for yourself. But here it is different. For the past eighty years Islam was isolated, it didn't move forward. It is a village kind of Islam." The consequence of the isolation from the rest of the Muslim world was particularly clear in a conflict over the interpretation of the Muslim calendar in Ghorjomi, the village twenty kilometers east of Khulo. Here the local Muslim community stuck to a Muslim calendar created by the locally famous mullah, Osman, who played an important role in religious life in upper Ajaria between the 1930s and 1980s. Because at that time there was no reliable information about the times of prayer or the start of Ramadan, Mullah Osman constructed his own calendar based on the moon and the stars. When the restrictions on religion were lifted and the rest of Ajaria adopted the standard Sunni Muslim calendar, the inhabitants of Ghorjomi stuck to the calendar of Mullah Osman, with the result that they start their Ramadan two days earlier than the rest of the Muslim world. They refused to adopt the standard timetable because they considered it a recent and impure modification.[8]

---

8. The previous imam of Ghorjomi—a middle-aged man who had taken Qur'an courses in Turkey—tried to abolish this calendar but was forced to give up his position after disputes with elderly Muslims.

The local inventions made in response to the isolation of Islam in Ajaria were seen by their defenders as an attempt to stick to an authentic version of their faith. Fervor to create an authentic Islam also led to other innovations. During an informal meeting of Qur'anic teachers, Hoja Muhammad displayed his wish to remain true to Muslim traditions in a way that was shocking to several participants. The family with whom the group was having lunch had arranged tables and chairs in advance. But on seeing the arrangement, Hoja Muhammad ordered the men to remove all the furniture and to arrange the "table" on the ground instead, which, he explained, was more in keeping with Islamic tradition. When his wish was realized, Hoja Muhammad went to the kitchen and insisted on carrying the food into the room, thus ensuring that the women would not have to leave the kitchen. When it turned out that the men were supposed to eat with their hands instead of cutlery, one could feel their discomfort. Little jokes were whispered, and one young Islamic teacher remarked: "Hoja says it is more Islamic [to sit on the floor], but according to me it is more Asiatic." He continued, "Luckily they let us wash our hands with warm water; that is the minimum."

These and other situations made less-devout Muslims feel that Islam was pulling them backward. The version of Islam propagated by men like Muhammad was understood as inhibiting progress. Likewise, many people struggled with the decision to send their children to madrassas where they would learn to read Arabic, something they saw as being quite useless in daily life. Moreover, inhabitants of Khulo frequently mentioned that children from moun-

Muslim men quietly expressed their discontent at being seated on the floor rather than at a table, as is the custom in upper Ajaria. Khulo, July 2000.

tain villages with stricter Muslim lifestyles performed very poorly at school. As the judge Amiran summarized it, "I pity them; they are prisoners of their traditions." The reservations many Muslims had concerning the "old men's Islam" of the 1990s were understandable, and these were an important factor in the subsequent decline of Islam. However, among the younger generation there were those who found new ways to integrate competing discourses into their personal lives. Moreover, some of the younger imams offered new interpretations of Islam that were more compatible with the aspirations people held for their own and their children's lives.

Finding Ways Out

Muslim men in Ajaria struggled with how to reconcile Georgian expectations of hospitality and the religious demands of Islam. They had to decide how to present themselves in non-Muslim contexts when the "wrong" identity could squelch their opportunities. They were often forced to choose between their religious and national identity, or to create a tenuous reconciliation between the two. Their Muslim identity and its implications even produced crises when they were making decisions about their children. Their struggles to restore and maintain their Muslim identity had been most difficult in the arenas of "culture," "nationality," and dreams for the future. The men I encountered in Ajaria all dealt with these issues differently. The stories of Kemal, Alexander, and Teimuri are apt examples of the ways in which young men attempted to deal with the difficulty of being Muslim and Georgian in Ajaria.

Kemal—Reinterpretation

After the border with Turkey was opened and restrictions on religious expression were lifted, wealthy Turkish citizens became interested in helping Ajarians reestablish Islamic institutions. Besides making contributions to the construction of mosques and madrassas, the Turkish benefactors invited young Ajarian men to study at vocational schools in Turkey. At first the muftiate in Batumi handled these invitations, but in later years young men were recruited through more informal contacts.[9] Kemal was initially invited to study in Turkey for one year, though his stay lasted altogether seven years. According to his account, he had been selected because he was the best student at the madrassa. During the first two years of his study (1994–96), he lived with a family in Trabzon, learned Turkish, and attended preparatory courses required for admittance to Seljuk University in Konya in central Turkey. He was accepted and spent the next five years studying and completing a course in Islamic law. On his return to

---

9. The muftiate facilitated the participation of some two hundred men in Qur'an courses in Turkey between 1992 and 1994. This triggered harsh reactions from the political establishment in Batumi (Meiering Mikadze 1999).

Khulo in early 2001, Kemal was appointed imam, because with his university degree he had the highest religious education in the village.

The male domain of his house consisted of the visitors' room and a large study. Kemal was especially fond of his study room. There was a computer, which he had received from an Islamic organization in Turkey. His bookcases were filled with books in Arabic and Turkish. During one of my visits, he showed me his university yearbook, making sure that I noticed the high quality of the paper and the colorful layout, something that was very rare in Georgia. He went through the pages of photographs of students and talked extensively about his professors. He also had me admire the advertisements that had enabled the production of this book, something he considered a wonderful combination of business and good deeds.

In our conversations, Kemal often made comparisons between Georgia and Turkey. Perhaps what struck him as the biggest difference was the way people were engaged in economic life. While Turkey (and especially Konya) had rapidly developed during the years he lived there, Georgia had not managed to overcome its deep economic crisis. To Kemal this was a sign of intense chaos not only in economics but also in the mental state of the inhabitants: "Do you know what the difference is between rich men here and in Turkey? In Turkey, when someone starts to make money, he won't show it off. Instead, he first wants to expand his business, to guarantee a secure income for himself and his family. But here, as soon as someone has earned a sum of money, he will immediately buy a car and spend the rest of the money on partying. People don't act the way they should."

Many examples followed that showed Kemal's positive attitude toward Turkey. For him, Turkey represented a model of progress and proof that it was possible to "modernize" an Islamic country. Well aware of the existing stereotypes in Georgia concerning Muslims, Kemal perceived the Turkish system as successful in tolerating difference without losing the unity of the state: "One of the problems we have here is that people mistakenly equate ethnicity with religion. For example, some people say that Ajarians are not Georgian because they are Muslim. But those are two separate things." In Turkey, by contrast, "there are many religious and ethnic groups, but they all see themselves as belonging to the Turkish nation." The implication was that if the Turkish model were followed, there would be no problem in being Georgian and Muslim at the same time.

Kemal's formal religious training had also changed his view on the religious practices that were commonplace in Ajaria. Although he was careful not to mention names, he regretted that most hojas had never been "properly" trained: "They learned about Islam only from their parents during the winter, behind closed doors." This older generation was, in Kemal's view, under the spell of certain superstitions, such as wearing amulets as protection against the evil eye and reciting Qur'anic verses to cure sickness.

Kemal managed to realign Islam with aspirations that many of his fellow townsmen held. He separated religion and nation, something that worked well in the Muslim community in upper Ajaria but, as we have seen, was challenged outside the local community. Moreover his "modern" picture of Islam involved a rejection of those markers of Georgian identity (hospitality, consumption) that were vital in social life and that many Muslims in Ajaria explicitly used to stress their loyalty to the Georgian nation. His positive stance toward Turkey as a model of development was accepted by several young Muslims, but it also evoked suspicion from those who saw any potential influence from Turkey as a possible attack on the nation. Also, his modern depiction of Islam aroused the suspicion of several elderly Muslims, like Hoja Muhammad, who on one occasion expressed his doubts concerning the changes that Kemal had made in the organization of the mosque.

Alexander—The Best of Both Worlds

Alexander's life had not been easy. He was born in 1972 and his father died when he was sixteen years old. As the oldest son he became the head of the household, responsible for the well-being of his family during unstable times. Alexander had done reasonably well even so. He had managed to make good money by traveling and trading in Russia and Turkey.

I had not seen Alexander for about a year when I ran into him near his home in July 2001. It came as a surprise to find him working in the fields, cutting and stacking hay. On earlier occasions he had always insisted that there were easier and more lucrative ways to earn money. He smiled when he noticed my surprise and said that he had changed his lifestyle and that these days he harvested the fruits of *real* labor. Profits from earlier businesses had enabled him to purchase several plots of land. He declared that for now he had given up on trading: "It is no use anymore; you end up losing money because of all the bribes you have to pay."[10] Besides the changes in the way he earned a living, I noticed another change as well. Around his neck hung an amulet which, he told me with a laugh, his mother had urged him to wear.[11] That evening when I joined Alexander for dinner, there was no alcohol. To my surprise, Alexander seemed very comfortable with the fact that he had broken the Georgian custom. Instead of making apologies—which was almost standard practice when alcohol was absent—Alexander told me about a recent encounter that had made a big impression on him.

Six months previously Alexander had gone to Batumi to sort things out for a lumber-selling deal in which he was involved. He had bad luck and was unable to quickly find Turkish buyers. After searching in vain for several days, he

10. Difficulties while traveling through the North Caucasus (paying huge bribes and being beaten up by police) convinced Alexander that it was no use to continue this kind of trade. Because his brother found a job in Abashidze's private militia, his family responsibilities had also lessened.

11. These amulets contain a piece of paper with a verse or phrase from the Qur'an, preferably written by an imam. They are believed to protect the wearer from the evil eye.

decided to ask his cousin Ismet for help and ended up living with him for an entire month. Many believed Alexander's cousin Ismet would become the future mufti of Ajaria as he had been studying off and on for six years at the prestigious Al-Azhar University in Cairo.

> I can tell you, living with him was quite an experience. You know how I used to live. I like women, company, drinking. Well, Ismet knew this, too, of course, and he immediately warned me that I would need to adjust my behavior if I wanted to stay in his house. There would be no drinking in his house. . . . Well, I agreed. But a few days later several friends passed by, wanting to thank me for a deal that had worked out well. I thought to myself, "Okay, this time I will do it right." I refused [the bottles of] vodka they offered me. Of course they didn't accept it, but I told them, "If you want to thank me, buy me a bar of chocolate." You should have seen their faces! [laughter] The next day I heard that they had been beaten up just after they had turned around the corner—something about a debt or so. So you understand that I was grateful to Ismet, for in a way he had saved me from this fight.

This was only the beginning of the story that Alexander wanted to tell me. He continued:

> One evening Ismet and I had a long conversation. Ismet demanded that I give up my sinful lifestyle. I told him, I never steal or cheat and I don't kill people. My only two sins are that I drink alcohol and that I sleep with women other than my wife. But as long as I am young, I can't give up the women. Ismet thought for a while and said: "Just be careful with women, but the drinking you definitely have to give up." After some talking back and forth I gave in, but I said that in that case he should help me with one question: How could I be sure about the existence of God? We talked about it, and in order to convince me Ismet asked what my strongest wish was. So I told him that I really, really wished to talk with my [deceased] father once more, to find out what had really happened to him when he died. [Ismet then instructed Kemal how to meet his father in his sleep.] I never had such a vivid dream as I did that night. I really saw my father. He told me not to worry about it, that there was nothing to find out and that I should go on with my life. . . . How can you not believe after such an experience?

After that encounter, I saw Alexander once more. A week before my departure from Ajaria I met him in one of the cafés in Batumi. Alexander was in the company of some men, eating and drinking *ch'ach'a* (strong alcoholic drink). I joined them. We discussed international politics and raised toasts to Georgia, women, and good business. Nothing seemed to indicate his previous change in lifestyle. But this was Batumi and not Khulo. Alexander was a man with many faces. He definitely needed those different faces. To survive as a trader in a highly unstable region, it was not only vital to have good trading skills but also to be able to adjust to different social contexts. However, this did not seem to diminish the value of Islam for him, which gave him spiritual strength and a place of refuge back in the mountains.

Teimuri—Caught in the Middle

Khalid, the father of my research assistant, Teimuri, had made the hajj to Mecca in 1992 and was, partly because of this, well known and respected in the Muslim community. His two sons, Anzor and Teimuri, however, hardly observed any of the religious obligations. Because of this, Khalid worried about what had gone wrong in their upbringing, and sometimes he half jokingly told his sons that he had made a big mistake in allowing them to go to the university in Batumi. It is doubtful whether I should label Teimuri a Muslim, as he himself usually avoided answering the question. In fact, he had been in an almost continuous struggle about how to reconcile his religious and national identity. As he came to know more about my research, he jokingly suggested that I should simply take him as my research subject, because all the tensions in religious and national identifications came together in him.

At times he felt that he should convert to Christianity, especially since many of his friends in Batumi implicitly or explicitly had urged him to do so:

> I used to celebrate Easter with them, and when they would greet me with the words "Khristos voskres" [Christ is risen] I knew I was supposed to say "Voistinu voskres" [He is risen indeed]. But then, should I say that or not? I would feel very uncomfortable in such situations. On the one hand I spent an important part of my life with them—they have helped me with so many things—yet I reject their faith. But then on the other hand I have my family.

Making a conscious decision to convert to Christianity would be a slap in the face of his father. As a result, Teimuri called himself a lost cause and explained that what he felt was *udvoenie* (two-sidedness). He was not only incapable of choosing one religion over the other but of allowing any faith to enter his heart. He expressed some of his ambivalent feelings during a conversation we had about the position of Islam in Ajaria:

> Islam might be a good religion, but it is incompatible with the Georgian state. We finally have our independence and we can't give too much freedom to Islam because we are still in the process of constructing [our country]. Look at the Muslim children here, they can hardly write a correct sentence. Their parents send them to the madrassa and only care about their children being able to read Arabic. But what is that going to do for their lives here? Our entire language, our culture, is all connected with Christianity, so being Muslim immediately draws you away from it—it inhibits integration of Ajaria in our [Georgian] society, it inhibits the development of these people.

Teimuri stressed the aspect of "integration," and he did so on several occasions, because of his own experiences. Teimuri often spoke about disadvantages he encountered at the university, his difficulties being accepted into the lives of friends with non-Muslim backgrounds, and his unease about not knowing Christian—and thus Georgian—lifestyles. For his children, he told me, this would be different. He was determined to provide them with a better start. At home he taught his children Georgian history and also acquainted them with Christianity, so that they would be "free." This freedom, Teimuri explained, entailed not only the freedom to choose one religion over the other but especially the freedom to live in Georgian society. That this was problematic for someone with a Muslim background was very obvious to him, and actually he could not always understand why Muslims still perceived themselves as Georgian: "The Muslims here say that they are Georgian, but besides language, what is it that makes them feel Georgian? I don't understand that."

Despite all his doubts, over the past four years changes in his own life drew him closer to a "Muslim" life. In 1997, when I first met Teimuri, he was about to finish his *aspirantura* (postgraduate studies). He was full of hopes that finishing his thesis would give him a good start in establishing an academic career. However, four years later his hopes had largely vanished. After several delays, partly caused by the difficulty of combining writing a dissertation with obligations at home, he had finally finished his thesis in 2000. But because organizing a public defense of his dissertation in Georgia required making monetary or other contributions to the right persons, in 2001 Teimuri still had not managed to obtain his degree. During that time several vacancies to which he applied went to others, people whose financial resources and personal networks guaranteed them an academic career. Teimuri's lack of both diminished his hopes of making a living in Batumi. Teimuri no longer participated in the supras organized by his former friends and colleagues, partly because of the unease he felt at not being able to repay these social favors. Instead, after having lived in Batumi for six years, he had returned to his native town. Through hard work and with the help of his relatives he more or less managed to get his life on track. This change in lifestyle also meant that, even if not by choice, Teimuri adhered to religious demands and took part in Islamic rituals more actively than before.

Islam was important for the three men as it was part of social life in the local community to which they were tightly connected. For Alexander, the Muslim community was a place of refuge where he escaped from his hectic and dangerous life as a trader. For Teimuri, it was a place he would rather have left behind but to which he returned when his hopes for establishing a life in the city faded. For Kemal, the Muslim community was the place to which he returned after a prolonged stay in Turkey, and where he now held an important position. But all three had ambivalent feelings about the kind of Islam that was propagated in Ajaria during the 1990s, and they each responded to it differently. As such, the three men represented distinctive ways in which young men in Ajaria dealt with the complexity of realigning religious and national identity. Each of their strategies had limitations that became apparent when acted out in public life. The "reinterpretations" of Kemal could be seen as an attempt to provide new meanings to Islam, but they involved the risk of alienation both from society at large and from the more conservative local Muslims. Teimuri's "two-sidedness" referred to accepting both the messages of Georgian nationalism and Islamic tradition. This meant that he was constantly confronted with the contradictions between the two discourses, leading to withdrawal from direct involvement in religious life. Alexander partially by-passed such contradictions between national and religious discourses—by keeping his Georgian and Muslim identity separated in different spheres of life. Actually, this last "strategy" seemed to me the most promising, with the only risk being that this interpretation of Islam would not be acceptable to more devout Muslims.

Breaches in the Frontier

Paradoxically, post-Soviet "religious freedom" led to a further marginalization of Islam in Ajaria. Increased expectations of what being a Muslim entailed ran counter to increased demands for displaying loyalty to the Georgian nation. Thus, it was often difficult for Muslims to observe Islamic requirements. Moreover, the asymmetries involved in the construction of religious and national narratives meant that Muslims found it highly difficult to relate their religious beliefs to their aspirations for the future.

The initial upswing of Islam in Ajaria, as shaped by elderly Muslim men, was informed by images of a "pre-Soviet Islam." The portrayal of Muslim life advanced by these elders involved a rejection of the inclusive language of Georgian nationalism. They held on to a distinction between Georgian (Kartveli) and Ajarian (Ach'areli) on the basis that Georgians were Christian and Ajarians Muslim. This narrative of difference was difficult to accept for those young Muslims who saw themselves as Georgians and whose careers were tightly interwoven with the Georgian state. Young males with more moderate views of Islam displayed a preference for a depoliticized and de-ethnicized version of Islam. They claimed that religion and nation were different things and that therefore there was no problem in being simultaneously Muslim and Georgian. This depoliticized version of Islam attempted to soften contradictions in the combination of Georgian and Muslim identities. But, as we have seen, it only worked in the Ajarian highlands and only in exclusively Muslim circles. The combination of religious and national identity lost its cogency and was suspect to criticism when confronted with Georgian nationalist discourse. Moreover, because these Muslims incorporated part of a national Georgian ideology, it limited the practice of Islam in their daily lives.

The tragedy of Islam in the first decade after socialism was that it did not manage to advance a worldview powerful enough to function as an acceptable alternative to Georgian nationalist ideology. The view of the elders was contrary to ideas of Georgian nationality, but it did not offer an acceptable alternative to the younger generation. The moderate view of younger Muslims, on the other hand, did not solve the incompatibility of Muslim obligations with expectations of "Georgian" behavior in daily life, thus resulting in dilemmas that over time often became untenable. In part, this was a result of the specificities of Soviet rule in Ajaria. During the Soviet period, representations of culture and ethnicity were stripped of all Islamic symbolism and meanings. The lifestyles of Muslims were reinterpreted as "village traditions" or leftovers of a despised Ottoman Turkish past. This meant that Muslims, especially those who had (partly) embraced the promise of "modernity" as modeled on the national Georgian ideal, could no longer legitimize their way of life through the language of ethnicity and culture.

The stories in this chapter reflect the dilemmas stemming from the way Ajarians were partly included and partly excluded from the Georgian national imagery. In this imagery, Ajarian Muslims were not complete "others" but were rather "incomplete selves"; they were simultaneously brother and potential enemy. One of the responses to this ambiguous position was to adjust presentations of self to changing circumstances. However, these adaptations did not necessarily *ease* the problems of reconciling conflicting identities and loyalties; rather, they resulted often in an uncomfortable oscillation between different (imagined and real) communities. The case of Teimuri showed this vividly. In upper Ajaria, he called himself a Muslim, while in Batumi he presented himself as Georgian. The way he talked about these different settings revealed that he felt caught between rural Muslim space on the one hand and urban Christian space on the other. Moreover, his ambiguous position tended to result in a "powerless" Islam.

Teimuri was, to an extent, representative of a generation that imagined its future within the bounds of the Georgian state. Yet because of the constraints the Georgian nation put on Muslim men's processes of self-identification, some opted for alternative frames of reference where they could imagine and construe their lives. Kemal focused on religious centers in the Muslim world, while Alexander looked toward transnational trading networks. The opening of the border with Turkey was an important factor in the creation of such new points of reference. On this point, Shami provides interesting insights in her discussion of post-Soviet identities in the North Caucasus. About the Circassians, she writes, "More than the fall of Soviet communism per se, it is the sudden porousness of borders and accessibility of territories that had been largely closed to them, that has been of transformative importance to concepts of ethnic identity" (1999, 43). Although I do not want to go as far as Shami does in attributing a radical transformative power to the opening of the border, it certainly influenced the scope of possibilities for articulating religious identities. As Kemal's story demonstrated, new transnational contacts offered a vision of Islam that was more compatible with certain aspirations. Moreover, the opening of the border produced ways to circumvent the straitjacket of the state that so tightly bound a Muslim's possibility for self-identification and religious expression. Alexander's story illustrated that this process of circumvention was not limited to eluding official structures; it entailed evading expectations of religious and national loyalties as well. For Alexander, the nation-state had become less important. It was a place of temporary residence, while his interests, and perhaps even his loyalties, lay elsewhere. Because of the centrality of Christianity in the national imagery, if there is a future for Islam in Ajaria it is through such shifts in points of reference, which help Muslims conceive of their identities outside the bounds of the Georgian nation-state.

6 Ancestors and Enemies in Conversion to Christianity

In the late 1980s, when restrictions on religion were lifted, Ajarians seemed to be converting en masse to Christianity. A local newspaper of that time reported that five thousand people had been baptized in Batumi in a single day and that the recently opened churches were unable to seat all the worshipers who had finally been able to "return to their ancestral faith," Georgian Orthodoxy (*Sovetskaia Adzhariia*, 29 May 1989). Bishop Dimitri recalled those days with delight, remembering that "we baptized from early morning to late at night, one after the other, and still there were people waiting." These mass baptisms were not only taking place in lower Ajaria, with its heterogeneous population, but also in upper Ajaria, where the position of Islam was much stronger. In June 1989, Patriarch Ilia II paid a visit to the medieval church in Skhalta, a small mountainous village in upper Ajaria.[1] During his visit the patriarch held a requiem for those who had died in landslides and floods earlier that year. He then delivered a speech in which he expressed gratitude that, after centuries of oppression, it was once again possible to pray at this sanctified place (*Sovetskaia Adzhariia*, 1 June 1989). "He admonished the Ajarians to return to Christianity [and] told them that the catastrophe that had befallen them was obviously the punishment of God for their unfaithfulness to the Savior" (Lilienfeld 1993, 227). Afterward, the patriarch carried out baptisms near the walls of the old church. The arrival of the patriarch caused a stir among the population. Rumors circulated that every person he baptized would receive a cross of pure gold. Whether or not for this purpose, during that day no fewer than fifty villagers were baptized, among whom were several village notables including the kolkhoz director, the village council chairman,

---

1. The church in Skhalta, which was built in the thirteenth century, is the only medieval church in Ajaria that survived both the Ottoman and Soviet periods.

and other state functionaries.[2] However, according to one of the converts from this village, only a few of those who were baptized ever attended a service in the years following their baptism. What is more, about ten baptized families started to attend the Friday prayers at the local mosque when it was reopened a year later in 1990.

Although the church may have interpreted the numerous baptisms (estimates of the actual number vary greatly) as a confirmation of its hope that Ajarians would rapidly "return" to Christianity, it was difficult not to see these baptisms as opportunistic adaptations to the time or as symbolic gestures toward the nationalist movement. Moreover, economic and political considerations may have influenced people's decision to be baptized more than religious concerns did. That is at least what the stories of gold and the predominance of the village elite among the "converts" suggests.[3] The events offer a glimpse at the unstable political and economic atmosphere in Ajaria at the time. It is unclear, however, how these events relate to religious change, the direction of which was indeed far from obvious in the early 1990s. In subsequent years, however, it became clear that there was another current, a slower but more permanent process of conversion to Christianity, which is the focus of this chapter. This process of "permanent" conversion proceeded steadily in the lowlands—sometimes including the population of entire villages—but was much slower and less predictable in upper Ajaria, where Islam retained an important role in social life.[4]

In the previous chapters I outlined some of the basic factors that made the adoption of Christianity understandable. These included the amalgamation of religious and ethnic identity in nationalist discourses and the difficulties of observing Islam while living in a state that privileged Christianity both through state policies and through the dissemination of Georgian "high" culture. I build on these observations and argue that conversion to Christianity in upper Ajaria in the 1990s can largely be understood as an attempt by new Christians to realign history and community. The converts pursued a restoration of perceived unity between Georgiannesss and Christianity that also held the promise of a "modern" future. The role of religious conversion in the pursuit of modernity reflected Werth's important observation that "rather than coding religion as indisputably traditional and construing modernity in terms

---

2. I based the estimate of fifty converts on the accounts of villagers. It is significantly lower than the estimate of three thousand mentioned in the local newspaper *Sovetskaia Adzhariia*, 1 June 1989.

3. During the period of social and political turmoil, village notables might have gauged it to be in their interest to adjust to the new political realities by responding to the rhetoric of the first government of independent Georgia that Christianity is an "indivisible part of the Georgian nation." This does not mean, however, that baptism offered any direct benefits or that conversion to Orthodox Christianity was somehow imposed on them.

4. Obviously, the term "permanent conversion" is relative, as it applies only to a period of five to ten years.

of religion's demise and transcendence . . . religion, especially in a colonial context, can serve as a vehicle for inducting subjects into modernity" (2000, 514). In upper Ajaria conversion was motivated by notions of modernity and had an emancipating effect in "Georgian" contexts. Nevertheless, it complicated the position of converts in their "Muslim" community, spurring new attempts to demarcate spheres of belonging.

Talking about Conversion

Insight into the complex motivations and effects of conversion can be gained by looking at the way new Christians talked about their conversions. In what follows, I present four conversion stories. I recorded these stories, as well as the other verbal accounts that are the basis of this chapter, in Khulo, the administrative center in upper Ajaria. The town had important functions for Muslims in the region: it hosted one of the largest mosques in Ajaria, and the deputy mufti and several influential families of Muslim teachers lived there. At the same time, Khulo also functioned as a bridgehead for Christian missionary work. In the 1990s the Georgian Orthodox Church regarded Khulo as a prime location for its missionary activity in upper Ajaria. In 2000 and 2001 the Christian community was still only a fraction of the town's total population. The church had three hundred members or 5 percent of the population.

The accounts were recorded during interview sessions in which I specifically asked about how new Christians came to be baptized. In most cases this material was supplemented by circumstantial information recorded at other occasions. The reason for including four stories at length is to provide an idea of how people talk about and explain their conversions and to provide a basis for my discussion of the meanings of conversion. Because presenting lengthy stories automatically favors those who are willing to talk about conversion— by implication the more outspoken converts—in the subsequent discussion I will not only refer to these four texts but also include shorter comments by new Christians who were less talkative about their own conversion.

Tamaz

Tamaz had been teaching at the Christian lyceum since 1991 and he was the only one in his family who opted for Christianity. His quest for a satisfactory worldview, which eventually led him away from Islam and toward Christianity, had been long and, in view of his continued ambivalence about his decision, difficult. Born in 1958, Tamaz grew up in what he called a "true atheistic period," although his parents continued to observe Muslim rites even then. Tamaz himself, however, refused to participate in these practices, and his parents sometimes half-jokingly called him "our little heathen." After Tamaz completed high school, he entered the pedagogical institute in Batumi. He did not see this period as having influenced his later conversion, because "at the institute we didn't even talk about religion; it was severely forbidden. And besides, it was not interesting to me." After four years, Tamaz returned to Khulo and married a girl from a neighboring village.

> Shortly after my wedding in 1982 my wife and I visited Tbilisi. By chance we passed the Church of David. The doors of the church were open and the sounds of the choir filled the air. It struck me as very beautiful, and I told my wife that I would have a look inside. It was one of those exciting moments. I didn't even know what rules to observe, and upon entering I was completely taken aback by the peace and beauty of the scene. It was as if I had found peace and I understood that this was what I had been looking for all my life, that this was part of my life, *my* culture.

However, on their return to Khulo, his sudden interest in Christianity slackened. In 1991, however, the local boarding school was turned into the Spiritual Lyceum of the Apostle Andrew. Tamaz found employment in the lyceum as a teacher of Russian. Although teachers were not required to adopt Christianity, working at the lyceum, of course, involved being exposed to Christianity:

> During the period that I worked here, I came to a point—and I don't say this to portray myself as better than others—that step by step I returned to the old religion to which my forefathers three centuries ago had adhered. The final decision to be baptized was not an easy step, but the [historical] works and sources I read convinced me that my forefathers had been Christians. In 1999, with the help of Father Iosebi I finally managed to break the barrier. With his assistance I managed to rid myself of the Muslim rites and customs that were in my skin and in my flesh, and I returned to my native religion. . . . My father on the whole agreed with my decision, more so than my mother and wife. Of course there was some resistance from their side, but I explained that my forefathers had also been Christians. Within my family they talked badly about me, saying that I had been behaving differently since I started working at the lyceum . . . but I remained true to my own path.

Badri

When I met Badri for a dinner at his house in the upper part of Khulo, the room for guests (st'umari otakhi) had not been prepared yet, so Badri decided to show me around his neighborhood. During our walk we stopped to look at the neighbor's baby, who was just being put in her crib. Badri zealously explained the tradition of the crib:

> This crib is made in the traditional style that allowed it to be picked up and carried away whenever there was a threat of danger. Another custom was to hide a large knife under the mattress, so that the women could defend themselves against the Turks. You see, the Turks could have attacked at any moment and people had to be constantly prepared.[5] Our people struggled for centuries to defend not only their families but also their faith. As you see, although my neighbors are Muslim, they still hate the Turks and have preserved our Christian traditions.

---

5. It is more likely, though, that the knife was intended as protection against the "evil eye."

Through this story of the crib, Badri revealed his convictions about religion as well as some of his reasons for adopting Christianity, even before I had a chance to ask him about his conversion. Later that evening, Badri and I discussed his conversion. He spoke about when he was a student of veterinary medicine in Tbilisi in the early 1980s:

> At that time I visited churches as if they were museums. I did not know anything and I did not have strong beliefs, neither in Islam nor in Christianity. Once, my friends made plans to go out. I joined them without asking where we were going until it became clear we were going to attend a church service. At the time this was, of course, strictly forbidden. The KGB kept an eye on everything. After we had entered [the church] I watched how the others received blessings. I found out how I had to act and decided to go myself as well. I was insecure of course; I didn't know if what I was doing was allowed. But the priest did not ask me any questions and drew a cross on my forehead with wax. After this event I went more often, also without my friends, and every time I became more intrigued. I also started to read literature about Christianity.

After his studies, Badri returned to Khulo and had no further opportunity to continue the quest he had started. He became a teacher at the Christian lyceum in 1991, but he was not baptized until the church in Khulo was opened in 1996:

> I didn't get baptized earlier because of my neighbors. They can't even comprehend such a move; it is not part of their understanding. From their perspective, Islam is the proper [*sobstvennaia*] religion. I felt that they were giving me strange looks. Don't think that it was an easy decision; there were unpleasant responses from neighbors who told me that I had made a big mistake. But I always replied that I had made the right decision, that I had chosen the path of our forefathers. My father had no problem with it, he was and still is a staunch Communist, and although his parents were Muslim, he himself is practically an atheist.[6]

Badri envisioned an important role for the Georgian Orthodox Church in Ajaria. In his view the Church should do everything in its powers to fix the problems in society. "Only the Orthodox Church can do that," he insisted.

On subsequent occasions, Badri often complained about his illiterate neighbors who did not understand historical truth. "They can't see," he explained to me, "that Islam is only here because the Turks imposed it on us." Badri wanted to rid himself of this Muslim past, and his baptism can be seen as an act of ritual cleansing of what he saw as foreign, inauthentic influences. Convinced that Ajaria's future would be Christian, he enrolled his two children in the Christian lyceum and later decided to have them baptized, without

---

6. Badri's grandparents and several of his uncles were arrested in the 1930s. They were sent to jail in Batumi and possibly deported to the gulag, but nothing further is known about their fate.

consulting his relatives. Not everyone was completely happy with his actions, but Badri easily dismissed the differing views. Concerning his wife's reaction, he told me that she "started to cry when she heard that I had [our children] Giorgi and Nino baptized. She was upset because she feared that no one would want to marry our children. As if I would accept a son-in-law who is Muslim! It actually made the whole issue easier; this way only proper marriage candidates will come forward to marry them."

Ketevan

Ketevan was still very young when her father died. She was raised by her mother and grandmother. She was about eleven years old when a neighbor (of Georgian-Christian origin) told Ketevan and her mother that she wanted to baptize Ketevan. Despite the fact that her mother declined the request, Ketevan presented the event as a turning point in her life. After this, she stressed, she became very interested in Christianity. When she was in the eleventh grade Ketevan wanted to be baptized. However, her grandmother was against it and there was no way Ketevan could make such a decision without her grandmother's consent. Nevertheless, during those years she began to weigh the religions against each other: "Although I was more inclined toward Christianity, something kept me away from it. It probably had to do with my upbringing. My grandmother played a role in this, of course, but it was only recently that I came to understand that it was my past that was sitting in my heart, keeping me away from my religion." Significantly, while talking about these experiences she merged two historical perspectives: the family history as symbolized in the grandmother and a more nationalist perspective on history, symbolized in "my religion."

Only later, after Ketevan enrolled in the school of music in Batumi and had lived with relatives in the city for several years, did she start to think more concretely about adopting Christianity:

> My friends, although not all of them were Christians, shared that same lifestyle. At school we often sang religious songs, and because of the acoustics we often practiced in the church. Then I realized that I wanted to lead this life with these friends, but that would be impossible without being baptized. I then remembered what my neighbor had said ten years before. For me it was a confusing period. I even started to have dreams in which I entered the church to be baptized, but I always woke up before the ceremony was completed. I was unaware of it then, but now I know that these were messages from God. . . . When I was in the second year we talked about the issue in my family. Mother was not against it, or at least she didn't say that she disagreed.

Her grandmother, however, was against Ketevan's plan from the first moment. "Although she didn't threaten me with reprisals, she never gave her approval. But she has come to accept it, and now she merely says that I shouldn't forget about our religion," which for Ketevan's grandmother is obviously Islam:

Of course there are things I can't say at home. My grandmother is very pious; she observes Ramadan and she prays. For her it is too difficult to abandon Islam. I respect her, and therefore I hide my icons. In my bedroom I have a corner with religious items, but I only pray there when grandmother is not at home or late at night when they are asleep. My mother is not baptized, but when she sees how I pray from the heart, she sometimes wishes that she too would be Christian. Maybe when grandmother is gone she too will be baptized.

Marina

Marina explained to me that she had recently gone through a difficult period in her life. Since her conversion in 1998 she had been separated from her husband, but they were planning to get back together. She emphasized that her marital problems were, to a large extent, caused by the Muslim clergy: "They have tried everything to get us divorced, simply because they fear that [if we stayed married] it would speed up the decline of Islam; they are afraid to lose their control over the community.[7] But you know what is so interesting? My husband is now himself preparing to be baptized. He tells me that he is ready for it now." Marina was one of the first people in Khulo who converted. This, in addition to the difficulties she experienced following her conversion, made her a kind of heroine for other converts. During a two-hour session we spoke about her experiences, but when we got to the point of her own decision to convert, she seemed a bit nervous, as though afraid that I would not understand it correctly:

> Of course it did not just come out of the blue. When I was young I often had to travel and I remember very well visiting a church in Sverdlovsk [in the late 1980s]. Then I already understood that only Christianity saves one's soul. Later, when they opened the lyceum and Father Grigori came here [he became the director of the Christian lyceum], I got more involved. [Besides him] there were also a few nuns, and I often talked about my feelings with one of them. She would give me things to read and we discussed them. But at that time I still could not decide to make that step.

Marina hesitated for a second before she told me about the incident that prompted her decision. She had joined the priests from Khulo on a trip to the church in Skhalta, where sermons were being given. After the sermon had ended she went out for a short walk:

> It was March, still very cold and a bit foggy. You know, the forest there starts almost next to the churchyard. So I was walking around, captured in my own thoughts, when I saw something between two trees. It was as if there suddenly was a wide,

7. She probably intimated that individual conversions of marginalized (divorced) individuals would be less threatening to the Muslim community than accepted conversions within families.

shining path through the forest. On the middle of that road I saw an old man in a black cassock. He stood there, or rather was waiting, with a staff in one hand and a cross in the other. He looked up to me and told me, "Don't wait any longer with what you have to do." He turned around and disappeared as suddenly as he had arrived. Then I became aware that he was my ancestor. It was even as if I had known his face all along. You see, my ancestors used to be priests. The last priest in Ajaria was one of my forefathers. I know that it was he who had sent me on the right track. The next day I was baptized.

Conversion Narratives: Continuity, Enemies, and Progress

These conversion accounts do not necessarily reflect the original motives that led Tamaz, Badri, Ketevan, and Marina to adopt Christianity, but they do tell us something of how new Christians explain and defend their decision to be baptized. Put differently, the language of the stories and the recurring signs and symbols in them suggest how conversions are imbedded in wider discourses. The goal in this section is not only to show *that* the conversion narratives are related to wider discourses but also to reveal the particular discursive mechanisms through which they are related. To achieve this, I focus on those recurring themes in the stories that are important for understanding what conversion entails in relation to national and private arenas.

Continuity

Although non-Christians in Ajaria frequently employed the verb "to convert" (*perekhodit'*) to describe the actions of new Christians, many converts did not use the word because of the unwanted connotation of change.[8] What they had experienced should, in their view, not be understood as a personal change or disruption but rather as a regaining of the true self in Christianity. Instead of a change, the ritual act of baptism was presented as a purification, as an expulsion of inauthentic influences. This was, for example, evident in the statement by Tamaz that "I managed to rid myself of the Muslim rites and customs that were in my skin and in my flesh." In other words, while ridding the new Christians of inauthentic influences, the conversion enabled a return to—not a new embrace of—Christianity. A young woman in Khulo expressed this notion directly, saying: "I don't have the feeling that I am switching from one to another religion. No! I have *returned* to my native religion."

---

8. New Christians talked about "being baptized." The Muslim clergy also did not use the term "conversion." Instead, they denoted new Christians as "misled people" or "apostates." Assuming that "conversion" does not have negative connotations to the reader, I will continue to use "conversion" as a relatively neutral term (more so than "return to Christianity" or "apostasy") to describe personal religious change as a process that neither starts nor ends with the ritual act of baptism.

What did this "return" to Christianity imply? In many stories it quite bluntly pointed to notions of primordial national, ethnic, and religious identity. Tamaz, for example, stressed that Ajaria was historically Christian and that Christianity was the religion to which his forefathers adhered. He portrayed his conversion not as a change to something new but as the continuation of Christianity that had remained part of his Georgian culture, even through periods of interruption. These notions were made meaningful by reference to the distant past, a past in which the local Ajarian population was Christian.

History clearly provided an important source of approval for the new Christians, who presented their conversions as a continuation of the original faith of their predecessors. This aspect of continuity was true not only for the accounts presented above but also recurred in fleeting comments made on the subject. During one short interaction, a new Christian said about his conversion: "It's simple: if you read history then you start to understand that our religion is Christianity. Everything of value in Ajaria, the bridges, castles, churches, they were all built in the twelfth century. And by whom were they built? By us—Georgians!" References to the heyday of the Bagratid kingdom (twelfth and thirteenth centuries AD) were made frequently. The relation between this distant past and the present was portrayed as self-evident. Verbally connecting the twelfth and the twenty-first centuries by placing them next to each other in one sentence was generally enough to get the message across. In many accounts, it seemed as if the twelfth century had ended only yesterday. How the eight centuries in between were explained away was not a matter of great interest, although some referred implicitly to the issue. For Vakhtangi, for example, the historical realities continued in a straight line up to the present: "It is the Georgian soul that pulls us to Christianity. Of course, most people say that they are Muslim, but that is just a cover: by way of their lifestyle and customs they are drawn toward Christianity. If you would be able to have a look in their soul you would find out that they truly are Christians." In other words, this Christian Georgian "reality" could never be erased, even though it had been repressed for centuries.

The idea that Islam had only had a superficial impact on the local population was also voiced by Badri, when, in the story presented previously, he pointed out to me all the signs of Christianity that had survived centuries of Ottoman rule and the "superficial" Islamization of the area. That the narrative of an ineradicable Christian past resonated with the ideas of the converts is obvious, as it provided affirmation for their decision to adopt Christianity. By implication this meant an adoption of national rhetoric as revealed in scholarly works about the history of the region. As a female convert commented, "I have read those books. I have read them all, and I discovered that our ancestors were Christians. A thinking person cannot ignore that."

The basic idea behind the numerous statements about historic truth was that the composite of Georgian culture and Christianity had been obscured—

but not essentially changed—by Ottoman rule. By the same standards, new Christians argued that in the "postatheist" context, the available historical knowledge made it possible to "uncover" this "covered reality," a reality that according to new Christians had been hiding behind the superfluous image of Islam. But whereas this historical narrative of "Christian continuity" was unproblematic in the larger part of Georgia, which is often presented as a Christian island *surrounded* by Islam, Ajaria had been a *part* of the Muslim realm for several centuries. This difference made the historical narrative sketched above simultaneously more problematic and more crucial for the people involved. Indeed, Ajaria's location on the frontier of the Muslim and Christian realms is an important factor in understanding why new Christians so zealously embraced nationalist historical rhetoric.

Enemies

When new Christians talked about history or culture, it was often in opposition to the "other." This "other" manifested itself in speech as "the Turk," "the Ottoman," or more broadly as "Muslims" and was presented as radically different from the "self." The "other" was simultaneously a religious and a cultural "other." This was well captured in the statement by a young woman who had been baptized several years earlier: "When I read the Qur'an I do not recognize anything: it is not about our people, not about Georgians. In contrast, when I started to read the Bible I recognized everything, everything struck me as familiar. The Bible is about people like me." In this short comment, Islam and Christianity were neatly opposed. The Bible was presented as a book about Georgians. It was contrasted with the Qur'an, whose messages were portrayed as alien.

Significantly, the comments were not only about difference but also about danger. Muslims were thought of as having done a great injustice to the Georgians generally and to the inhabitants of Ajaria specifically, as the next comment shows: "I used to have nothing to do with religion; I was a simple farmer, although once in a while I went to the old [closed] church out of curiosity. . . . But I did read a lot, for example that the Turks had cut off three hundred heads and thrown them into the Chorokhi [River] and then sent a message to Skhalta that the same thing would happen there if people didn't submit to Islam." Similar stories about the cruelties of the "Turks" or the "Ottoman Empire" were repeated over and over again. They were exchanged during dinners and discussed over wine.[9] In addition to the historical injustice that the "other" had inflicted, the "other" was also perceived as a present-day threat, judging from stories about the danger of renewed influence of "the Turk":

9. I heard the story about the Turks cutting off the heads of those unwilling to submit to Islam from at least five respondents. The storytellers usually adjusted the names of rivers and villages to local circumstances, and some added that the rivers had been red with blood for days on end.

[One day] a whole group arrived from Turkey; they called themselves hojas, but in fact they were secret agents. They studied the situation here, about how people related to religion and the state. Of course the Muslims here are interested in religion in Turkey, but it turned out that the [hojas] were agents; they wanted to restart the process that took place here four hundred years ago.[10]

Although this particular story was known by many, the numerous references that were made to publications and scholarly works on the subject point to the active role of Soviet ideology in the creation of an enemy. Whereas part of this Soviet ideology was denounced as propaganda, the rhetoric about the "cruel Muslim past" had remained an active and important part of collective memory.

Defining the "other" is problematic because the stories were hardly ever about personal encounters with the typical "other," that is, Turks. Indeed, few of the converts who made these comments had ever been to Turkey or had met with citizens of Turkey. The fact that the story of the "hoja-agents" was so well known in the Christian community made me wonder what the unspoken messages of the story might be. Why was this story repeated, distributed, and celebrated? Perhaps it was the little note in the above comment saying "of course the Muslims here are interested in religion in Turkey," which indirectly suggested that the "other" could also come from the inside, from the Muslims living in Ajaria.

Further insight might be gained if we examine how ideas of the "other" related to conversion. Another look at the story of Badri might justify the hypothesis that the act of being baptized was a form of ritual cleansing from "a past contaminated by Turks." He stressed that even his Muslim neighbors acted in a Christian way and hated the Turks just as much as he did. As he saw it, their mistake was that they failed to reject Islam as a religion of disliked foreigners, the Turks. In other words, the statements suggested that the "other" was very near and, in fact, resided in one's own household, family, or street. Doubts about who the "other" was can also be found in the following statement from Marina: "The most important thing is that we never married Turks. It tells a lot about how people here related to the Turks, about the fact that we were always one indivisible nation." She was referring here to nineteenth-century and Soviet publications about that period. Although Marina was probably correct that the local community did not, on the whole, marry Turks (who were not living in the area anyway), what she left out and what needed to be left out was that the "we"—parents and grandparents—had been Muslims. Moreover, this view omitted the fact that the inhabitants of Ajaria had partly abandoned the Georgian language in favor of Turkish by the

10. The likely original source of the story claimed to know that the hojas were secret agents because he had seen them spend the night in the mosque, which in his view was against Muslim law.

end of the nineteenth century and that they had fought with great fervor against the "heathen" Christians, as we saw in chapter 4.

The problem that new Christians faced was that the historical intertwining of different, sometimes opposing, points of reference in Ajaria undermined definitions of the ideal cultural, ethnic, and religious "other." Having their roots in a community that had been Muslim for generations and opting to become "true" Christian Georgians, it seemed as if converts had to exorcize the "other" from their *own* past and their *own* community. Instead of just getting rid of some alien influences, it was this sense of "self" that needed to be purified. I would suggest that part of the reason for the demonizing of the "other" stemmed from the ambiguous position that the new Christians had in relation to their local communities, on the one hand, and the Georgian nation, on the other. I will pursue this point further, but not before commenting on the theme of progress, which is even more clearly related to the experiences of families that converted than the two themes discussed so far.

Progress

In the previous sections I argued that conversion was imagined as a return to a glorious Christian past and that the stories that were told about becoming Christian underlined the converts' national affiliation through an oppositional "other." Important as these aspects were for legitimizing the *personal* adoption of Christianity, the "past" and the "other" also played an important role in ideas about the region as a *whole*. New Christians endorsed the idea that the "backwardness" of Ajaria could be eliminated by the "return" to Christianity. Through imaginings of the progressive nature of Christianity and its favorable comparison with the "backward Turks," Christianity contained a promise, one of progress and unambiguous (re)connection of Ajaria with "civilized" Georgian society.

New Christians, but also people without clear religious predilections, worried about the possible strength of Islam in upper Ajaria. One person told me: "There simply can't [shouldn't] be a future for Islam. It is a dark, dark religion. It turns people into slaves of Allah." A lecturer from the University of Batumi similarly invoked the idea of Islam's backwardness. After we had an encounter with an imam, he expressed his worries about the activities of Muslim leaders: "You know what would happen if they were in control? They would send us straight back to the Arabia of the seventh century, to Muhammad and his camels." The alleged regressive characteristics of Islam were placed in unambiguous contrast to the achievements of Christianity. Once, when visiting one of the medieval bridges across the river Ach'aristsqali, a Christian acquaintance told me the following: "Can you imagine, they [the Ottomans] ruled here for four centuries and during that period not a single bridge or monument was constructed, whereas these ingenious bridges were already built in the twelfth century when Ajaria was Christian. Architects would not be able to construct them even today." The medieval monuments and bridges were symbols of a desirable and unambiguous connection with the rest of Georgia. What the new Christians aimed for was to be part of "civilized" Georgian society. For converts the "return" to a Christian past contained promises for the future.

The new Christians clearly saw themselves as forerunners of an unavoidable process that over time would encompass all Ajarians. As Inga, a young woman of twenty-five, commented: "For me Christianity started as a kind of hobby, but now I want to make it official. That is just natural; I think that in a few years everyone will be Christian and it is better that way." For Inga, Christianity was natural and better, and better not only because Christianity was, to her, indivisible from the Georgian character but also because of the civilizing role it supposedly had played. For many converts, the return to Christianity was vital to alleviate the region's backwardness.

The clergy actively appropriated these ideas in their missionary efforts in Ajaria. But, as a result of this appropriation, the clergy saw themselves in a difficult position, as the idea of progress was not easily compatible with the message of Orthodoxy. As Father Miriani explained:

> Many people here think that Christianity is progressive. Well, from a certain perspective they may be right. In the third and fourth century we had already constructed splendid churches, cathedrals, and monasteries, while when you look at southern Georgia during the three centuries of Ottoman rule, the area remained backward. For the people here this proves Christianity's progressive nature. But, in essence, Georgian Orthodoxy is about the original message of the Bible.

Father Miriani's statement illustrated a tension between the clergy, who stressed the authentic roots of their faith, and the new converts, who stressed the modern and civilizing role of the Church.[11] It is important to note that this tension was hardly felt by new Christians, who quite readily infused Orthodox Christianity with ideas of modernity.

My colleague, Teimuri, also witnessed the "modernizing" force of Christianity in aspects of daily life, such as the way people dressed. On a walk through the center of town, Teimuri remarked, "Wow, it is just like Paris here," referring to an attractive woman whose shirt accentuated her breasts. Jokingly he added, "No wonder people are converting to Christianity, if you compare this to the dark clothes that they have to wear in the [Muslim] villages." Whether it was his imagination or not, the idea that Christianity enabled the wearing of "modern" clothes and the adoption of a "modern" lifestyle was an idea that several new Christians held. This was obvious in the warnings people gave me when I visited a village higher in the mountains.

---

11. In one case this tension led to a rift between a priest and one prominent church member, who demanded that the church take more action to alleviate the "backwardness" of Ajaria, preferably through forced conversions.

There, several people in Khulo told me, life was backward. When I returned, many people (especially women) wanted to know whether the women in the mountains really wore veils and whether or not these women really did not speak to men outside their families. "Well, at least here we have some civilization," Ketevan mentioned once when I returned to Khulo. "For you it may not seem much, but for me [it is different]. I am really glad that here at least I can talk with who I want and dress the way I like."

The modernizing force of conversion and the important role of education were clearly related in this line of argumentation. Most converts were from educated families and stressed that they had read not only works of history but also the Russian and German classics. The argument of how education and Christianity were linked worked in two ways. On the one hand, education was supposed to raise awareness that Christianity was the true religion (for Georgians) and to help Ajarians discover that they had been living with a false consciousness.[12] On the other hand, education was meant to provide people with freedom and to allow children to make choices for themselves.

The theme of progress was also evoked when Christians stressed that better education would automatically precipitate conversion: "If a person is educated and so is his family, then they shouldn't have a problem arriving at certain conclusions when reviewing our history. And if they are educated and understanding, then they shouldn't forbid their children to become Christian." Likewise, baptized Ajarians said that although their conversion had provoked negative reactions, "the educated people" had supported them. According to the converts, educated people recognized the importance of Christianity in the project of modernization. These ideas of progress, of "modern" lifestyles, and of catching up with the rest of Georgia did not find resonance with everyone. Rather, these topics were of particular relevance to a specific group.

Baptisms and Biography

The numerous comments on the antiquity of the Georgian nation, the references to centuries of Ottoman oppression, and the claims that the Bible was a book about Georgians illustrated the importance of nationalist (and Soviet) discourses in legitimizing converts' decisions to adopt Christianity. However, they fail to explain why these discourses found resonance with those who converted, nor why some people appropriated these discourses while others clearly rejected them.

This unresolved dilemma intrigued not only me but also my colleague Teimuri. What was the meaning of all these stories about tradition and his-

---

12. Bishop Dmitri, for example, stated: "People have been living in ignorance for centuries; they were suppressed by the Turks and later by the Communists. Now they are free to learn about their true selves."

tory? Why were people so obsessed with them? At a certain point, Teimuri got frustrated, arguing that collecting all those stories would not get us anywhere:

> They all say that in the Bible it is written like this, but when you confront a Muslim with those ideas he simply points to his Qur'an and tells you that there it is written in another way, the right way. The Christian will say, "Our ancestors were also Christian," and then the Muslim will say, "My grandfather and grandmother have taught me like this [the opposite]." Perhaps a Muslim might confirm that his ancestors were Christian, but he doesn't feel it, he only knows it. For him it is just historical reality, nothing more.

The basic problem was that by collecting stories and verbal statements, I learned nothing about what made people choose between opposing discourses, only about how they legitimated their choices. Asking explicitly about the reasons did not resolve the issue. On the contrary, when attempting to do so, all I got were circular arguments concerning historical truth like "I was baptized because the first Georgians were Christians, and thus Christianity is our religion."

However, the obsession with continuity started to make sense when compared with statements of those new Christians whose conversion had not been problematic within their family or neighborhood. For example, when I interviewed a new Christian who was baptized six years after his father had adopted Christianity, all he had to say about it was, "What I can say is that everyone in our family is Christian and that is how I became convinced that Christianity is the true religion. But even if he [my father] hadn't made that choice I would have gone in the same direction, because Orthodoxy is the true faith." Similarly, converts in Sarpi and other parts of lower Ajaria, where the process of conversion had proceeded much further, were often more moderate in the way they mobilized history, using it merely as an affirmative rather than as an instigating force.[13] In short, the explicit appropriation of nationalist sentiment was less important in cases of conversion that did not disrupt social ties. If the social position of converts influenced how they talked about their conversion, then the reason for explicit appropriation of nationalist discourses and the obsession with continuity could well be located in the life trajectories of early converts in upper Ajaria.[14] By exploring how the themes of "return to the original faith," "demonizing the other," and the stress on the "progressive nature of Christianity" are related to personal lives, we might find more clues as to why specific people made the decision to be baptized.

13. However, in Sarpi the mobilization of history was crucial in other areas, notably in defining ethnic and cultural boundaries.

14. When I write "early convert" I have in mind practically all converts in Khulo, precisely because they formed a minority. The exceptions are children whose parents had already been baptized.

The center of Khulo, July 2000.

The New Christians in Khulo

Although the conversion accounts aptly illustrate how ideas about nation, state, and religion were integrated into personal biographies, the new believers did not represent the "average" Ajarian and, in fact, were partly outsiders in their own communities. Some additional information on Khulo, the distribution of new Christians over its territory, and their social position in the town is needed at this point.

The four persons whose stories have been presented at length—Tamaz, Badri, Ketevan, and Marina—lived in two of the twelve neighborhoods of Khulo, and were, as such, representative of the uneven distribution of new Christians in the town. In fact, almost all new Christians lived in just three neighborhoods, Daba Khulo (center), Dekanashvilebi, and Kedlebi. These three neighborhoods bordered on each other, forming a kind of triangle extending from the center northward. Apart from being located in or near the center, with its more dynamic pace of life, these neighborhoods had other characteristics that made them different from the nine remaining ones. Whereas most other neighborhoods consisted of a few family groups who had lived there for at least five generations, the more central districts showed a different pattern. Although in Daba Khulo, Dekanashvilebi, and Kedlebi there were several families who prided themselves on having lived there for many generations, most inhabitants were families or individuals who had moved from mountain villages to the district center between the 1930s and the 1970s, when Khulo was expanding as an administrative center for the region.

The means of livelihood in Daba Khulo, Dekanashvilebi, and Kedlebi were also different from the other neighborhoods. Although there used to be kolkhozes in the latter two neighborhoods, most people were employed elsewhere, either in the two clothing factories, the service sector, or the town administration.[15] This pattern was even more evident when reviewing the social backgrounds of new Christians. Among the sixty-four adult Christians about whom I collected sufficient information, there were twenty-two teachers, six civil servants working at the town or the district (raion) administration, five nurses, and four physicians and other medical specialists; the remaining twenty-seven people had occupations such as housewife or bookkeeper, or had formerly held a position (mostly middle management) at one of the clothing factories in town. They were almost exclusively representatives of the educated "middle class," while farmers and technicians (former kolkhozniki) were virtually absent among the new Christians.

The middle-class families valued education and sent their children to Batumi, Tbilisi, or other cities to attend the university. Members of these families took up positions in state structures and often lived part of their lives outside Khulo, mostly in urban areas in Georgia. Moreover, they all had seen their social and economic positions deteriorate in the last ten years. The factories closed their doors not long after the Soviet collapse. And although a large percentage managed to retain their positions in the district administration or in the medical and educational institutes, their wages decreased so dramatically that they necessarily fell back on income- generating strategies that combined their official positions with other activities such as local small-scale trading.[16]

In short, the new Christians were often people who moved "in" and "up" during the Soviet period. They were, in a sense, the embodiment of the new "modern" life that started in the Soviet period and obtained explicit Christian characteristics in the wake of Soviet disintegration. But this "modern" life had become problematic for the involved families, since many, after moving "in" and "up" during the Soviet period, had subsequently fallen "down" when the Soviet state collapsed. Seen from this perspective, their conversions may be

---

15. In the other neighborhoods, the majority of the population was employed in the kolkhozes.

16. The decline in living standards had been more abrupt for this group than for most former kolkhozniki (especially in less densely populated neighborhoods), who were able to reclaim their grandparents' land and manage to sustain a modest livelihood.

partly understood as attempts to retain or regain their middle-class position, even if conversion itself entailed few material rewards.

Life Courses

One more look at the conversion narratives of Tamaz, Badri, and Ketevan may help us further understand the patterns sketched above. In their stories, the decision to adopt Christianity was presented as a turning point in their individual lives, as the moment when people saw the light that brought them onto the righteous path. But what is more relevant for our purpose here is to note that the conversions coincided with, or were preceded by, other crucial episodes in the biographies of those involved. Tamaz, Badri, and Ketevan had each lived for a considerable time outside their own community, whether it was in Tbilisi or Batumi. During those periods they were initiated into a different social environment. Although Tamaz rightfully observed that when he lived in Batumi an atheist atmosphere predominated, his stay in the city nevertheless implied a way of life that was radically different from that of the small community in which he was raised.

Whereas perhaps only for Ketevan did the period outside Khulo mean an actual encounter with Christianity, all three were exposed to city life that embodied Georgian culture and that later was tightly reconnected to Christianity, a life they wanted to be part of. Negative attitudes held by other Georgians concerning Ajaria and Ajarians sometimes also played an important role, as revealed by the following remark of an Ajarian man who had studied in Tbilisi in the 1980s:

> Someone suggested we visit a church, and at that exact moment I felt that everyone was looking at me with strange eyes, [after which] the topic was changed. Then I said, "If you think that I keep Islam somewhere inside of me, then you are just flat wrong. As if I don't respect Christianity! I am probably more Georgian than you are." So we went to visit a church.

The emphasis that converts put on encounters and social environment does not negate the sincerity of their belief in Christianity—and there is, for example, no reason to doubt Ketevan's belief in the Christian God—but it suggests that their life courses made them more susceptible to the Christian message. In other words, because of their experiences they found a connection with Christianity that enabled them to make this religion their own. The prevalent idea among some converts that once people became educated they would adopt Christianity was therefore true enough, albeit in a slightly different way than they saw it. It was not education as such but the content of this education (with a strong focus on Georgian history) and the context in which this education took place (higher education was always located on Georgian

"Christian" territory) that made "educated people" more receptive to the Christian message.

There were a few other common characteristics in these genealogies that at first glance did not seem to relate to one another. In several cases the families with baptized members had also been victims of the purges of the Stalin period, and in a significant number of cases one or more parents of the new Christians had died prematurely. Ketevan had grown up in a family without a father or a grandfather, whereas Badri's grandfather and uncles were arrested in the 1930s, never to return home. That deportations and arrests might have had some influence on later religious change was also suggested by the data on the social background of the converts. Of thirty-six converts about whom I had extensive biographical information, ten turned out to be members of repressed families.

This finding was in itself not that surprising, since it was especially the middle class that fell victim to the purges in the 1930s and 1950s. But apart from the overlap between repressed families and middle-class families, who were more exposed to national rhetoric, there are several other ways in which repression might have influenced later conversion. Akaki, a sixty-year-old history teacher who converted several years ago, said: "My grandfather, father, and three uncles were imprisoned in 1937. My grandfather was killed there, while my uncles and father returned home. . . . Father was always scared. He knew Turkish and Arabic, but he never prayed, he didn't carry out any rituals. He wanted to make sure that nothing would inhibit his children from having a prosperous life." In this account, but also in the case of Badri, who described his father as a staunch Stalinist, this fear about possible imprisonment resulted in a strict atheist atmosphere at home and explicit adoption of Soviet lifestyles. What it suggests as well is that education and repression both caused the family to be only partly integrated into the local community. Whether the convert's parents had fallen victim to the purges or whether the convert had gone to the city for study, it meant that they were partly outsiders in their community and thus had a relatively large social and conceptual "freedom" to explore alternative paths. Or, arguing from the opposite angle, the converts experienced less pressure to comply with local values and norms. As for repressed families, they were often stigmatized by covillagers long after their rehabilitation. This, and perhaps also the feeling among the repressed that the local community had betrayed them, in a way pushed them out of the local moral community.[17]

Here I have identified three factors that contributed to religious change: education, lack of compactness of the genealogical group, and the social and

---

17. One nuclear family confirmed this hypothesis too well to pass unmentioned. In this family, three out of five daughters had married priests. The family stood not only "outside" the community but was also disrespected because the mother had divorced two husbands and, according to rumors, had been highly promiscuous.

geographical mobility of its members. The resulting weak communal ties meant that the converts were in a sense less inclined to comply with local customs and traditions—which were largely Muslim—and more apt to conform to what was seen as "modern" or "civilized" Georgian society. Education basically meant stronger integration with and more direct exposure to Georgian, and thus Christian, lifestyles. But while making religious change more likely, this ambiguous position in the local community, and sometimes even in relation to family members, was only intensified by the act of baptism, thus further challenging the social status of the new Christians.

Baptized Georgian: Mobilizing Ancestors and Other Kin

In the previous section I elaborated on how national discourses and personal lives converged. There is one theme, however, that recurred in almost every narrative but upon which I have not commented yet: ancestors. They mattered so much because they enabled new Christians to link the national discourses with their personal lives in a very poignant way. Perhaps the most striking example was in the story of Marina, who decided to be baptized after she received a message from her ancestor that the time had come for her to make a decision about her faith. Although this was a particularly striking incident, it was not the only case in which ancestors showed the way to Christianity. Rezo, a Christian with rather radical ideas about the need for forceful proselytizing, had similar experiences with his great-grandmother. In his youth she would often talk to him about his forefather's move from a Christian Georgian region to Khulo. Many years later, when Rezo had reached adulthood, his grandmother appeared to him in a dream: "She asked me: 'What are you waiting for? Go to Tsioni' [the central cathedral in Tbilisi]. The next day I went there and was baptized." Whereas in Marina's story the forefather was a priest, in Rezo's account the grandmother talked about their roots in Christian Georgia, thus connecting the family to a Christian tradition. Yet another respondent, Vakhtangi, made a similar claim, stating, "From childhood onward I was oriented toward Christianity because of my grandmother, who had told me that we had Christian predecessors."

What was it that made ancestors such important metaphors for, and symbolic actors in, shifts of religious affiliation? Given the emphasis on history and the negative experiences with the local community, it was not hard to see why ancestors were so important. On one level, ancestors proved that Christianity was not something new but something that had always existed. This was not only important for the converts themselves but also for the Church, which had to counter local accusations that it manipulated the youth and talked them into converting. It is thus not accidental that the clergy often prided themselves on having been able to convert the elderly. Bishop Dimitri told me: "Every day we have new baptisms; sometimes even people aged seventy or eighty rediscover their true [*istinnaia*] religion." Later I was shown a video that featured the baptism of an eighty-year-old man from Khulo. Following the ritual act the man was interviewed: "I am very happy that I was baptized today, the way that my ancestors were also baptized. I have dreamt about being baptized Georgian for a long time, and when I die I will die as Georgians used to die, as a Christian." His words were quite similar to what others might have said, although his statement of being "baptized Georgian" was a very explicit example of the connection between national and religious sentiment. For the clergy, however, the power of this fragment—the reason that they recorded and proudly showed it—was the man's age, which reduced the gap between the past and the present.

Grandparents were also useful in reassuring converts that their decision was correct. When I joined Nugzar—a professor of ethnology—on his visit to the bishop, a conversation unfolded between them in which Nugzar told the bishop that his grandfather had been a hoja and had been shot by the Communists. Hereupon the bishop replied: "I am sure that your decision [to baptize] would have made your grandfather very happy. He himself didn't have that opportunity at the time, you know." Investing old people, and more distantly ancestors, with the wish to have been able to carry out their true Christian nature reduces historical religious disruption. Ancestors thus very powerfully convey the message of the continuity of the Christian faith, and they link the issue of faith to that of nationality. Ancestors root people in particular soils and give a moral and historical weight to nationalist and religious claims. In essence, they make nationalist—and religious—claims more tangible and concrete by linking family relations to national ideals.[18] They personalize a nationalist narrative of history. By stating that it was *our* family that was Christian, *our* family that was forced to become Muslim, and by referring to grandmothers who reminisced about the family being Christian, the martyrdom of the Georgian nation was reconceptualized on the level of kinship.

For the new Christians, ancestors also had more concrete roles to play. For one, ancestors provided a legitimization of the choice to be baptized. Teimuri rightly observed that historical knowledge did not suffice to effect religious conversion. But when "historical knowledge" was framed in a narrative of family and tradition, a convert's decision at least started to become meaningful. Ancestors were indeed not only important as historical figures but also as familial figures that bound family and community together. They, in essence, gave weight to the claim that converts were reincorporated into the original communities rather than being renegades. Ancestors accomplished what ideology could not accomplish—they rooted people in time and restored interrupted genealogies.

18. This line of reasoning is taken from Verdery (1999, 41), who argues that ancestors are vital to national ideology. Similarly, Gingrich (1998) discusses the predominance of ancestors in stories about Islamic Turkish influence in the Balkans.

The ancestor was thus the ideal figure to repair disruptions in locality. They were not alone in this task, but were often assisted by other kin (especially older ones such as parents and grandparents) who were similarly employed to soften the disruptions caused by the act of baptism. One woman told me, "Mother would also have adopted Christianity, but she is afraid that for her things will end if she does. But at the same time she has icons hanging in her room and she has a picture in which she stands surrounded by her icons. She reads Arabic and has read Muslim books, but she is more inclined toward Christianity." As in this example, stories about individual baptisms were often accompanied by statements about relatives and friends that indicated that the convert did not stand alone in his actions or ideas concerning religion. The importance of this theme was also obvious in the stories presented earlier. Ketevan, for example, mentioned that her mother "sometimes wished to be Christian," while one of the first things that Marina told me was that her husband was now "ready to be baptized." Similarly, Badri stressed that his neighbors, despite being Muslim, really hated Turks. Whether these statements really matched the intentions or attitudes of the family members cannot be answered, but they illustrated how important it was for Christians to find a new place in a community that had disapproved of their decision to convert—preferably through changing that community.

The Dynamics of Religious Change

What do the conversions to Christianity discussed in this chapter and the appropriations of Islam discussed in the previous one reveal about the dynamics of religious change taking place in Ajaria? Contrary to the predicted return to pre-Soviet religious traditions, the Ajarian case showed that the forms in which religion reentered the public sphere were not (or were only indirectly) related to the pre-Soviet past. I argued that to understand postsocialist religious renewal one has to take into account the profound impact of Soviet modernization as well as the gradual dissemination of Georgian national ideology. Furthermore I asserted that although these changes were instigated from the federal and national centers (Moscow and Tbilisi) and transmitted to the periphery (Ajaria), the relation between these poles was more complex than such a simple model would suggest. To see religious change as part of a process extending from the national center to its periphery risks underestimating the complexities and ambiguities that characterize religious change at the frontier. This complexity of religious change can be illustrated by first summarizing the main trends and then commenting on the ambiguities and seeming contradictions that I observed at the micro level.

The dominant trend—the gradual shift from Islam toward Christianity—can be understood by referring to the workings of institutional structures and the dissemination of national ideology during the Soviet era. Although the "assimilation" of Ajarians was not completed, the mechanisms through which it was advanced severely handicapped the post-1990 Islamic renewal. During the Soviet period, nationalist Georgian discourse was so effective in Ajaria *because* Georgian national identity was (at least partly) disconnected from religion. In other words, because religion was banned from the public sphere, Ajarians had come to see themselves as Georgians. They could be Georgians in public while remaining Muslim at home. This state of affairs changed in the late 1980s when Georgian nationality was tightly reconnected to Christianity. In the emerging nationalist discourse, Georgian and Muslim identities became incompatible, creating a dilemma for Ajarians who saw themselves as both. This effectively muted Muslim voices and curtailed Islamic renewal in Ajaria. Moreover, because of the incompatibility of pursuing both professional careers and an Islamic lifestyle, Islam had become increasingly a religion of the lower echelons, of kolkhozniki and unskilled workers. This trend isolated Muslim groups from the economic, political, and intellectual elite of Ajaria and consequently resulted in a further marginalization of Islam.

In contrast, proponents of Christianity could cash in on societal changes facilitated by Soviet rule and on a nationalist ideology that imagined Georgia as a coherent Christian nation surrounded by dangerous and "foreign" Muslim peoples. The fact that regional elites either had been Christians all along or relatively quickly converted to Christianity further contributed to the "Christianization" of the public sphere. These elites used their influence to establish Christian schools and to introduce Bible studies as an obligatory subject in "secular" education. Moreover, they excluded Muslim voices from the media and scholarly writings. Recently converted Ajarians effectively appropriated the nationalist discourse and in doing so contributed to the acceleration of Christian expansion. Conversion followed distinct patterns and was embedded in changing social and political configurations. In Khulo, the first converts to Christianity were representatives of the middle class, and conversion was especially common among those families that lacked strong cohesion and were weakly integrated in the local community. Because of the crucial positions these families held in public institutions, the conversion of their members added to an ideological environment in which many people, especially the youth, abstained from identifying with Islam and increasingly turned to Christianity.

Although this broad outline may render the direction of religious change understandable, it is crucial to note that things were more ambiguous at the micro level. The religious discourses could not be applied smoothly to the level of personal and familial experiences. This was true for Christians and Muslims alike. New Christians needed to "restore" the disruptive aspects of their conversion by re-creating genealogical lines and by downplaying their neighbors' or ancestors' loyalty to Islamic traditions. For Muslims, on the other hand, the "new" demands of Islam ran counter to the ways they had led their lives until recently. The resulting contradictions pushed them to find new ways of reconciling religious and national identities. This intertwining of religious and national forms of belonging raises questions concerning the meanings of the categories "Muslim" and "Christian." What did these religious labels mean to the inhabitants of Ajaria after seventy years of state atheism, and how did their appropriations of these labels change during the 1990s and early 2000s? The question may help us understand how different layers of social identification—religious, ethnic, national, familial, professional—are interlinked and thus can illuminate changes taking place on the religious frontier.

The provocative writings of Mikhail Epstein, a postmodern Russian literary philosopher, show the danger of using religious labels as analytical concepts in the post-Soviet context.[19] In a sweeping depiction of post-Soviet spirituality, he argues that Soviet atheism has "produced a type of believer who is impossible to identify in denominational terms. He is simply a believer, a *veruiushchii*" (1995, 363). Epstein rightly questions the meaning of denominations for people who had been "resolutely cut off from all religious traditions" (363). His writings form an implicit and devastating critique of (Western) social scientists who use formal (clerical) sets of beliefs to measure the postatheist religious revival (see, for example, Greeley 1994; Kääriäinen 1999). The use of such formal sets of beliefs is problematic, of course, because it assumes (interrupted) continuity between postsocialist religious forms and their presocialist referents. But whereas Epstein sees an amorphous sea of "believers" indicating a turn to postatheist and postmodern forms of spirituality, I would suggest that, by itself, the ambiguity of the relation between believers and denominations reveals only that state atheism had profoundly shattered religious life. What Epstein fails to consider is how the "belief dimension" is related to more recent social and political processes. Focusing on predefined indicators of adherence to a "denomination," on the one hand, or undefined "spirituality," on the other, bypasses the important and interesting question of how these two aspects are actually interlinked.

The meanings of religion for people who had grown up without (or with only restricted) involvement in religious life cannot be disconnected from its public dimensions. In Ajaria, religion entered a contested public space and was from the outset imbued with political messages. During the early 1990s mass baptisms were organized by the clergy and rumors circulated that Ajarians would be forced to convert to Christianity. The period also witnessed sudden and massive constructions of mosques and strong local opposition to the increasing influence of Christianity. But this eruption of religious activity simultaneously revealed that religious loyalties were often weak. The serial conversions of people who were baptized one day but the following month were attending the Friday prayers in the mosque attested to this. Often, conversion to Christianity seemed a symbolic act of support for the independence move-

---

19. I rely here on a short article by Epstein (1995) as well as discussions of his work by Borenstein (1999) and Miller-Pogacar (1995).

ment and had little to do with personal religious convictions. Likewise, although in many villages the population participated in the construction or reconstruction of mosques, this did not always mean that people were planning to attend prayers, and a number of these mosques subsequently remained empty. Religion had suddenly returned to social life in Ajaria, but its contents were not as yet defined.

However, this does not mean that people in Ajaria were not actively constructing boundaries for their beliefs. As people confronted the social and political implications of Islam and Christianity, their ideas about specific denominations gradually took more concrete form. The influence of religious leaders was particularly relevant for this process. Muslim and Christian clergy began performing crucial roles in rites of passage such as weddings and funerals and as such stimulated discussion of what is acceptable and desired social behavior. Young men who finished their education in Turkey returned to upper Ajaria, bringing new knowledge of "proper" interpretations of Islam. Similar processes took place in Orthodox Christianity. New priests were added to the Batumi and Skhalta diocese, and in the late 1990s the Church became more active in upper Ajaria as well. The effect seemed similar to what Motika concluded about religious processes in Azerbaijan. He argued that although the relationship between Shiite and Sunni Islam was "still dominated by ecumenical and sometimes eclectic spirit, the 'old' categories are given new relevance by foreign missionaries" (Motika 2001, 122). The relation between "believers" and "denominations" should thus be understood not only in terms of "spirituality" but also in terms of the political-economic webs in which religious elites play an important role.

One of the most interesting aspects of the religious dynamics in Ajaria is that the first decade after socialism showed a gradual tendency toward a more active appropriation of religious labels. The categories "Muslim" and "Christian" were increasingly becoming part of new and distinct lifestyles. This was largely because the politicized situation on the frontier led to explicit definitions of "self" and "other." Indeed, religious categories were not only applied in reference to a strictly defined list of religious demands—as externally defined denominations—but were also important in reference to identification with familial, regional, ethnic, and national categories.

Religious affiliation can be seen to link up with various aspects of social identification (see table 2). This scheme would appear to be valid only for people who were unambiguously Muslims or Christians and to overlook those who were situated somewhere in the middle. As we saw throughout the previous chapters, many inhabitants showed considerable ambiguity in discussing religious affiliation. For example, as a villager commented about some political leaders in upper Ajaria: "Here in the mountains they base their authority on their Muslim identity, but as soon as they descend to the capital [Batumi] they will pretend to be Christians. For them there is no religion, only politics."

Table 2. Aspects of social and religious identification in upper Ajaria

	Christians	*Muslims*
Family	Saw conversion as return to their (distant) ancestor's religion and downplayed recent familial traditions	Stressed that immediate ancestors were Muslim and that they continued that tradition by remaining faithful to Islam
Region	Saw Ajaria as an inherent part of (Christian) Georgia and perceived its autonomy as an anomaly	Saw Ajarian autonomy as confirmation of the region's Muslim background
Ethnic "group"	Stressed that Ajarians were ethnic Georgians and that the term "Ajarian" had only geographical connotations	Differentiated between Ajarians and Georgians, but were careful not to make politically sensitive statements
Nation	Underlined the unity of religion and nation	Avoided commenting on the relation between religion and nationality

Although this may be valid for those to whom "only politics" counts, the aforementioned aspects of social identification were, for most people, more than simple labels that could be taken up as the situation required. Indeed, it would be a mistake to assume that "nonbelievers" could form a neutral category. Even if inhabitants of Ajaria denied the existence of God or Allah and avoided calling themselves Christian or Muslim, this would not relieve them from adopting a stance in relation to the other aspects of social belonging. And others would quickly reconnect any elaboration on themes like nationality and ethnicity to issues of belief.

This schematic overview also shows why Muslims were more reserved than Christians about making public statements concerning "righteous" faith (table 2). Whereas Christians publicly claimed that Orthodox Christianity is the only true religion and that others have been misled or are fundamentally wrong, Muslims on the whole would say that the specific religion to which one adheres is only of secondary importance and that acknowledgement of the existence of God is more crucial. The reason for this is that statements concerning Muslim identity immediately prompted connotations with other social and political issues, to which most Muslims had at least ambivalent attitudes. The differences in how strongly the truthfulness of personal convictions could be expressed illustrates the asymmetries in the balance of power at the frontier. Besides playing a constitutive role in national ideologies, religion also served as an important part of people's conceptions of personhood. The confrontation of Islam and Christianity not only challenged a person's own faith but also the faith of his or her predecessors and offspring. Moreover, since religion could not be confined to one sphere of life, it was not only faith that was contested. Local customs and traditions, indeed people's entire way of life, was challenged in the process. Religious identification, like any form of social affiliation, is formed around notions of difference and commonality. Being Muslim or Christian in upper Ajaria involved continually trying to relate personal experience to larger narratives of nation and state, thereby simultaneously setting new boundaries between "us" and "them."

PART III
Postsocialist Borderlands

Introduction

Treacherous Markets

In February 1997, just before my first visit to Ajaria, I had been in a rush to make all the necessary purchases for my fieldwork. Anticipating that fieldwork would involve extensive walking I decided to buy new shoes. Eventually I bought relatively inexpensive shoes (approximately $50), Italian Dolcis. They seemed well suited for the rough conditions, and I expected that they would last at least until I returned. However, three weeks of walking on unpaved village paths and plenty of rain and mud were obviously not the conditions for which the shoes were designed. Only a month after I had bought them they were practically useless. The sole had cracked open and the padding was pulverized. I was a little angry with myself, for my "Dutch wisdom" told me never to buy cheap. Anyway, the next walk through the mud revealed that I had to replace my shoes. Since it was impossible to purchase new ones anywhere nearby, I had to tell Teimuri about my shoes, although I felt embarrassed to do so.

Teimuri was astonished when he learned my solid-looking shoes had worn out so fast. He was even more baffled when I told him what I had paid for them (to him an extraordinarily high price). But it did not take long before everything was crystal clear to him. According to Teimuri, the shoes I had bought were not of Italian origin at all. I showed him the brand name and the "Made in Italy," but this made no impression on him. He shook his head and said, "I am sure that these shoes were not made in Italy. Probably they were manufactured in Turkey or somewhere, and the seller has simply duped you." For him this was another example of how the Turkish "Mafia" operates. He showed me his own shoes, "Do you see these? I bought them seven years ago when I was in Moscow. Maybe they don't look beautiful, but they are very strong, made in Russia." With disappointment in his voice he added, "Unfortunately they don't make them any more."

When I asked Teimuri about a good place to buy shoes he was unsure how to answer. "These days it is difficult to know where to go to. It is probably better to ask Mzia [my host mother in Batumi]. She knows the town better than I do." It was decided that Teimuri would stay in the village while I went to Batumi. After I had arrived I discussed the issue with Mzia. She told me that there were several possibilities depending on how much money I wanted to spend. First, there were the new boutiques, and Mzia seemed eager to accompany me there, perhaps because she had never bought anything in those shops with their expensive import goods. And then there was the Hopa bazaar, named after the first Turkish town across the border. Noting my interest in the bazaar, she raised doubts as to whether I would be able to find any good shoes there.

Mzia arranged a ride for me with her neighbor Malkhaz, a successful businessman and owner of two telephone shops. Once we were on our way in his Mercedes, Malkhaz made clear that he thought the whole expedition was a joke, a Dutchman buying Turkish goods. He was sure I was the first person from the West to shop at the Hopa bazaar. When I stepped out of the car he gave me a last bit of advice: "If you really want to buy shoes here, you might just as well buy a second pair straight away; otherwise, tomorrow you will have to go back there barefoot." The $8 shoes I eventually bought lasted until social expectations back in the Netherlands induced me to buy new ones.

Without being aware of it, my shoes and I had behaved in unexpected ways, triggering responses that provided insights into locally held ideas about the opening of the border and the rapid social and economic changes. The regret with which Teimuri talked about his Russian shoes betrayed nostalgia for times in which you could be certain about the quality of goods. That era stood in sharp contrast with the uncertainties of the present, in which deception was common. Mzia's and Malkhaz's comments pointed in the same direction and revealed the sense that present-day markets were treacherous. These markets symbolized the disillusionment with capitalist change and the massive influx of new consumer goods (cf. Humphrey 1995). In this context my behavior had been highly inappropriate, as it disregarded the hard lessons learned by inhabitants of Batumi. I had ignored Mzia's advice to buy shoes in one of the new boutiques that sold high-quality import goods and, instead, had purchased my shoes in a disliked place where most Batumi residents would buy their clothes only out of sheer necessity.

But there was another underlying theme that explained my acquaintances' astonishment about my and my shoes' behavior, and which indicated continuing expectations about the future. In Ajaria, along with much of the post-Soviet world in the 1990s, there was a general expectation that economic decline was only a temporary phenomenon, a necessary phase of a transition to a "modern" end stage. Terms like "democratic," "capitalist," "civilized," "Western," and "European" all served to index a future in which there would be a higher standard of living, no unemployment, less corruption, and general order.[1] Both in everyday speech and in political discourse this "transition" was imagined as a return to Europe, which combined the promise of an abundant future with the possibility of holding on to "authentic" Georgian traditions. For Teimuri, my Italian shoes had represented the end stage of this imagined transition, the destiny of his dream of modernity. My expensive Italian shoes should therefore have been good looking and of high quality, but they lost both characteristics after a few walks through the rain. Instead of acknowledging that "even" European goods may be of bad quality, he denied my shoes' European origin and suggested that they were produced in Turkey. This particular channeling of discontent allowed for the continuation of the dream of a better future. In the next two chapters, I argue that the reenactment of the dream of modernity involved not only popular responses to the uncertainties of the present era but was also actively cultivated and propagated by the political elite, who had a vested interest in demonstrating that it was bringing Ajaria "back" to Europe.

1. Although these terms may have different connotations to the reader, this was not necessarily the case in Georgia. Darchiashvili and Pataraia, for example, showed that "the West" and "Europe" have the same connotations for the Georgian political elite (2001, 65). The political philosopher Nodia, moreover, argued that whereas Western scholars hasten to distinguish between "modernization" and "Westernization," these notions are almost synonyms in Georgia, and "Western" is used interchangeably with "advanced," "modernized," or "civilized" (2001, 32).

7 Channeling Discontent

The fall of the iron curtain between Georgia and Turkey brought about a tremendous flow of goods and people across the border. It offered Georgians access to Western consumer goods and hard currency; both were extremely valuable there at the time. Transnational trade rapidly increased in volume and continued to be important for the region as a whole, affording many residents a means of living. Although the positive effects of the border opening seemed obvious, inhabitants of Ajaria increasingly tended to ascribe negative qualities to it. My acquaintances said the border opening had been responsible for the spread of diseases and for chaos in the markets. They also perceived it as a threat to local values.

At first glance, these negative reactions confirm observations made throughout the former socialist bloc. When people were exposed to the destabilizing qualities of global economic forces, the high hopes of life after socialism were replaced by "anger, resignation and selective nostalgia for the socialist era" (Hann 2002, 94). Moreover, as Hann and others observed, these resentments were increasingly channeled toward "the West" as the new threatening "other" (Hann 2002, 94).[1] This disillusionment caused by unfulfilled hopes was equally present in Batumi, but it led many Batumi residents to different conclusions. Despite the decline in the standard of living experienced by the majority, and despite the great inequalities that emerged, "the West" retained many of its mythical qualities, fueling hope that "the transition" might eventually be completed.

In this chapter I aim to explain this unexpected coexistence of widespread

---

1. See also Pine, who stated that in Poland "the state and the public domain came to carry connotations of the oppressive 'other,' this time in conjunction not with Russia but with the 'West'" (2002, 108).

disillusionment about the changes with continued confidence in a "modern" future by focusing on the new flow of commodities across the border. As numerous anthropologists have noticed, changes in the world of goods have been central as signifiers of postsocialist change (Berdahl 1999; Caldwell 2002; Creed 2002; Patico 2003). The obvious reason for this is that in the late Communist period the West was perceived as an earthly paradise, as a world imagined to be replete with material goods.[2] After the collapse of Communism, these fantasies were confronted with capitalist realities. While Veenis in her study of former East Germany argues that the confrontation of "capitalist dreams" with reality resulted in disillusionment and the disappearance of this dream (1999), Creed argues that, at his Bulgarian field site, "the world of goods continues to be significant precisely because it has *not* materialized" (2002, 119, emphasis added). The logic seems clear: as long as the products are out of reach, the dream can be maintained, whereas their availability incites the reconsideration or even rejection of the dreams of "modernity." What is important to note, though, is that the goods themselves lacked a stable meaning. I believe that by attaching new meanings to goods, people in Batumi could continue dreaming of modernity. By reevaluating the goods they could preserve their confidence in a "modern future" and direct their frustrations to real or imagined evils, symbolized by "the Mafia" and "Turkey." Moreover, this particular channeling of discontent personalized "the economy," providing locally convincing explanations for why Batumi residents were denied the expected fruits of the post-Soviet era. By comparing these interpretations to actual economic changes—particularly in relation to cross-border trade—the significance of these shifts of meaning will become clearer.

The Opening of the Border

In 1988, when the border was opened, surprisingly little happened at first. A few visas were granted for family visits and transit trade, and a few tour operators started organizing cross-border trips (Nişanyan 1990, 111). This "serenity" suddenly ended in 1991 when the governments of Georgia and Turkey loosened restrictions on traffic. The border village of Sarpi became one of the few open gates to the capitalist West. In 1992 an astonishing eight hundred thousand people—arriving from Georgia, Russia, Azerbaijan, and other republics—passed the border gate in Sarpi.[3] Besides the rush to obtain Western consumer goods across the border, the opening also offered the possibility of

2. As Creed emphasizes, these fantasies were constructed "from the vantage point of cash availability and limited choice [in which] the capitalist world of goods seemed like a paradise" (2002, 121–22).

3. According to the newspaper *Adzhariia* (29 March 1995), every fifth inhabitant of Georgia made one or more trips to Turkey. Hale estimated that in 1992 some three million visitors from the socialist bloc entered Turkey. The majority made shopping expeditions (1996, 4).

exporting Soviet goods, which was extremely profitable because of the huge discrepancy in prices between the Georgian and Turkish side. Georgia was still in the ruble zone, and the prices of many commodities were still set by the state. Moreover, because the newly independent republic experienced severe economic decline and staggering inflation, people badly needed hard currency. Meanwhile, Turkish goods started to enter Georgia and filled the gap in the distribution of consumer goods. Batumi was strategically situated to profit from the new transnational movements, and the city became a major trading center on the crossroads between Turkey and the Caucasus (see also Aves 1996).

Residents of Batumi vividly remember the first hectic years. The road from Batumi to the border—until then a dead end accessible only with special permits—became a major highway almost overnight. It was a very slow highway, however, since time-consuming procedures at the understaffed customs office meant that travelers had to wait for days before crossing the border. An acquaintance who used to work in Gonio, a town located six kilometers from the border, told me, "Even there, cars, buses, and trucks piled up in an endless row. People waited along the road for two, even three days. There were no toilets, no restaurants, no hotels. So they were forced to spend the night in their vehicles. You can imagine what kind of hygiene there was. The beach literally became a huge public toilet, to the distress of the people living there."

For the villagers who lived along the "highway," the traffic jam was both a nuisance and a source of unlimited economic gain. They remembered the difficulty of traveling to Batumi and the shortcomings of the state in supplying both the villagers and the waiting crowd with food. But these nuisances, many villagers quickly learned, could be turned to their benefit. Those waiting in the line would buy anything that the villagers could lay their hands on—fruit, vegetables, cigarettes, vodka—at almost any price. Villagers thrived by setting up money exchange offices and kiosks selling drinks and food. During the night young men were involved in "car-moving," which, I was told, implied offering drivers the possibility of crossing the border within a few hours. If the driver agreed and was willing to pay, the villagers could use their residence permits to drive the car up to the gate.

Those engaged in cross-border trade used various methods to make their trips worthwhile. An early strategy was to capitalize on the discrepancy between official currency rates and those that existed on the black market. Until 1991 the ruble was officially still rated higher than the dollar. The trick was to obtain an international passport, which allowed the conversion of rubles into dollars at the official rate. As a Batumi resident explained, "With dollars you could buy anything in Turkey. But it only lasted for a few years. The ruble declined, and thereafter people only had coupons, which couldn't be used for any purpose." Around 1992 the most simple and effective way to generate profits, the method used by most traders, was to export cheaply obtained goods to Turkey. A common strategy was to buy goods in the state shops at subsidized prices or to mobilize personal networks to procure these products directly from factories and then to sell them at huge profits across the border. Selling was no problem, because "as soon as you crossed the border the Turks rushed up to you to buy your goods." This form of trade took on massive proportions, to the extent, as a Georgian geographer phrased it, that all the cheap (state-subsidized) goods "disappeared from shops all over the Caucasus as if a vacuum cleaner had gone through it" (Gachechiladze 1995, 3).

Batumi residents who were not professionally engaged in this trade still seized the opportunity to add income to their decimated wages. As the economic crisis in Georgia persisted, the exodus of goods to Turkey rapidly increased. Old clothes, furniture, Soviet medals, bicycles, binoculars and cameras, among other items, found their way to the "Russian" bazaars in Turkey.[4] Sometimes personal belongings were sold in Turkey with the conviction that later they could be replaced cheaply through the state shops, a hope that was never realized. One person told me that he had sold his portable stove, which he thought he would not need. But when the central heating system of Batumi permanently collapsed one year later, he was forced to buy a Turkish stove that was more expensive and of lesser quality.

The petty trade engaged in by thousands of individual traders was equaled, at least in volume, by the large-scale exports undertaken by representatives of state institutions. Export permits were granted to institutions to enable them to generate funds for paying employees their suspended wages, but the bulk of the money probably ended up in the pockets of managers and others who held strategic positions. Timber from the forest reserves began to move to Turkey; metal was stripped from industrial enterprises (and even from tramlines) to be transported across the border. This period later became known as the "grand liquidation of Georgia," in which much state property was sold to Turkey.[5]

At the time, public sentiment was generally positive about the opportunities for trading. The newspaper *Adzhariia* interviewed people about their experiences. A mother was quoted as saying, "If not for the new possibilities of trading, my daughters and I would have perished." Another interviewee pointed out that he had been able to renovate his apartment from his profits; and one man even mentioned the educational value of petty trading because it gave his sons the chance to practice business skills that would be needed in the new market economy (*Adzhariia*, 13 April 1993). Those who were well

---

4. For a discussion of these "Russian" bazaars in Turkey, see Hann and Bellér-Hann (1992, 1998).

5. The first trials concerning these illegal sales were reluctantly brought to the Georgian courts in 2000. Although some ministers resigned, no major sentences were imposed during the Shevardnadze era.

situated to participate in this trade, such as many residents of Sarpi, were able to buy Western cars and vans, and they partly renovated their houses and apartments. Other evidence of people's trading trips to Turkey were the audiovisual devices (televisions, video recorders, and radios) bought from initial profits. But several years later, in the late 1990s, the expensive items often seemed out of place in apartments that otherwise betrayed impoverished lives.

Attempts to fulfill "capitalist dreams" remained abortive for most residents of Batumi. In an interview by the local newspaper an attentive student foresaw what later would become a general sentiment: "For some the trip across the border is like a dream that will never come true. Children see the fashionable clothes in shops and the tasty looking food. But their parents are not able to buy those goods" (*Adzhariia*, 13 April 1993). Popular attitudes toward the border opening were shifting and grew more negative as the benefits of trade faded in the mid-1990s. An elderly man from Sarpi gave a dense summary of what he observed as the general trend:

> [In the beginning] young people made lots of money. But they didn't keep it in their pockets. *Tuda, siuda* ["that way, this way"] and the money was gone. They just spent it all, mostly on girls, in Turkey or over here. But then the [traffic] line became shorter and they [authorities] brought order in the line and the opportunities disappeared. After that we became hungry again. So after the disintegration of the Soviet Union we expected that life would become better, but unfortunately that didn't happen.

Indeed, for most ordinary citizens the initial opportunities of transnational trade only lasted several years. This was partly the inevitable outcome of the fact that the sell-off of Soviet state property had been completed and that trade became dominated by professionals, which made it more difficult for "amateurs" to participate. Equally important, in the mid-1990s local power holders tightened their grip on cross-border trade and thereby limited opportunities for small-scale trading. These diminished trading opportunities for ordinary citizens, combined with the general deterioration of the economy in the 1990s, are key to understanding why public opinion about the border opening grew increasingly negative.

Diminished Opportunities and Inverted Flows

Data on the transnational trade between Turkey and Georgia show large discrepancies, mainly because a large part of it was carried out by thousands of unregistered tourist-traders (see also Hale 1996, 59; Hann and Bellér-Hann 1992). Despite the absence of reliable figures it is safe to say that while during the first years after 1990 the net flow of goods was directed toward Turkey in later years the flow was reversed.[6] Another significant change was that although the volume of registered trade increased, in subsequent years the cross-border movements of people sharply decreased. While in 1992 almost 800,000 people crossed the border, in 1996 only some 170,000 border crossings were registered.[7] In other words, the flow of goods was not only reversed but the trade was carried out by a group of people that had greatly diminished in size.

Concentration of Trade

The indicators presented above point to the changed nature of cross-border trade. During the early 1990s the trading activities were mostly conducted by individual tourist-traders who exchanged whatever they could in return for cash and consumer goods. But in 1997, when I made my first research trip, little remained of the hectic situation that had characterized the first years. Cross-border traffic consisted predominantly of large trucks, while smaller vehicles were largely absent. A few bus companies still ran daily lines between Trabzon and cities in Georgia, but their passengers went to Turkey mostly for occupational reasons. They were employed in hotels, worked as seasonal laborers on tea and hazelnut plantations, or traded at the Rus pazarı (Russian bazaar) in Trabzon and other Turkish cities. The goods sold in these "Russian" bazaars, however, were no longer of Soviet origin but were produced in China or Taiwan and purchased by Georgian traders in Istanbul or other large Turkish cities and then resold in Trabzon at a profit.[8]

What had happened was that the Ajarian authorities had extended their control over the trade. New regulations made the trip across the border more expensive, and it was prohibited to trade in certain goods.[9] As residents told me, these included the most profitable goods such as beverages, cigarettes, and liquid fuel. Further control over cross-border trade was achieved by a massive replacement of border personnel in 1995, which strengthened the ties between

6. The estimated value of exports to Turkey totaled $800 million in 1993, while hardly anything went in the opposite direction (Derluguian 1995, 27). In 1996 imports from Turkey to Georgia totaled $780 million, 25 percent more than the total for exports (*Resonansi*, 11 June 1997).

7. Data were retrieved only for the first ten months of 1996, when 144,596 people crossed the border (Republic of Turkey, Office of the Prime Minister, State Institute of Statistics, at http://www.die.gov.tr/English/Sonist/turizm).

8. This information is based on conversations with Georgians who lived "temporarily" (between two and five years) at and around the Rus pazarı in Trabzon, April and August 1997.

9. In 1995 the fee for a Turkish visa was raised from $10 to $30. Official fees on the Georgian side, including insurance vouchers, bank statements, and computer registration, amounted to $40 for one person with a car, apart from taxes and/or bribes for transported goods. Also in 1995, the Ajarian government monopolized cross-border trade in 15 to 20 percent of all commodities (*Adzhariia*, 29 March 1995).

customs and the Ajarian political elite.[10] This reorganization did not end corruption at the border but rather ensured that informal payments were channeled more effectively toward the political elite. The Ajarian leadership refused outright to implement a directive from the central government in Tbilisi that demanded (in order to secure the cash flow to the central budget) that control over the customs office be handed to a British firm. This provides a hint at the importance of the clandestine profits generated through cross-border trade. A report by Freedom House underlined the link between transnational trade and the position of local power holders, stating that in Ajaria "illegal monopolies exist in the most profitable liquid fuel and cigarette markets, protected by top state officials and often owned by close relatives" (2001, 297).

The tightening of patronage networks within the Ajarian political-economic environment meant that most trade became concentrated in the hands of a small group of people. To ordinary citizens it became evident that only this minority would be allowed to share in the wealth. Of course, it had been clear from the beginning that people profited unequally from the trade. Everyone had known about the self-enrichment of customs officers in the early 1990s. A typical guess was that between 1992 and 1994 a customs officer had "a very bad day when he earned less than two thousand dollars." The accuracy of such guesses was supported by the sight of large mansions built in Batumi by customs officers. But whereas in the early 1990s ordinary citizens were—if only marginally—able to engage in this trade, in the late 1990s even these possibilities had vanished.

Hayder, who had made numerous trips to Turkey with his son in the early 1990s, gave the following typical summary:

> In the beginning there was little control. All we paid was a small tip to the customs officers, and in return they allowed us to export cars filled with electronic goods, even though this was officially prohibited. . . . Over the last couple of years we haven't gone to Turkey any more. There simply are no goods left to sell. Besides, we can no longer pay the *karmannyi nalog* ["pocket taxes"] they demand at the border.

When I interviewed Hayder in 1997 he and his son were still involved in the trading business. As they were no longer able to go to Turkey they worked as street peddlers, reselling jeans and shirts that the "big shots" imported from Turkey. For these men, and for Batumi residents like them, the trade continued to be important. Many were engaged in the transport of goods to other parts of Georgia; others made an income by reselling goods on the streets or capitalizing on small price differences between various importers. But the

---

10. The Russian press bureau TASS mentioned that the government of Ajaria dismissed all three hundred employees of the regional customs department, citing their unsatisfactory performance.

most lucrative part of the trade, the part that involved cross-border movement, had become out of reach for most Batumi residents.

The first image that people evoked when talking about the diminished possibilities was that of "the Mafia." People explained that the Mafia fully controlled the trade and collected all substantial profits. In ordinary conversations the identity of Mafia members was not usually specified, although when pressed people would say that the Mafia were "they" (*isini* in Georgian), a statement sometimes accompanied with a gesture into the air indicating that the Mafia was made up of those in power. Only sometimes were my respondents more concrete. They indicated that the political leaders constituted the core of the Mafia, as in the reply of one middle-aged man: "Who is the Mafia? I don't know . . . Shevardnadze, Abashidze, they are all the same. All the money ends up in their pockets." The concept "Mafia" in this context referred to the extensive lines of patronage that dominated economic (as well as political) activities in Ajaria and that linked the political leaders to all sorts of economic enterprises, including the customs and the police. In themselves, these patronage networks were not condemned as morally wrong. On the contrary, the informal links that structured economic and political arenas were in other contexts described as the "cement" of Georgian society and as the basis of many valued social practices. However, in the common opinion, "the Mafia" had misused these informal links and in doing so had deprived others of the chance of economic prosperity.

The Mafia as a symbol derived its popularity from its ability to "symbolically express many of people's difficulties in the transition," as Verdery notes for "mafia-talk" in Romania (1996, 219). The "Mafia" provided concrete reasons that people had not been able to see their dreams fulfilled. At the same time, the Mafia was more than an image, as it very forcefully pointed to actual practices in the political and economic domain. In reference to the double meaning of "Mafia," Verdery argued that it is important not to confuse the "conceptual mafia" with the "real thing" (1996, 219). In Ajaria, people usually did not refer to the "real Mafia" but rather applied the metaphor of Mafia to what Ries calls the government Mafia—"those who are seen as invisibly, conspiratorially, and effectively mastering social resources and power to the detriment of the people 'down here'" (Ries 2002, 308).[11] When people mentioned the role of the Mafia they thus simultaneously critiqued the greediness of those in power as well as their deprived status within the new economy. The Mafia evoked a differentiation between "them," who benefited from the trade, and "us," who became victims of the recent changes. As such, the concept was closely connected to the restructuring of economic flows.

---

11. Ries argues that in Russia the Mafia sometimes started to be seen as demonstrating "the means by which avarice and corruption might be reined in" (2002, 305). In Ajaria, however, the Mafia continued to be perceived as perpetuating the negative, and particularly the uneven, effects of postsocialist change.

Reversed Flows: Winners and Losers

The previous section showed that reinforced regulation at the border and a tightening of political-economic networks reduced opportunities for most citizens and led to highly visible social inequalities in Batumi. Discontent with these changes was blamed on "the Mafia." However, when commenting more generally on the plummeting economy people often evoked another evil, Turkey. It suited the status of wrongdoer particularly well because it was perceived as a cultural and religious "other" and it was seen as a continuing threat to the Georgian nation, notions that were easily transposed to stories about the new trade. But to understand how and why Turkey was blamed for economic dislocations, we first need to explore the wider context in which the border opening occurred.

The new possibilities of trade occurred simultaneously with the collapse of the overall economy of Georgia.[12] The decline hit almost every economic sector in Ajaria. As a prestigious holiday resort, Batumi had attracted tourists from diverse parts of the Soviet Union. This influx of tourists abruptly ended with the disintegration of the Soviet Union, and it remained unlikely that the beaches of Ajaria would attract substantial flows of tourists in the near future, since tourists from the former Soviet Union found more exotic, sunnier, and better equipped resorts in Europe and the Turkish Mediterranean. Besides tourism, Batumi also lost its car manufacturing and most of its oil refining industries that had formed central pillars of the local economy. The factories were abandoned, dismantled, and partly sold across the border as scrap metal. Although after 1996 the economic situation stabilized and a gradual economic recovery was observed, it will be a long time before pre-1991 levels of production will be regained.

The impact of changed geopolitical circumstances can be effectively illustrated by changes in the agricultural sector, especially in the production of tobacco, tea, and citrus fruits. The decline in the production levels and market value of these crops also explains why negative sentiments about the border opening were particularly strong among those who depended on the cultivation, processing, and trade of these commodities. In the 1980s the coastal region of Ajaria was considered one of the most prosperous agricultural regions in the Soviet Union. The subtropical climate and the protection from competitors offered by the iron curtain meant that Ajaria (along with the rest of western Georgia) had a virtual monopoly on the supply of subtropical crops to the socialist bloc. These crops secured a steady income for kolkhozniki and provided employment in retailing and processing. Moreover, the citrus fruits cultivated on private plots could be sold at tremendous profit at kolkhoz markets throughout the Soviet Union.

12. Between 1991 and 1995 the gross national product of Georgia declined by 75 percent. In 1996 65 percent of the population was estimated to live below the poverty line (UNDP 1998).

This unique economic position was lost after the collapse of the Soviet Union and the opening of the border with Turkey. As a result of civil strife and continuing unrest in Abkhazia and the North Caucasus, the most important market, the Russian one, became inaccessible by land. Moreover, while transport from Ajaria to Russia was seriously hindered, trading relations between Turkey and Russia quickly expanded. Ajaria had to compete with the superior produce of Turkey, while lacking an adequate infrastructure for processing or marketing agricultural crops. The production of tea fell 93 percent between 1991 and 1995, while the production of citrus fruits dropped by 50 percent (*Adzhariia*, 16 November 1996). In the fields, tea was gradually replaced by subsistence crops such as corn, potatoes, and beans. For the inhabitants of Ajaria this collapse of the rural economy was tragic enough in itself, but discontent was further intensified when these same commodities started to be imported from abroad. Shops in Batumi sold English and Indian but no Ajarian tea, the Tbilisi Coca-Cola factory imported Turkish oranges for its sodas, and virtually all cigarettes consumed in town were manufactured in Turkey.

The new trading opportunities may have been vital for Batumi residents to make ends meet in difficult times, but the trade did not make up for the general economic decline. Moreover, while standards of living in Ajaria had dropped significantly since Soviet times, Turkey's neighboring region had prospered. Since the 1970s Turkey had expanded its cultivation of hazelnuts and tea, which according to Bellér-Hann and Hann was the foremost factor "responsible for the prosperity of modern Lazistan" (2001, 76). The new opportunities for trade with Russia and the Caucasus further enhanced the region's economic development. The Turkish press spoke of the "golden era" of trade with the former Soviet Union, which created an economic boom in the Turkish border towns.[13] The increasing economic asymmetries between Turkey and Georgia did not remain unobserved in Batumi. The following comment was typical of public opinion there concerning the widening gap in economic performance:

> If you had been in Turkey some ten years ago, you would have seen how poor they were. There was nothing there, maybe a few wooden houses, while now they have beautiful office buildings and banks, luxurious shops and hotels, really everything. Turkey has been able to develop itself at our cost [literally, "on our necks"]. But for us the opening of the border meant nothing but misery. . . . We sold everything, and look what we have now—nothing at all.

People in Batumi had ample "evidence" that Turkey benefited disproportionately from the trade. This evidence concerned the initial sell-off of state prop-

---

13. As stated in *Adzhariia*, 17 June 1995. See also Hale (1996, 57–61). Bellér-Hann and Hann (2001, 76–85) provide a more nuanced picture, arguing that although the opening of the border was generally beneficial to the region, local shopkeepers initially tended to lose from the sudden influx of cheap commodities.

erty to Turkey and, even more, the reversal in the flow of goods. As a customs officer put it, "The trade was at its height between 1992 and 1994. In that period Georgians sold many things in Turkey, but they sold it then much too cheaply. Now it is the other way around, but we still have the same problem. Georgia sells wood to Turkey at thirty dollars per cubic meter. In Turkey they make furniture out of it and sell it back to us at five times the original value of the wood." The new patterns of trade were perceived as a grand liquidation of Georgia that enriched Turkey and left Georgia without possessions, products, machinery, or raw materials. "We have sold our country," several residents of Batumi told me. "In the beginning, the Turks paid almost nothing for our belongings, and now they sell goods you can only use once [*odno-razovye tovary*] at high prices." The new trading relations with Turkey were perceived as exploiting ordinary citizens. After having commented on the poor quality of Turkish imports, a middle-aged teacher exclaimed: "But what can we do? For us there is no other way out. If we had other neighbors, if we could go to Western Europe, we wouldn't even care about Turkey."

Evil and Sacred Commodities

In the preceding section I argued that the proximity of Turkey and prevalent ideas about the Mafia provided conceptual tools to keep the dream of the West alive, despite the great dislocations produced by "the transition." People retained their dreams of modernity by denying the capitalist nature of contemporary changes. The way the changes in the economy intertwine with images of modernity can be indexed by focusing on the goods that entered Batumi and found their way into the households of most residents. In Batumi, the disruption of the state distribution system and the influx of new goods from across the border resulted in radical changes in the availability and affordability of consumer goods. Compounding this sense of uncontrollable flux was the fact that the goods themselves changed status. The resulting frustrations and confusion felt by consumers were suggestive of the difficulties of arranging goods into new coherent frameworks. In this section I examine shifts in the meaning of commodities (cf. Kopytoff 1986, 64) to reveal aspects of the moral economy behind the visible transactions.

Consumerism and the Trajectory from Socialism

The most pervasive cold war images of consumption in the Soviet Union are those of shortage, empty shelves, and long lines in front of state shops. The images, whether accurate or not, hinder proper understanding of the changes in consumption, because they produce a false comprehension of consumer behavior in the Soviet Union. Besides the fact that the images were more applicable to the cities of central Russia than to subtropical Batumi with its rich kolkhoz markets, they rest on the assumption that in the Soviet Union people were as dependent on shops as they are in the West. This neglects the importance of subsistence production and the pervasiveness of personal networks in the Georgian Soviet economy. Anthropologists Mars and Altman (1984) convincingly argued that personal networks were the pillars of the economy and were the means through which access to jobs and services as well as consumer goods was gained (see also Dragadze 1988; Fairbanks 1996). In such an environment the picture of empty shelves had a different meaning than we tend to attach to it, and it was radically opposed to the way local inhabitants remembered consumption opportunities during the Soviet era. Consider for example Teimuri's comments on the availability of consumer goods:

> We used to have European goods over here, from Czechoslovakia, Yugoslavia, and even from the Netherlands and England. The government exchanged oil and metal for cloth and other products, so that we could buy coats and trousers. And then, of course, the sailors smuggled many products. They bought coats, liquor, and cigarettes in the West and sold them in Batumi. Customs posed no problem, for this is a small town where everybody knows one another. . . . You could get everything, although you had to put some effort into it. Back then you needn't worry about most things. You could always buy bread, tea, food, and clothes. Maybe it was difficult to obtain luxury goods, but that was not too serious a problem. And once you got it you were happy. People didn't have as many pretensions as [they have] now.

It might be tempting to interpret this statement as selective nostalgia that omits the lack of consumer goods. But the difficulties of gaining access to commodities—especially basic goods—should not be overstated. As a port city and holiday resort, Batumi had a relatively rich supply of goods. Moreover, the diverse rural economy of Ajaria meant that the kolkhoz markets used to be well stocked with fruits, vegetables, and dairy products and that real shortages in the food supply hardly ever occurred.[14] But, more important, the comments pointed to the change from a period in which not money but access to goods was the crucial factor, to a new period in which all the goods became available but were often beyond the means of ordinary residents.

The opening of the border definitely brought about a tremendous increase in the availability and variety of consumer goods. In the center of Batumi in the late 1990s, numerous luxury shops had been opened and small grocery stores could be found on almost every street corner. The five large open markets were bustling with activity and displayed a rich array of goods, ranging from clothes and makeup to construction materials and computer software. But only the elite could really take advantage of this abundance. For most people the appearance of new consumer goods was hardly an improvement, as they couldn't afford them anyway. The new commodity flows posed formid-

---

14. An indication of the importance of the kolkhoz markets in Soviet Georgia is a study from 1979, which revealed that in Tbilisi almost 40 percent of food purchases were made in kolkhoz markets (cited in Gachechiladze 1995, 126).

able challenges for Batumi residents. They needed not only to deal with the rising costs of most commodities but also with the difficulty of establishing a fair price in an unstable market. In the 1990s, quality and price differences became much more pronounced than they had been during the Soviet period, and—as everyone in Batumi could testify—it became often very difficult to find out what was an imitation and what was the real thing.

Reordering Goods: Unstable Taxonomies of Production

In Soviet Batumi the most reliable way to gain information about consumer goods was to inquire about their origin. There was a more or less stable hierarchy of value based on site of production. At the top stood goods like trousers, shoes, and paint from East Germany, Czechoslovakia, and other Eastern European countries, followed by goods produced in Russia and Ukraine. The lowest values were attributed to goods produced in Central Asia. Floating above this rudimentary taxonomy were "foreign" products that only irregularly entered Batumi households. Middle-aged and elderly town dwellers regularly evoked the times when they ate Dutch cheese, drank coffee from Brazil, or watched Indian movies, memories that betrayed the mystery these goods represented.

Many of my acquaintances continued to be preoccupied with the origin of commodities, even as the relation between origin and quality became more difficult to determine. A rudimentary classification of goods based on their presumed origins in the late 1990s can be summarized as follows: Western products were expensive, but beautiful and of good quality.[15] Russian products were cheap and of good quality, although the aesthetic value was low. Turkish products were also cheap and looked relatively good, but they were of extremely poor quality. Georgian products, finally, were mainly restricted to domestic production and consumption. These predominantly agricultural products were valued for their purity and functioned sometimes as a source of national pride.

The values attached to commodities of different origins become clearer in their mutual relationships. Turkish commodities were contrasted with the better-quality Russian goods that had mostly disappeared from the markets. At the bargain markets in town it was not unusual to see kiosks with signs advertising *Russkie tovary* [Russian goods], whereas the Turkish origin of goods was usually concealed. In a typical response comparing Turkish and Russian goods, one of my acquaintances commented, "Maybe the Russian stuff doesn't look very beautiful, but the quality is good. Compare for example blouses. If you wash and iron a Turkish blouse two times it will fall apart, while Russian clothes will remain in good condition for years." Nevertheless,

---

15. The category "Western" was used loosely and included Western European, North American, and sometimes high-quality Asian (Japanese and Korean) products.

Midday at one of the bazaars in Batumi, June 1997.

most people agreed that Turkish products at least looked better. This is illustrated by the following comment: "The chocolate from Turkey is worthless and it is old, but you can sit down behind the wrapping and look at it for hours—as if it were television." Significantly, in this intentionally comical remark beauty was hardly considered a favorable point, for it cast the appearance of Turkish goods as misleading.

The assessment of foreign products was not simply a balancing of the pros and cons. The people I talked with mostly gave a total valuation of the commodities and thereby stressed certain characteristics while neglecting others. Thus, that Russian products had a low aesthetic value was less important than their high quality and low cost. Western products were forgiven their expense because they lasted and had a high aesthetic value. By contrast, the beauty and low price of Turkish products were considered misleading properties. Instead, they were seen as "expensive" because they lacked quality.

Western goods enjoyed tremendous popularity in Batumi. Coca-Cola and Fanta were indispensable drinks at Georgian banquets. Mercedes cars were valued not only for their good quality but also because they were considered powerful and masculine cars. New beauty shops and boutiques attracted their customers with images of the European Mediterranean. In fact, many of my acquaintances had a far greater knowledge than I did about the relative quality and prices of various brands of electronics, European cars, cell phones, computers, and cigarettes. However, the problem of deception noted in reference to Turkish goods was equally present in the case of Western commodities in that it was often hard to distinguish between "real" and "counterfeit" Western goods.[16]

A case in point was that of cigarettes. At the beginning of the 1990s numerous cigarette brands entered the Batumi market. Soon cigarettes with names such as Kennedy, Taste of America, Party Cigarettes, or President replaced the Soviet brands. When people asked me whether these cigarettes were sold in the Netherlands, they took my denial as further proof that Georgia was being used to dump bad quality products. According to several Batumi residents, general shifts had occurred in what were considered good quality cigarettes. At first any Western-looking brand would do, but when people found out that these brands were counterfeit, they turned to (still relatively cheap) Parliament cigarettes, which later lost in popularity to L&M. But these cigarettes were not the "real thing" either, and several people pointed out that L&M were second-rate cigarettes manufactured by Philip Morris, specially produced in Turkey for the former socialist bloc. Those who were aware of this (and who could afford it) increasingly turned to Marlboros. But even these popular cigarettes, which were sold for two lari (one dollar) a pack in 1999, were not necessarily "real," as I discovered during a dinner. When I tried to light a Marlboro, a rich customs officer grabbed it away, adding, "Here, take one of these. They are imported from America." He proudly remarked that they had cost him eight dollars a pack and showed me the original American packaging of his expensive cigarettes.

By classifying goods through their presumed origin—even when the origin could not be known for sure or when the product was manufactured in more than one country (as many "new" goods were)—people managed to attach meaning to changes in the world of goods and the local economy. The attachment of the label "Turkish" to all commodities that were considered worthless, and preservation of the label "European" for those products that were highly valued, strengthened peoples' conceptual map of both the past and the future. This time dimension was in itself revealing. Whereas Russian products symbolized the past, Turkish goods referred to the disliked present, while Western products continued to trigger hopeful images of the future. Many inhabitants of Batumi expressed nostalgia about the Soviet Union by referring to the price and quality of goods. By stressing the solid and reliable nature of Russian goods, people communicated the discomfort connected to deteriorating standards of living and loss of security. In contrast to Turkish goods, European products represented a dream of a better and more colorful life.

Conspiracies and the Market

The new goods that entered the Batumi markets were arranged according to origin, quality, and price. As we have seen above, Turkish goods were generally

---

16. The problem of distinguishing "counterfeit" from "genuine" Western commodities was not restricted to Georgia. For observations from Russia, see Ries (2002, 288).

disliked. They were considered trash and described as useless (*bezpolezno*), of poor quality, and even harmful to one's health. In part these valuations can be understood as expressions of frustration with the deterioration of life in the post-Soviet era, directed at Georgia's historical and—since the opening of the border—immediate "other." Disillusionment with the new flow of goods and the dependency on trade with Turkey reinforced existing stereotypes. But the stories about Turkish and other goods went beyond the merely representative. When my acquaintances discussed the relative quality of goods or the increased prices, they were not simply making an observation of a fact but were raising the issues because they needed answers. In other words, the changes in the economy were not *simply* taking place, they were seen as having specific causes.

To understand the dilemmas and questions that Batumi residents raised and answered, it is important to note that discussions about the negative aspects of economic change were simultaneously discursive confrontations between, and amalgamations of, "Marxist" and "capitalist" views of the economy. Batumi residents were usually well informed about presumed mechanisms of the market and concepts such as supply and demand, competition, and inflation. Besides their own experiences with trading, and more broadly with the changes of the previous ten years, they also had been supplied with media reports about the workings of "the market" and the necessity of market reform. However, these market theories often proved inadequate to explain why the prices and quality of goods had changed so radically. In what follows I present accounts of inhabitants who experienced a deterioration in their standard of living, that is, of those for whom the questions concerning the changing economy were most pertinent. I have structured my argument around three typical questions that were raised in discussions about economic change.

Why Did Prices Rise beyond Expectations?

The reasons behind the staggering prices bewildered many of my acquaintances. This was not surprising given that in Batumi, as elsewhere in the Soviet Union, the prices of basic consumer goods, transport, and accommodations had remained stable for decades until the 1990s. Moreover, the sudden price increases challenged the widespread and attractive notion that ideally the pricing of goods should conform to the costs of production. In other words, every product was assumed to have a "real" price that served as the basis from which people evaluated the changes. Murman, a fifty-five-year-old mechanic, evoked these ideas when explaining to me why prices were rising:

> We used to have well-stocked shops on each corner. But they closed them and now the Mafia controls everything. First they wanted to make a little bit of profit, maybe one lari. But now it already came to a stage that they say that a sack of flour costs fifty lari, simply because they want to have more money. They want to

have ten lari profit; one [lari] isn't enough for them. Why would the price of flour be fifty lari? During the days of the Soviet Union a sack of flour was six rubles in our Russian money, so approximately ten dollars, and now it is twenty-five dollars.

To Murman it was clear that the Mafia manipulated the price levels and could simply "say that a sack of flour costs fifty lari," even though the "real" price was much lower. The conviction that goods have a "real" price points back to the Marxist dogma that prices of goods should be equal to production plus labor costs. But Murman was not unaware of the dynamics of "the market." The standard "market" answer would have been that the price increases were caused by inflation. To account for this possible factor Murman traced the respective prices back to their supposedly inflation-free value in dollars.[17] The comparison taught him that the price of flour had nevertheless more than doubled. Another respondent referred to the same issue, stating that "in Turkey there may be inflation, but it is inflation of the [Turkish] lira, while in dollars the prices remain the same. But here in Georgia we have an inflation of the dollar as well. Everything has become more expensive." Such comparisons may not be valid from the perspective of an economist. What they ignored was that in the Soviet Union the prices of consumer goods (as well as exchange rates) were set by the state and were not directly related to economic costs or international exchange rates. But for many Batumi residents the comparison was very real proof that market concepts were insufficient to account for the rising prices.

What was particularly significant was that Murman was suggesting a less abstract cause for the price increases. Arguing that "the market" was unable by itself to have caused the changes, he logically concluded that prices were manipulated. He explained it as the greed of the Mafia, who increased the prices because "one lari is not enough" profit for them. His discomfort concerned his uncertainty as to where this manipulation would lead. After all, "they" could simply decide they wanted to make more money and increase prices at any moment. "They" controlled the prices and little could be done about it.

Who Manipulates the Quality of Goods and Why?

Discontent with the increased cost of living was matched by concern about the quality of the new goods that entered Batumi. The following statement by a female bread seller shows the fears people had concerning the forces hiding behind the flow of goods:

17. Murman was carefully trying to identify the causes of the price increases, rather than making a rhetorical point or underlining economic hardship. Had the latter been the case he could have contrasted—as was commonly done—the spending power of former and present wages to reveal a far more dramatic difference.

When I was sitting in the bus I overheard a man say that his kids got rashes from Turkish flour. [People] say that the Turks add chemicals to their flour and physicians are aware of this problem. And when you use Turkish washing soap your skin starts to peel off. The children start to scratch their itches and this is very difficult to treat. They say that the Turks want to harm the Georgian women with washing powders, that they export sweets to injure the children and they damage the men through cigarettes and vodka.

People often mentioned the use of chemicals when discussing the negative quality of Turkish goods. Because of their invisibility, the idea of added chemicals stirred up anxieties regarding the new goods, the quality of which was difficult to determine and the appearance of which was deceiving. But stories about the manipulation of consumer goods also reflected frustration with, and incomprehension of, the fact that Turkish goods had pushed locally produced crops and goods out of the market. I encountered this concern when invited to a drinking session. When the host offered Yup (instant lemonade) to go with the vodka, his thirty-eight-year-old son Lasha immediately exclaimed: "What is this! Taste in a little bag!?" and, turning to me, he continued: "Now you see what the Turks are doing to us. They sell powders, and 'plop' you have fruit juice . . . or 'plop' and you have vodka." We all laughed, but Lasha continued in a more serious tone: "Because of Turkey it is hardly profitable for farmers to grow crops. If potatoes are actually worth forty cents, then they [the Turks] come with their fake potatoes so that the price drops to thirty cents. The same with cucumbers, they are all counterfeit. They add some chemicals to the plant so that they can grow a whole cucumber in a single day, while here it takes an entire month."

The message seems to be that through deception and the falsification of products Turkey pushed local producers out of the market. In this context, it was not only the prices that were manipulated but the quality of the goods. The same concern was present in the following account: "Macaroni, for example. If they have spoiled grain, they just put it through the mill and sell it anyway. If a [Georgian] sack costs thirty rubles, someone without money will buy the Turkish sack for ten rubles. Such a life we have now: it is a very difficult time for us." In this anecdote there was both a "real" quality and a "real" price to a sack of macaroni. The price was set at thirty rubles (actually lari) for a sack of "real" macaroni. But as the anecdote shows, through falsification and the use of bad quality material, traders could sell "fake" macaroni below the "real" price. Interestingly, the argument prompted by the respondents quoted in the previous section was reversed here. Whereas there it was argued that the Mafia drove up the prices, here it was argued that the prices of Turkish products were too low for local producers to compete with.

The contradiction between stories arguing that prices had gone up steeply and others claiming that Turkey sold products below the "real" price can partly be explained by looking at the intent of the narratives and the different roles of the storytellers. Obviously, "consumers" were most concerned with the rising prices. These concerns arose when people talked about the difficulty of making ends meet. Alternately, the alleged manipulations of quality and their lowering effects on prices were mentioned by "producers," who aimed to explain why it was so difficult in Ajaria to set up a viable business as a farmer or a manufacturer of goods. If in real life people were often both consumer and producer at the same time, this did not mean that the incongruities between these two explanations were of any concern to them. As an acquaintance commented when we discussed the incongruities: "Well, you know, this entire *perekhodnyi period* [transitional period] has been a contradiction." Indeed, for many ordinary inhabitants of Ajaria it was simply a fact that they were neither able to compete successfully with Turkish commodities nor to purchase sufficient goods to meet their daily needs.

Why Are the Dislocations of the New Era Happening?

The stories about rising prices and conspiracies were told by people who were pressed to the margins by postsocialist change. They rendered their own misfortune meaningful and explained how others (such as customs officers and other state functionaries with modest *official* wages) could have turned into millionaires. The stories were also intended to explain why post-Soviet change had not lived up to expectations and why the Georgian economy remained in a state of crisis. It is here that the notions of the Mafia and popular ideas about the opening of the border converge. The following example is from Rolandi, a businessman who lost most of his money after he set up a small mandarin juice processing factory but was unable to sell his product profitably. His comments show both frustration with his own misfortune and regret about the economic situation in general:

> Why would you buy Turkish flour if you are able to grow it yourself? Why would we need to buy clothes from Turkey if we had those factories in our own country? Why? You know why? Because for the Mafia it is profitable if the factories don't operate. Because [then] they can buy goods cheaply in Turkey and sell them more expensively over here. . . . They are like vultures that eat dead corpses. Like vultures they have destroyed and sold our factories. I tell you, this didn't happen anywhere else, not in Ukraine or in Russia, not in Latvia. They only did it here. And they allow no one else to set up businesses. . . . In Tbilisi a cigarette factory was opened, [but] three times production has already been shut down because of fires in the factory. The Mafia set fire to it, because they can make much more money by importing than by producing, because that would mean competition and then the profits would be lower.

Rolandi was convinced, along with many others, that the decline of the economy was explained by the direct involvement of the Mafia. They argued that the Mafia in Georgia was not like the one in Italy, because over there the Mafia was actually part of the economy, while in Georgia it was simply claiming everything for itself. The destructive force attributed to the Mafia, or simply to those in power, was also evident in a popular anecdote. Someone would say that he hoped that "they" would destroy everything even faster than they had done so far. The explanation of this unexpected statement would be that "they" wouldn't need an honest worker as long as they hadn't destroyed everything, but once they reached that point they would surely ask him to help rebuild the country.

The conspiracy theories of my respondents did not give "objective" explanations as to why prices rose or why local farmers and manufacturers were unable to compete successfully with imported goods. What they did do, however, was draw attention to the unintended and unanticipated outcomes of the recent economic transformations. Rolandi's insistence that it was more profitable for the elite to trade in goods than to set up "honest" businesses resembled Burawoy and Krotov's provocative statement (1992) that the post-Soviet era saw the rise of a form of "mercantile capitalism." It may be that in the neoliberal imagination such stories at best illuminated the "side effects" of the transition. But the centrality of these "side effects" in local narratives implicitly indicated—and rightly so, in my opinion—that these unanticipated changes were actually the *core* effects of "transition."

The predominance of the "Mafia" and "Turkey" in the stories presented above may be seen as misdirected discontent over what were actually the destabilizing effects of global economic forces. But, and this is a crucial aspect, "the market" was not sufficient to explain the present economic situation. In fact, inhabitants cited several elusive forces in order to comprehend economic realities. Unequal access to the "free market" and the patronage-based actions of power holders converged in what was called the Mafia. The commentaries of ordinary people were not far off the mark, and they certainly reflected post-Soviet realities in Ajaria better than the insistence of the government that gradual progress was being made to complete the transition to a market democracy. But the stories were also about the relative lack of power of those who told them. The Mafia, as a metaphor for asymmetrical market forces, had robbed them of their past status and undermined their hopes of future advancement.

Katherine Verdery observed in Romania that for many citizens " 'the economy' was beginning to become an impersonal, unregulated social fact, something to be taken for granted because it worked" (1996, 184). In Batumi, few people would attribute self-regulating qualities to "the economy," and they would not agree that it "worked," at least not for them. Instead they saw—quite realistically—economic processes as tightly interwoven with webs of power that were exclusive and unpredictable. Their use of the term Mafia should be understood in this context. For Batumi residents, the relevance of the term was not only that it characterized certain practices but also that it set a line between "us" who suffered and "them" who benefited from the collapse of the Soviet Union. Moreover, the Mafia served as an image in explanations of why the transition had failed. The Mafia was the embodiment of elusive and destabilizing economic change; its evocation also alluded to the fact that the recent changes had relatively little to do with economic models assuming an automatic transition from socialism to the "free market." Because the Mafia provided a specific cause for economic dislocations, hopes that the ideals of a "modern" and wealthy end stage would eventually be reached could be preserved.

Preserving the Dream

Though I have suggested that many people in Ajaria held on to the dream of modernity, this did not imply that they saw their own situation as having in any way approached that dream. As was extensively illustrated, many inhabitants experienced the changes as pushing them in the exact opposite direction—toward backwardness and poverty. In a discussion of trader-tourism (i.e., small-scale trading activities under the guise of tourism) between Bulgaria and Turkey, Konstantinov argued that while capitalism was for a long time perceived as the final "safe haven," this image started to be replaced by the realities—insecurity, inferiority, immorality—of the trade route itself (1996). With the fall of the iron curtain Ajarians faced similar realities, but they continued to see themselves as traveling to the final "safe haven." They did not need to abandon their goal and their fantasies about their future life, for they could blame more immediate and personal forces for the dislocations that were taking place. The hope that these dangers could be defeated had not disappeared. And answers about how to reach the bright future were actively being produced.

The issue that remains is how the feelings of insecurity, inferiority, and immorality are counteracted, in essence, how the "safe haven" can be reached. In this respect, a comment by Humphrey about perceptions of chaos in Russia seems equally applicable to Ajaria: "The nightmare of chaos, in this way of thinking, is counteracted by the exercise of power. This is different from the strand of Western European thought which conceives of the state in reified form as 'that which has always existed'" (Humphrey 2002a, 28, citing Herzfeld 1986). In applying this idea to Ajaria, it becomes clear that the socioeconomic dislocations reinforced two strands of thought: on the one hand, a continued longing for "the West," and on the other, a wish for the reinstitution of rightful order, one that is able to check the injustices done to ordinary citizens and to Ajaria and Georgia in general. The Abashidze regime of Ajaria skillfully appropriated these two longings. It did so by presenting its rule as a form of authoritarian democracy, which would guarantee the "revival" of Ajaria and its "reconnection" to Europe.

8 The Social Life of Empty Buildings

The rapid changes following the demise of socialism challenged familiar spaces and shook social relations. In Batumi, these changes were intimately related to the breakdown of the centralized economy and, equally important, to the fall of the nearby iron curtain with Turkey. As mentioned in earlier chapters, the impact of these events should be understood in relation to changes in the position of Ajaria within the Georgian republic. Although its status as "autonomous republic" had its origin in the early days of Soviet rule, this status meant fairly little during most of the twentieth century, when Ajaria was an integrated part of the Georgian Soviet Socialist Republic. During the decade following the collapse of the Soviet Union, however, its position changed rapidly. Of central importance to this change were the power struggles in the national center and civil strife in various parts of Georgia between 1990 and 1993, which enabled the regional political elite of Ajaria, centered around Aslan Abashidze, to extend its power base (see also Aves 1996, 41).[1]

Aslan Abahidze, a descendent of a family that had been influential in pre-Soviet Ajaria, had held various bureaucratic positions until he was installed as the chairman of the Supreme Council of Ajaria by Georgian president Gamsakhurdia. Steadily consolidating his power basis throughout the 1990s, he continued to present himself as a democratic leader and as a champion of the free market. He was said to have personally initiated a prestigious "center of democracy and regionalism," and he and his political supporters were always keen to stress the importance of establishing a "free economic zone," because, he argued, "free competition" would provide a boost to the local and country-

---

1. For more extensive discussions of the consolidation of economic and political control by the Revival Party, see Derluguian (1995) and Hin (2000). The Revival Party dissolved itself in 2004, after leader Aslan Abashidze had fled to Russia.

wide economy. But beyond this rhetoric, it was clear that the Abashidze government was growing increasingly authoritarian. During the second half of the 1990s the Ajarian government managed to gain control over the most important economic assets of Ajaria and to suppress all political opposition within the autonomous republic. Bearing this in mind, it would be logical to conclude that transition rhetoric as used by the political elite bore no relation to actual economic and political processes in Ajaria—except to veil the political and economic interests of the elite.

The discrepancy between transition rhetoric and political and economic change forcefully points to the difficulties in analyzing "transitions." In the 1990s the dominant Western discourse was that the changes that followed the demise of socialism should be interpreted as a transition to market democracy. As has become abundantly clear since the mid-1990s, this master narrative often contrasted sharply with the processes of change in former Soviet republics. From various sides attempts have been made to account for the poor fit between the transition paradigm and postsocialist realities. Neoliberal economists and most international organizations tended to explain the discrepancies by referring to the "Soviet legacy" that hindered the transition, or by seeing them as temporary side effects of the transition period. Either way, authors writing within this framework have held that obstacles might *slow down* the transition but that changes were still pointing to an unavoidable end stage of Western-style democracies and free markets. Others, especially anthropologists and some sociologists, strongly criticized the ideologically informed transition theory held by neoliberal economists and development agencies.[2] They argued that one should consider the possibility that the unexpected outcomes were in fact the *core* effects of the transition, thus stressing the uncertainty of the direction of change. Provocatively denoting the changes as transitions to, for example, "feudalism" or "demodernized society," these authors challenged the received wisdom of the master narrative (Verdery 1996; Shlapentokh 1996; Platz 2000). Though these criticisms have rightly pointed out the fallacies of the master narrative, this should not lead to underestimating the impact of transition discourse on social life. Indeed, the ideology of transition has been woven into the language, ideals, and actions of the inhabitants of the former Soviet republics and thus has influenced the way they think about, act on, and understand economic and political situations.

The dilemma is similar to the one outlined by James Ferguson in his *Expectations of Modernity* (1999), which deals with a very different corner of the earth. Based on research in the Zambian copper belt, Ferguson provides a convincing critique of the myth of modernization—of which the transition

---

2. Among the earliest critics of transition theory was Humphrey (1991), who described a process of increased control by local potentates over their administrative regions, and Burawoy and Krotov (1992), who argued that the changes were the opposite of market formation and were better understood as heightened monopolies.

paradigm can be considered a condensed form—by making a useful distinction about the meaning of the word "myth." The first meaning corresponds with popular usage of the word and refers to a "false or factually inaccurate version of things that has come to be widely believed" (13). This aspect of myth forces Ferguson to attempt a deconstruction of the modernization myth, to show its fallacies and its ideological basis. The second meaning of myth refers to its social function, as "a cosmological blueprint that lays down fundamental categories and meanings for the organization and interpretation of experience" (13–14). Although as a theoretical construct the modernization myth needs to be deconstructed, as a cosmological blueprint it has continuing importance for social life. On the basis of this argument Ferguson points to the need to turn the modernization myth into an ethnographic object. Of Ferguson's two missions—to deconstruct grand narratives and to turn these into ethnographic objects—the latter one seems to be especially pertinent for studies of postsocialist change.[3]

The situation that took shape in Ajaria in the decade after socialism epitomized the discrepancy between transition rhetoric and socioeconomic reality, as well as the persistent obsession with the ideals of the transition on the part of inhabitants of Ajaria. To capture this relationship between imagination and social reality, I center my discussion on what I call "the social life of empty buildings."[4] In post-Soviet Ajaria not only were buildings the most conspicuous expressions of how groups envisaged the new era but also, because of their visibility and because of people's emotional attachment to them, they were very important in legitimizing and criticizing the present. Moreover, construction projects revealed how the appearance of "modernity" and the adoption of transition discourse influenced the processes and understandings of change in post-Soviet Ajaria.

Images of "Transition"

In the late 1990s, suggestions that Ajaria was becoming part of the global community confronted visitors right after they passed the Georgian-Turkish border. Road signs in English welcomed the traveler to the Autonomous Republic of Ajaria. Privately owned companies advertised their names in French or English, like the Black Sea Maritime Bank, the Montpellier Hotel, or the business center, Riviera. One of the few exceptions was the name *Didi banki*, left untranslated from Georgian, perhaps because Big Bank would sound too arrogant. The signs were often grammatically incorrect and sometimes unin-

---

3. Others, most notably Verdery (1996), Burawoy and Verdery (1999), and Wedel (2001), have written convincing critiques of the transition paradigm.

4. This phrase and thus the chapter title stem from Appadurai's seminal work, *The Social Life of Things* (1986). Like the approach advocated there I focus on how the empty buildings are "consumed" and how their "value" is negotiated in a process of politicized social exchange (56–57).

telligible even to English speakers, suggesting that the hint of "newness" the sign provided was more important than its information. State employees wore Gore-Tex jackets saying "Police," "Security," or "Customs" in English, despite angry reactions from nationalists who claimed that the jackets not only were a blow to the Georgian language but also that the alphabet used was unintelligible to most people.[5] New economic and political projects were celebrated as conforming to "European" or "international" standards, and the newest technological achievements in Ajaria were presented as steps toward the completion of "the transition." The daily news had previously been presented only in Georgian and in Russian, but after TV-Ajaria began to be transmitted by satellite in 2000 and, according to the political leaders, was watched all around the world, the news was also presented in English, German, and Italian.

The new dynamism of this former Soviet periphery was very obvious in terms of economic activities and consumption. Following the opening of the border with Turkey, Batumi was transformed into an important trading center between Turkey and the Caucasus. The opening of numerous clothing shops and grocery stores with imported goods seemed to prove that the new economy functioned properly, whereas their closure several months later appeared to reflect fierce market competition. Privatization of housing, the opening of markets, the adoption of European legal codes, and the installation of democratic state structures, all indicated a transition to a Western-style market democracy. But each of these indicators proved problematic when examined closely. The market was only "free" to those with the right connections, while privatization often meant expropriation of public property. And concerning the introduction of democratic principles of government, it should suffice to mention that the leading party of Ajaria received between 90 and 100 percent of the votes in all elections between 1994 and 2003.[6]

The darker sides of the "transition" were just as striking and just as new as the signs of progress. New indeed was the presence of mass poverty in the streets. The many people trading in loaves of bread, homemade pastries, or cigarettes, like the day laborers waiting on corners for the next job, constituted a phenomenon that was unknown before. On the outskirts of town, most streets were severely damaged and flanked by privatized apartment buildings that looked even shabbier than in socialist times. In between such buildings,

5. The differences between the Georgian, Cyrillic, Latin, and Arabic scripts made them useful for conveying various public messages. In Ajaria the Georgian script was used most widely. Russian (Cyrillic) was gradually disappearing but was still used in some economic and political domains. Arabic script, by contrast, had made a comeback in rural areas where Islam had experienced a partial revival. Latin script was used in business and trade and increasingly by state agencies.

6. During elections in 1999, residents of Batumi and Sarpi mentioned a lack of ballots (despite a 99 percent turnout), manipulation of election results by local election committees, and demands by government officials that village authorities guarantee a 100 percent turnout for Abashidze.

however, were newly constructed villas protected by high fences. The contrasts illustrated the increasing economic inequality between the majority and the new rich. However, these were only temporary side effects, or so the government claimed.

If the transition to a market democracy wasn't occurring, then what did the adoption of "Western" images and rhetoric by the state mean? Should they simply be seen as veils that obscured political and economic interests, invented by the regime to legitimate its interests? If so, what did the images mean for the citizens of Ajaria? What did they suggest for the changing sociopolitical contexts in which they were embedded? The situation in Ajaria vividly showed the paradox that I outlined in the introduction. On the one hand, new flows of images, ideals, goods, and people all suggested changes in political and economic life. On the other hand, the numerous indications of nepotism and state control suggested a continuity with Soviet practices.

This tension was most visible in the construction projects that were (or were claimed to be) carried out by the state. The importance of construction was already visible in the name of Abashidze's political party, the Union of Democratic Revival. Revival (*aghordzineba* in Georgian) had to be taken quite literally, or as one Batumi resident put it: "Revival means building up. With that name they like to show off. They say that while in other regions destruction continues, they do the reverse." In the party's brochures, "revival" was explicitly linked to long lists of new construction projects. The numbers of new churches, schools, houses of culture and hospitals were all mentioned, and the exact height and length of new bridges was proudly described. Pictures of the new soccer stadium, tennis courts, kindergarten, and factories were presented not only in the party brochures but on postcards sold on many street corners.[7] In some cases, construction seemed more important than the actual use of the buildings.

Emptiness

One building project that figured prominently in discussions about progress and development was a new kindergarten. Its central location, near the harbor and on one of the main roads, ensured that this "sign of progress" was highly visible to both the inhabitants of and visitors to Batumi. The kindergarten was only one of the projects being realized in this part of town. In the immediate vicinity many houses and other buildings had been torn down to make way for spacious parks or (still unrealized) new urban construction. The "ultramodern" kindergarten rose above ornate fences, catching the attention of those who passed it. I visited the site with Misha, the architect. The large playground was quiet and peaceful, perhaps because of the large old tree in the

---

7. A visual tour showing many of the mentioned images can be made on the "Official Website of the Ajar Autonomous Republic" at http://www.adjara.gov.ge/eng/gallery2.php>.

middle, perhaps because of the sterility of the new pavement. The building itself was bright white, white being the color of Batumi, as Misha reminded me. The interior was overwhelming. Standing inside the entrance hallway one could see up to the glass ceiling some twenty meters higher. Sunlight shone on the white walls, the marble staircases, and the floors of polished natural stone. In the center of the hallway were several neo-baroque sculptures: Roman images in white marble, decorated with silver and gold.

Both sides of the hallway led to rooms designed for play or sleep, as well as to some other facilities for the children. The dressing rooms had green, red, and yellow lockers for every child. The playroom had German wood floors and contained evenly spaced sets of tables and chairs. Vertical blinds hung in front of double-glass windows. The nap rooms were equally well equipped with wooden beds and colorful bedding. Misha then showed me the other facilities, first the kidney-shaped swimming pool with sea blue tiles, complete with a footbath to be used before entering the dressing rooms. The kitchen was equally well equipped. All the utensils and furnishings were shiny and new. They were imported from Europe, I was told. Misha led the way to the second building.

The second building was a renovated structure that used to be the old kindergarten. Its exterior was less ostentatious, but inside everything that used to be concrete and wood had been covered by marble and natural stone or replaced with plastic and aluminum. The rooms for computer education and the language lab, where children could practice foreign languages with the aid of earphones and instructors, were located here. Last, but not least, we entered the director's rooms. In the center of the main office was a heavy wood desk with a leather couch for the director. Chairs were placed on the sides of the room for visitors. The room led to a private bathroom. Misha explained that the director's room was planned to have its own shower, but that it had been decided that this was not really necessary. Still, the small kitchen and the guestroom made it hard to pity the future director.

According to Misha, the kindergarten was meant as a pedagogical experiment, a place where children could fully develop themselves. The transparency of the building—the large windows and the glass ceiling—were intended to lessen the divide between the rooms and the street, so that children could interact with their surroundings. "This kindergarten," Misha told me when we left the site, "will make sure that the children will be well prepared for life in the new world."

The kindergarten incorporated the newest technology and had many assets intended to prepare children for life in the modern world. This claim was discomforting, however, and my first impression was that the luxuriousness of the rooms, the staff cabinets, and the entrance hall would be more appropriate for an office building than a kindergarten. The computer rooms and the language labs, moreover, hardly seemed useful for children aged four to six. These are all just side remarks and are unimportant due to the simple fact that the kindergarten was devoid of children. None had been admitted since the

Construction on the "ultramodern" kindergarten in Batumi was completed in 1999. The structure nevertheless remained unused when I toured it in August 2001.

construction was completed two years earlier and there were no signs that this
situation would change.[8]

The kindergarten was representative of much of the new construction that
was going on in Ajaria. In all three Ajarian villages where I spent time I stum-
bled on new, yet empty, buildings. In the border village of Sarpi a new shopping center had been erected in 1997 to replace the shabby-looking stalls formerly used by villagers for trading. However, the larger part of this shopping
center remained empty and, due to lack of maintenance, two years later the
first signs of decay were already visible. In the mountain village of Ghorjomi I
regularly passed the new k'ult'uris sakhli (house of culture), which was inaugurated by Aslan Abashidze in 1999 but had never been used since then. In Khulo,
the district center, a new hospital and birth center proudly showed the emblem
of the Revival Party, but medical services continued to be provided in the old
building next to it. In Batumi, not only the kindergarten but also the renovated
university and the "prestigious" business center, Riviera, remained empty.

The emptiness of these buildings was difficult to grasp. Millions of dollars

8. The construction was completed in the summer of 1999. The description is based on visits to the kindergarten in September 2001.

had been spent, but the buildings had no apparent function. Sometimes, the empty buildings seemed simply a result of bad top-down planning. The kindergarten, for example, was not only empty but seemed also unfit for children of the proposed age. Were these buildings then to be understood as the result of centralized decision structures that were in part inherited from the old regime? Even if in some cases one could point to concrete reasons for the delay of their usage, the sheer number of empty buildings prevented one from seeing them simply in terms of bad planning and organizational problems.

Biographies of Emptiness

Construction of the kindergarten started during the summer of 1998 and was completed one year later. Some say the former kindergarten was getting too old or too small to meet the demand. The old kindergarten, which continued to function until 1998, had room for 100 children, only slightly fewer than the 130 children that were supposed to fill the new one. Because the old building housed the most prestigious kindergarten in Batumi, the city council urged the architect to spare it. Misha would have preferred to tear down that building as well, but instead it was renovated. The result was nevertheless satisfactory to him. The new building was constructed where there once was a canteen for workers and several small houses, "more like huts than real houses," Misha added, "so this is a great improvement for the city."

Whose Emptiness?

My first visit to the kindergarten (July 2000) was part of an organized tour for foreign visitors that was intended to show the progress being made in Ajaria and to present its political leadership in the most favorable light. While we walked through the rooms, the tour guide presented her fascinatingly propagandistic explanation. The kindergarten, she said, "is built by our leadership to improve the level of education in Ajaria. As you can see, everything is built according to international standards, using only materials of the highest quality. . . . It represents the great love of our leader, Mister (*Batoni* in Georgian) Aslan Abashidze, for children." In the brochures of the Revival Party, the kindergarten was presented as one of the accomplishments of its rule, thus leaving little doubt as to who should be credited with this achievement. Most people whom I asked about it also told me that it was Abashidze who had financed it, sometimes adding, "Who else has such money anyway?"

However, the issue of financial flow and control over these buildings was more complicated than the answers suggested. In another case, I tried to find out who had financed the renovation of the (not entirely empty) synagogue.[9]

---

9. The synagogue was built at the end of the nineteenth century when Batumi had a Jewish community of approximately one thousand. Because of emigration to Israel and other countries, the Jewish community had decreased to 180 members by 2001.

A hall in the newly renovated University of Batumi. Plastic covers ensure that everything continued to look brand-new, August 2001.

The president of the Jewish association told me that Aslan Abashidze had financed the construction. I asked him carefully if it was Abashidze's money or money from the state budget, or if others may have contributed. His harsh reply made the inappropriateness of that question clear: "Listen, when a friend gives you a wonderful present, would you ask him how he got the money to buy it? Or who had helped him to buy it? Of course not, that would be an insult." The reply indicated that it was better not to ask certain questions in Ajaria, and it also pointed to the personalized nature of politics. This last aspect was even clearer in his subsequent comment: "Besides, even if others would have paid for it, nothing would have been accomplished anyway."

In the case of the kindergarten I was more successful in finding people who were willing to talk about financial matters. Misha had been involved in the whole process of construction and knew the approximate cost of the kindergarten. The project cost a bit over two million dollars. This estimate did not include the price of the land, as the property had been allocated by the city authorities. To my surprise, however, Misha told me that the kindergarten was not financed by the state but had been paid for by the director of the harbor and was intended for the children of harbor employees. The kindergarten, which everyone referred to as a state project, was not financed by the state. In short, it seemed to be a privately owned school.

Despite my own surprise at this discrepancy, those who told me that Abashidze had paid for the school did not act surprised when they learned I had heard evidence to the contrary. It did not seem to matter all that much. A subsequent discussion with a political opponent of Abashidze, whom I had become friends with, made their reactions somewhat clearer to me:

> Maybe the harbor did indeed pay for it, but that tells you very little. What do you think? That the children of the dockworkers and other simple workers will go there? Of course not. Sure, some of the children of the most important people working at the harbor—the director and his staff—will go there, but for the rest they will simply be people of *his* [meaning Abadshidze's] clan. . . . You should understand how this kind of financing works. In the harbor all kinds of rules are violated, and the bosses earn lots of money.[10] Aslan knows that and can therefore easily force them to contribute to this or that project.

This answer was valuable not only because it provided insight into how "state" projects were run but also, and especially, because it called attention to the fuzziness of boundaries between the state and the private sector, and the banality of "using public office for private gain," to quote a classic definition of corruption. Moreover, the official Ajarian state budget was only a fraction of the money circulating through unofficial channels of finance. As a philosopher, who I also befriended, told me:

> On the one hand, we say that there is no money in the budget to finance simple renovations in schools, while, on the other hand, huge amounts are being spent. You know, in a transition period such practices may sometimes be legitimate. [Because] taxes are not being paid, the lost money somehow has to be retrieved. So actually it is money that Aslan Abashidze managed to accumulate outside the budget.

But rather than a temporary transitional practice, the personal relationships seemed to have become the backbone of the state. Nearly all key positions in the state structures were filled through these relationships. This system of allocation was made simpler because the key political and economic institutions—the harbor, the customs offices, and the state security forces—were controlled by a small group of families. Moreover, these families were closely related to one another in a larger kinship-based patronage network; the director of the harbor, for example, was Aslan Abashidze's brother-in-law. In such an environment it is very difficult to determine what belongs to the political and what to the economic domain, something which suggests that the generally problematic differentiation between economics and politics was even less tenable in Ajaria.

So whose emptiness was it? Who controlled the empty kindergarten? Was it the state, the harbor, or Batoni Aslan Abashidze himself? In a way each of the

10. An "oil checker" in the Batumi harbor gave an indication of the scale of profit making. He claimed that in general the measuring of oil shipments allows for 0.5 percent leeway. By measuring very carefully, oil checkers in Batumi were able to make sure that they would always provide 0.5 percent less than stated. The difference added up to approximately $25,000 per ship or $30 million per year.

three answers was partially true. Although officially it was the harbor that paid for the kindergarten, the building was widely recognized to be a state project—in a context where the state was organized along personal lines. One could say that for the time being the buildings were controlled by Aslan Abashidze, but any change in the political environment could bring renewed claims by political structures or by the harbor.[11] This discussion partly reveals how empty buildings need to be understood. Their status or ownership was as unclear as the political-economic context, and as uncertain as the direction of the transition. The emptiness might be understood as a result of an unclear division of responsibilities, or more explicitly as a manifestation of the struggle over political and economic assets.

Why Empty?

The first answers I received to this question were quite predictable. The tour guide told me in 2000 that they were just about to open the kindergarten, thus successfully precluding any further questioning. A year later, the architect claimed that there had been difficulties in finding missing equipment and that a few shortcomings in the design needed to be fixed. Besides that, he argued: "This is Georgia. Here it isn't so easy to find the right materials to finish things off." The architect's answers might seem plausible, but the issue was a bit more complex. First, the same answers had been given a year earlier, when I first became interested in the kindergarten; nevertheless, it had remained empty. Second, if more than two million dollars had been spent on the construction of the kindergarten—which had been completed within a year— why then would it take more than two years to find an additional fifty thousand dollars or so to complete the last details and a few minor repairs?[12] Even if there were reasons for delay, the building itself was obviously more important than its stated future use as a kindergarten.

The nonuse of new public buildings was rarely criticized publicly, but informally people discussed and condemned such practices of the regime.[13] The local intelligentsia and members of the political opposition were most explicit in their criticisms, and it is worthwhile to explore how they explained the fact that public buildings remained empty. The first comment is from Mindia, a history teacher and a fervent, though careful, critic of the regime:

> Actually they wanted to open it last year. But the problem is that this kindergarten will be private. Parents will have to pay five hundred dollars [a year] for their child to attend. Can you imagine? As a teacher I only make three hundred dollars a year.

11. I have no information on what happened to the kindergarten after Aslan Abashidze was ousted from power in May 2004.

12. The absurdity of "missing details" is especially striking when considering the deplorable condition of the vast majority of schools and kindergartens in Ajaria.

13. There was no independent press in Ajaria at the time. The two regional television stations and all regional newspapers were closely linked to the Revival Party.

So the thing is that if they open it, people would realize that this was not built for them but only for his [Abashidze's] own clan.[14] They [the political elite] are afraid of the unrest that this would cause. That is why they keep it closed.

Similar criticisms were common among the former intelligentsia, who had to live on insufficient wages. This group had experienced perhaps the sharpest decline in economic and social status. They used to be able to send their children to the best schools. In their criticisms, bitterness over—and at the same time a fascination with—the new buildings can be detected. Consider the answer of Gia, a lecturer at Batumi University, to the question of why the kindergarten remained closed:

Very simple, they are waiting for his [Abashidze's] grandson Ricardo to reach the age for entering kindergarten. He is now three, so next year they will bring him and open the kindergarten at the same time. The kindergarten has all the modern facilities, so the rich people will all seek to put their children there. Only they can pay the money anyway.

In other words, the emptiness pointed to wealth and the distribution of power in postsocialist Ajaria. What the comment also suggested is that this unequal distribution of power and wealth was seen as inhibiting people from gaining access to the "modern"—and keenly desired—facilities represented by the kindergarten. Irakli, a former spokesman for one of the (marginalized) opposition parties, connected the example more tightly to the issue of morality:

It is empty because it is not built for the people: it is simply there to show off. But, that is between the two of us, don't write about it.[15] Maybe I am not right, but if we take for example the kindergarten, they won't allow us to send our children there because . . . they built it only for themselves. . . . They are provoking us. And because they are afraid that this provocation will turn into rebellion, they keep it empty.

Other critical voices did not try to explain the emptiness but used the issue as just another opportunity to mock the regime. For those who were hit hardest by the recent political and economic changes, the empty buildings symbolized the immorality of the political elite.

All these criticisms were directed at the fact that some benefited unduly from the new projects, but no one criticized the decision to build them in the

---

14. Mindia's use of the Russian word *klan* (clan) did not indicate the existence of a unilineal descent group. He used it to point to the kinship and marriage ties between members of the political and economic elite in Ajaria.

15. Later in our conversation I asked Irakli why the discussion should be kept secret. It struck me as strange because my tape recorder was recording everything with his permission. "It is not for me," he answered, "but for you! You should be thinking about your own perspective as a future specialist on Georgia. Why care about one small article when *he* can make your future work impossible."

first place. None suggested that the money should instead have been divided among the existing kindergartens, to raise the wages of employees or any other alternative. In the end, even the most severe critics agreed with the images to which these new projects pointed. The same Irakli who criticized the government for nepotism told me on another occasion: "Well, at least they are constructing. How and why they build is perhaps less important than the fact that something is being done." Or as Gia told me about the empty hospital and birth center in Khulo, "It is really smart that they constructed a birth center there, because the birth rate is very high in the mountains. I think *that* at least is a real improvement." So, although the manifestation of emptiness raised criticism, the emptiness did not seem to rob the "modern" images of their attractiveness.

However, most of my respondents were not critical at all. They would point out that at least Abashidze tried, that he had given new hope to the population, and that he could not be blamed for the fact that Ajaria was still in a crisis. Besides, people would tell me, "the wages may be low, but at least we receive them at the end of the month, whereas in Tbilisi people wait for years and don't receive anything." Several Batumi residents told me that they felt proud when they walked along the boulevard or through the center. As a school teacher put it: "Here new roads are being built, things are moving forward, and that cannot be said for the rest of Georgia." It almost seemed as if he was convinced that it was just a matter of time before he would benefit from the new economic dynamics as well. His answer resembled a claim that can be heard in almost any discussion of the subject—that "Ajaria is now in a *perekhodnyi period*," a transition period or literally "a period that will pass." Discussions would follow on the riches of their region, the availability of mineral water, the production of citrus fruits and tea—all suggesting that better times could not be far off.[16]

The new buildings were early signs of that turn for the better, of a future of fulfilled dreams. That the buildings were empty was perhaps even a *precondition* for the maintenance of that dream, because as long as they were empty they belonged to the realm of the future and therefore remained potentially accessible to everyone. Empty buildings—emptiness itself—would leave the unevenness of "progress" unseen: empty buildings would not reveal that the kindergarten was only for a select group of people, or that one would have to pay higher fees for medical service than before, or that it was really much more profitable to trade in your own run-down kiosk than to rent brand-new shops owned by the state or by someone allegedly representing it. Indeed, by keeping the future bright and open, emptiness muted criticism of the regime.

---

16. To understand the emphasis on agricultural crops—usually not what first comes to mind when talking about economic riches—tea and citrus fruits had brought wealth during Soviet times, when inhabitants could capitalize on their monopoly of production within the Soviet Union of these luxury items.

The ineffectiveness of criticism was reinforced by another peculiarity. Discussing various stories about and multiple meanings of "emptiness" means by implication that the buildings were not *completely* empty—they were *almost* empty.[17] This consideration was true also in a more literal sense. Although the kindergarten was devoid of the children for whom it purportedly was intended, it was filled with furnishings. The tables and chairs were ready to be used; the beds were neatly arranged and covered with colorful sheets that were aired once in a while by future employees. This seemed to suggest that the children could be expected any day. Aside from the security guards who were always present, the other employees were in the kindergarten only at specific times, to take care of some chores or, probably more important, to guard their own future position in the kindergarten. And of course they were present when it really mattered, when visitors would come to admire the building. The kindergarten thus was *almost* empty, and this reinforced the image of progress. It gave weight to the idea that any day its gates could be opened, and it effectively silenced any criticism of the new construction projects. Keeping the kindergarten *almost* empty thus not only managed to keep the future bright and accessible for everyone, it also tied this future closely to the present. In other words, the imagined transition was going to be completed tomorrow.

Imagining the Future through the Past

The new buildings had overt imaginary qualities, which were important in the creation and continuation of dreams about a future of abundance and leisure. In Ajaria this future often took the form of an imagined return to Europe, where Europe was a symbol of both technological progress and old traditions. Ajarian newspapers frequently talked about European standards that were being met, and the most important square and street of Batumi were renamed ERA Square and ERA Street, referring to the Assembly of European Regions, of which Ajaria had become a member as "the first region in the Caucasus, thus setting an example for the rest of the country."[18] The issues also came up in even the most fleeting conversations. People would ask me when I thought the transition would be completed, whether it would take ten or twenty years. Or they would make apologies for whatever minor inconvenience I might have endured. "Here we don't have civilization yet like in your country," people would tell me. The word *tsivilizatsiia* (civilization) was here employed as a synonym for technological progress. This usage of the word was common among villagers but not among the local intelligentsia, who used the term to refer to the glorious and lengthy past of the Georgian nation. However, both

17. I am indebted to Bonno Thoden van Velzen for suggesting this line of thought to me.
18. From a 1999 brochure of the Center of Democracy and Regionalism in Batumi.

meanings of the word "civilization" seemed to converge in an imagined "return to Europe."

Was it just me who had imagined these dreams? Was it because of my presence that people talked so much about Europe? During conversations with architects about their new building projects I expressed my doubts and asked them why so many new buildings seemed to be influenced by, or were even copies of, European architectural traditions. For them it was not at all an issue. In one interview with two architects I was told the following:

> This has nothing to do with deliberately copying European styles, you know. Simply, when you grow up here you come to appreciate the beauty of certain styles. We use new materials and techniques, but at the same time we want to continue the tradition of the city, and Batumi *is* a European city. . . . If you look at what is being built at the moment you will see much neo-baroque, neoclassical, and also ultramodern building designs. Those are tastes with which we have grown up.

The implicit linking of nineteenth-century Batumi with the present suggests both the eclipsing of time—the neutralization of the Soviet period by reaching back to this European Batumi—as well as a selective reading of the past. In this reading, historical Batumi had come to be only that part of town that was constructed by European oil companies in the 1880s to early 1900s,[19] while the architectural influences of the significant Persian minority and the indigenous Muslim population had been omitted.[20] The new buildings were not simply about economic development but were also about retaining valued Georgian traditions. Europe was an important model for both aspirations: to imagine a future of plenty, and to neutralize or negate Ajaria's Muslim past. These imaginings were represented in the exterior as well as interior designs of the buildings. The architecture showed a reconstruction of a new Europe in Batumi that made it possible to be part of a "modern" and globalizing world without having to accept the inherent plethora of cultural influences that threatened to undermine the sense of collective belonging to which many inhabitants clung. They illustrated a progressive use of "invented tradition" as a means to "reconcile ways in which the past is used as part of political agendas with the way in which people mobilize the past in developing their sense of place and belonging" (Sezneva 2001, 1).

The combination of the elements of imagined abundance and selective readings of the past was easily visible in yet another new building complex. This complex, Riviera, was located not far from the kindergarten in the presti-

---

19. During this period Batumi served as the main conduit for oil exports from the oilfields of Baku and attracted much investment from European companies.

20. This selective reading has been made possible by equally selective destruction during early Soviet rule, which spared the buildings of the European bourgeoisie but tore down those buildings that betrayed Turkish or Persian influences.

The "prestigious" business center and residential complex Riviera was designed to be a showpiece of the success of the Revival Party. Construction was halted because the soil could not support the weight of the complex, August 2001.

gious part of town, at the point where the beach takes a sharp turn and connects to the harbor.[21] The project was financed by the Turkish company Aksoy, but it had been designed by a number of architects from Batumi.

Construction started in 1998, but due to rising costs and sinking soil (caused by the weight of the complex) the construction activities had temporarily been halted. Nevertheless, the huge size of the complex triggered imaginations even in its unfinished stage. No one seemed to be quite certain what Riviera's function would be. Some people said that it was going to be a stock exchange; others believed it would be a showplace commercial center. According to Zviadi, one of the architects, it was going to be a large shopping mall with luxury stores, with the inner part containing apartment buildings for the president (as he used to call Abashidze), his daughter, and those who could afford to buy such apartments.

21. Plans for this project started in 1996 when a contest was held to design a complex that would be representative of the new era. The never-realized prize-winning plans contained futuristic designs combined with exuberant monuments in praise of Abashidze. The final design was developed in 1998 by a group of Batumian architects.

Although it was highly uncertain when or if this "dreamland" would be realized, this did not undermine the reality of the images connected to it. Indeed, just like the "state" projects that had been realized, Riviera had already been completed on postcards, illustrations in books about Batumi, and of course in the brochures of the Revival Party. The complex combined elements of leisure and affluence with architectural forms derived from neoclassicism. The ground level consisted of a kilometer-long, five-sided colonnade that would provide space for shops, restaurants, and cafés. At the side where the complex almost touched the sea the construction of a marina had been planned. Inside the pentagon, above ground level, luxurious and spacious apartment buildings were envisioned. The individual apartments consisted of eight or more rooms, numbers that must have seemed fantastic to most ordinary Batumians.[22] But most interesting perhaps was the portrayal of abundance in the sketches. Every apartment building had its own fitness center and swimming pool, while the open space between the buildings was occupied by a subtropical heaven, an area where you could sunbathe, play tennis or badminton, or drink your cocktails. The people in the drawings of these future dreamlands are especially interesting. The women are suntanned and clad in sexy bikinis; some of them are portrayed with cocktails in their hands or relaxing beside the swimming pool. The men are wearing dark sunglasses and talking on their cell phones, while they or their chauffeurs drive flashy cars of the latest model.

It is difficult not to see these images as the embodiment of the myth of transition, of the dreams of a "modern" life. What made them particularly disturbing—at least from an outsider's perspective—was that this new "modernity" only served the goals of the elite. But because the project was not completed, Riviera and the dreams it represented were still accessible to everyone, an imagined future life of leisure, luxury, and abundance. Most likely, this dream would vanish as soon as the images became reality, except of course for the few who would really be able to drink their cocktails beside the swimming pool between neoclassical castles.

Almost Empty Buildings and the Transition

The new architecture in Ajaria embodied the many facades of modernity and Westernness that spread throughout the post-Soviet republics. But what did these images mean? In post-Soviet Ajaria the transition discourse—with its strong resemblances to the myth of modernity—remained relatively unchallenged. This was true for both the political elite that attempted to use the discourse for its own purposes and the critics who witnessed only corruption, nepotism, and inequality. What the critics challenged was the *discrepancy* between the political reality and the discourse, not the dream of modernity itself.

---

22. Most Batumi residents lived in one- or two-room apartments. Apartments with three or more rooms were considered a luxury.

There was a strong link between the outward transition to modernity and the opacity of social reality. What we saw in Ajaria was "hollow" rhetoric combined with opaqueness concerning political and economic change, which made it possible to present dictatorships as democracy and civil society, and personal monopolies as the forces of the market. What was called transition was actually a process in which the space between images and realities was reconfigured. This uncomfortable space, and the many links that connect the two, needs to be explored to grasp the dynamics of change that took place after socialism.

Mitchell points exactly to such contradictions in his discussion of neoliberalism as a triumph of the political imagination:

> [Neoliberalism's] achievement is double: while narrowing the window of political debate, it promises from this window a prospect without limits. On the one hand it frames public discussion in the ecliptic language of neoclassical economics. . . . On the other, neglecting the actual concern of any concrete local or collective community, neoliberalism encourages the most exuberant dreams of private accumulation—and a chaotic reallocation of collective resources. (1999, 28)

Whereas Mitchell's comments typically deal with the dark side of actual neoliberal policies, in Ajaria it seemed that even the rhetorical and visual adaptation, the seeming adjustment to neoliberal standards, triggered similar results. Chaotic reallocation of collective resources and exuberant private accumulation took place without unraveling the mask of appearance, without destroying the dream of transition.

In this chapter I have looked at the hollowness of new state projects and presented them as the embodiment of this uncomfortable space between reality and discourse. Although the buildings remained empty, their emptiness served important goals and was filled with multiple meanings. Visual forms are, as Handelman has argued, powerful instruments for legitimating authoritarian forms of government (1990), and they fit well with constructing images of modernity. The facades were important for the regime to present Ajaria as a "modern region" moving in the direction of Europe, reviving from its ashes and ready to join the world of "international standards." But although these representations were often accepted, the "emptiness" helped substantiate ideas of conspiracy and corruption in the state, and these were instrumentalized in criticisms of power holders.

However, we have also seen that many people adjusted to these realities and continued to see the buildings as signs of a promising future. Villagers who came to town would see the grandeur of new buildings; town dwellers knew about the hospitals and culture houses built in the mountains. "At least something is being done, at least there is progress. In the future things will be better," many people seemed to be thinking. Moreover, although raising their eyebrows about the uses of the new buildings, many approved the direction of change, which was held to be in the direction of an imagined Europe. Michael Herzfeld discusses a similar issue in his book *Anthropology* (2001), where he stresses both the need and the danger of studying visual forms: "It remains useful—indeed, vital—to remind ourselves that spectacular performances may indeed provide authoritarian regimes with the means to enact an especially pernicious form of visualism—as long as we also remember to look behind the scenes and to catch the knowing winks and cynical frowns of spectators" (2001, 16).

Critics of the regime employed emptiness as a useful tool for pointing at the social and economic inequalities in Ajaria and at the corruptness of the regime. It was highly questionable, though, how effective these "winks and frowns" were in challenging political practices in Ajaria when they were framed within the same ideological language as the facades and hollowness to which they referred. Clearly, the discussions of almost empty buildings could not forecast the future of Ajaria. As we have seen, the emptiness was open to multiple—but not unlimited—interpretations. Potentially it was possible that the buildings would continue to represent an imagined future of abundance, though the emptiness could also become the symbol of the theft of that same dream. It was unclear yet which interpretation eventually would become accepted. Emptiness can be filled and refilled in various ways. In Batumi, it was permeated with contradictory messages and imaginations.

Conclusion:
Borders in Time and Space

The irony of these times . . . is that as actual places and localities become ever more blurred and indeterminate, *ideas* of culturally and ethnically distinct places become perhaps even more salient.
AKHIL GUPTA and JAMES FERGUSON, "Beyond 'Culture': Space, Identity, and the Politics of Difference"

A view from the border highlights the contradictions and imperfections in the grand narratives of nations and states. It shows that the rhetoric of the state becomes problematic at its edges and that along borders nationalizing policies are regularly defeated, ignored, or redirected. The fact that the ideals of the nation are contested at its borders may also be the precise reason for vigorous attempts by the state to "tame" borders and to intensify the dissemination of state ideologies. The changing balance and interlocking of these characteristics—that borders tend to escape state control and therefore attract the close attention of power centers—are crucial in understanding the nature of the divide between (Soviet) Georgia and Turkey, as well as the social and cultural identities that formed around it. To complicate matters, such dialectics also pertain to the relation between the physical and conceptual aspects of borders, as the epigraph indicates. The fall of the iron curtain and renewed movement across the border went hand in hand with increased attempts to defend ideas about self and homeland. Such ironies are reminiscent of Berdahl's statement that in the borderlands ambiguity tends to create clarity (1999, 232). Additionally, and more important, the biography of the Georgian-Turkish border also allows us to analyze how ambiguity and clarity are created, how they act on each other, and moreover, how the paradoxes involved are grounded in lived experience on the border.

The Rigidity of the Iron Curtain

Even when state borders are territorially fixed, their borderlands remain in a state of flux (Driessen 1998, 101; Douglass 1998, 88). These fluctuations in the wider border region have an impact on the nature of the state border with regard to both its physical permeability and its ideological rigidity. Border regions are often described as places where national rhetoric is challenged and where the political penetration of the state is limited. Moreover, according to this view, a state's border tends to be permeable despite the state's efforts to strictly control movement across it. The processes on the Soviet border, however, were markedly different from such depictions. Here the collision of two opposing states and the interaction of state representatives with the border dwellers unleashed forces that made the border virtually impermeable and subjected the lives of local inhabitants to strict control by the state. Consequently, the currently fashionable approach to treat the two sides of a border as an organic whole that differs from the respective centers (Martínez 1994; Baud and Van Schendel 1997, 216) has only limited applicability to the Soviet border.

Border studies have rightly challenged static depictions of national borders by drawing attention to the discrepancy between the rhetoric of central authorities and the actual practices of border dwellers. Whereas central authorities usually present their borders as inviolable dividing lines, border dwellers frequently defeat the geographical and ideological dimensions of borders. This suggests that it may be more fruitful to speak of a "zone of interaction rather than a divide" (Driessen 1992, 190). The discrepancy between border rhetoric and actual behavior can be detected within state structures as well. State authorities may claim to control movement across the border, but in practice they often abstain from exercising such control because of economic or strategic interests (cf. Kearney 1998). In short, whereas national authorities promote the view that the border is a line where different nations, states, or civilizations face each other, in-depth studies reveal that the border is often rather a zone where these "entities" overlap. Related to this discussion is the argument that political penetration is often relatively weak at the edges of the state. Kopytoff argues that there are limits to the "political penetration that the center could achieve both in geographical extent, and locally, in depth" (1987, 29). In some cases this weak hold on border regions may be due to their marginal economic relevance or geographical distance; in other cases the effective control of border regions by authorities is hindered because inhabitants can manipulate and lean on networks that crosscut official boundaries (Blok 1995; Carsten 1998, 232). By crossing the border or by shifting allegiances, border dwellers try to get the best out of the respective states. Such interdependence has perhaps been best expressed by border dwellers living along the Benin-Nigeria border who stated "we are the border" (Flynn 1997).

The often observed ambiguity of state policies concerning border maintenance, the discrepancy between border rhetoric and everyday practice, and the contested nature of state influence hardly applied to the Soviet Georgian–Turkish border. Here, the subversive actions of border dwellers prompted further fortifications of the divide and motivated the state to intensify attempts to mold the region into its own image. The ability and willingness of the Soviet state to exercise brutal force against its citizens was one reason why this divide lost the flexibility and Janus-faced nature often ascribed to borders. It is important to stress, though, that this closure was not the result of a straightforward and uni-directional exercise of power. The actions and reactions of border dwellers played a crucial role in developing the ultimate rigidity of the border.

When the border was initially delineated in the 1920s, the people living in its vicinity were not deeply affected by it. Up to the late 1930s the Ajarians maintained extensive ties with economic and religious centers in Turkey. The Laz of Sarpi continued to marry Turkish citizens, to work their land across the border, and to engage in small-scale cross-border trading. In some ways the border dwellers managed to make use of the differences between the two sides of the political divide. The possibility of doing so stemmed partly from the ambivalent attitudes of political elites toward the border and its inhabi-tants. The Soviet leadership had ambitions of reclaiming the territory the tsarist empire had lost to Turkey after World War I and had therefore an inter-est in keeping the border permeable for propaganda and intelligence activities. Even after the border was closed by the authorities in 1937, the villagers in So-viet Sarpi employed various strategies to maintain contact with the other side. Turkish citizens who married into Soviet Sarpi retained their Turkish pass-ports; others tried to maintain contact by singing and wailing. But these activ-ities backfired on the villagers. Paradoxically, through their subversive actions the border dwellers triggered new responses by the authorities that further de-fined and circumscribed the limits of the possible (cf. Berdahl 1999, 44–71).

The local population was simultaneously an instrument of, and a threat to, state authorities. The combination of instrumentality and suspiciousness re-sulted in extreme anxiety on the part of central authorities about this border and provoked ongoing surveillance of local inhabitants. When ambitions to reclaim part of Turkish territory were abandoned after World War II, Soviet leaders no longer had any interest in keeping the border permeable. The bor-der changed from a contact zone where the influence of the state was con-tested and where the local population retained some tactical power into an ideological divide, which was fortified with military personnel, detection de-vices, and checkpoints. This border impermeability was not simply achieved by decisions made from above. It was the combination of state force and local response as embedded in a culture of secrecy and fear that sealed the border. The unpredictability of the deportations and executions carried out by the state eventually resulted in villagers turning away from the border. The border dwellers avoided looking in the direction of Turkey and took part in civilian border militias that tried to detect and detain illegal border crossers. The resi-dents of Sarpi cooperated closely with the military, who were equally anxious to demonstrate control over the border by placing new fences and detection systems.

Between the 1950s and 1980s the border was, at least from the perspective of local inhabitants, no longer a place where two worlds met but an insurmountable barrier. The physical impermeability was accompanied by the involvement of the state in rewriting and reshaping the history and culture of the region. Moreover, these "impositions" did not remain external schemata detached from reality but became tightly interwoven with local life. The grounding of these "impositions" suggests why identities remained fixed after the socialist collapse.

Frozen Histories and Fixed Cultures

A persistent view in Western discourse, in the media as well as academia, is that Soviet rule held pre-Soviet identities in cold storage. In essence, this "cold storage" view asserts that previously held religious, ethnic, and national identities were repressed—but not eradicated—by Communist rule and that as soon as the "Soviet freeze" ended preexisting loyalties and tensions returned with renewed force.[1] For example, Castells writes that "Soviet experience is a testimony to the perdurability of nations beyond, and despite, the state" (1997, 41). Ironically, in his wide-ranging trilogy on *The Information Age* Castells draws explicitly on the Ajarian case to back his claim (39–41). For him, the "fact" that Ajarians did not on the whole aim at separation from Georgia proved his theory that "when people were finally able to express themselves in the 1980s" they returned to the "only source of identity that was kept in the collective memory: *national identity* (1997, 41, emphasis in original). The problem with this perspective is not only that it violates the history of Ajaria—inhabitants of Ajaria did not identify with the Georgian nation prior to 1917—but also that it fails to see how ethnic and national categories were created, molded, and contested by both the Soviet regime and its citizens.

Partly in reaction to the "cold storage" view, several social scientists have argued that the collapse of the Soviet Union left behind a cultural, social, and political "vacuum" that was filled with invented or reinvented histories. These social scientists see the rise of the primacy of cultural identity in the former Soviet Union as a way to "overcome socialism," and "invented histories" as strategic responses of elite groups to create and promote new national identities (Rupnik 1996, 53–54). The attraction of the pre-Soviet past is thus explained by the "ideological vacuum" that arose after Communism. The danger in this kind of explanation is that it presents the new era as an absolute new beginning, a view that violates the complex flow of memory, community, and culture in which people live their lives (cf. Lampland 2000, 210). Instead of assuming that forms of identity miraculously survived Soviet rule, or that they were willfully invented after the Soviet collapse, as the "cold storage" and "vac-

---

1. Phrases such as "the question of identity is clearly the most insistent to have surfaced after the long freeze" (Hooson 1994, 140) or arguments that describe conflict in the Caucasus as the "opening of old ethnic wounds" (Zverev 1996, 13) characterize this "cold storage" view.

uum" theories respectively do, it is crucial to analyze how these forms of identity were shaped and modified to fit changing social and political contexts.

The Ajarian paradox is that its inhabitants did *not* on the whole "return" to pre-Soviet identities, although they did mobilize pre-Soviet history to give meaning to the present. Many inhabitants of Sarpi and Khulo did not "return" to Islam—the religion of their parents and grandparents—but instead converted to Christianity. They justified this action, in part, by presenting it as a continuation of the missionary work that Saint Andrew commenced in the first century AD. The Laz of Sarpi did not attempt to reconstruct their community's appearance before Soviet rule but turned instead to much deeper pasts. Their "Colchian origins" and the presumed union of Laz and Georgians in classical times were crucial aspects in their discussions about what being Laz entailed. In Batumi, the ruling elite drew credibility for its claims to build a future of abundance by bolstering images of a nineteenth-century European Batumi. These "European" images shifted attention away from the economic and political asymmetries produced by the ruling elite. Moreover, the images fed on the dream of the region's reconnection to Europe. These and other "inventions of tradition" may indicate the richness of the past as a source for creating a meaningful present, but this should not prevent us from exploring how past and present are connected.

The "pre-Soviet" referents for identity had their own genealogies; they were, more often than not, actively produced and popularized during the Soviet period. Indeed, I suggest that the pre-Soviet past is important as a reference for identity not *despite* Soviet rule but, on the contrary, *because* of the Soviet need to classify, categorize, and construct its population along historical and territorial lines. To reiterate an argument that has been developed in earlier chapters, the attitude of the Soviet state to questions of culture and ethnicity reverberated between two trends—one of diversity, the other of uniformity. In public speeches, Communist leaders rarely failed to pay lip service to the Leninist expectation that Soviet rule would result in the creation of a distinct Soviet people, but it became clear with time that the government was not looking to erase all ethnic or cultural differences. Instead of fighting nationalism and ethnicity as organizing principles, Soviet rule attempted to mold cultural expressions and referents in specific ways. As Hann observes, "The discourses and practices of socialism and nationalism have often proved compatible" (1993), not least because identity politics were modified and changed while traveling from the federal center to local settings.

The stated intention of many cultural policies of the Soviet regime was that cultural manifestations could be "national in form" while being "socialist in content." That is, new rituals and ceremonies as well as literary and scholarly publications were allowed to feature national or ethnic characteristics, but these characteristics had to be embedded in the more important moral messages about the universal laws of history, the brotherhood of nations, and the leading role of the working class. This combination of nationalist and socialist rhetoric materialized in at least two different ways. As was pointed out in the discussion of the Colkhoba festival, local actors could appropriate socialist elements to dress up expressions of ethnic and national sentiment. In hindsight, they described the socialist aspects as obligatory formal procedures that had corrupted their "authentic" traditions. But whereas in some instances the combination of "nationalist" and "socialist" was employed to enhance local expressions of culture, this same combination was also instrumental in the enforcement and legitimization of extralocal nationalist assimilation policies. The Soviet ideal of state atheism was frequently used by regional and national authorities to combat cultural forms or expressions that were perceived as incompatible with Georgian nationality (especially those pertaining to Islam) as well as to rewrite the region's history along explicitly Georgian lines.

In short, the "national forms" did not reappear after a Soviet freeze but were actively shaped during the seventy years of socialism. Although the inhabitants of Ajaria created their identities, they did so under the constraints imposed by socialist rule and the limits set by an impermeable curtain. When, in the wake of the Soviet collapse, people reached back to images of a pre-Soviet past, they drew on messages of ethnic and cultural primordiality with which they had become thoroughly familiar in Soviet times.

As the Soviet Union recedes into the past and its messages are increasingly dismissed as a historical anomaly by local elites and Western observers alike, the impact of the Soviet period on cultural formations remains poorly understood (cf. Bonnett 2002). In this book I have shown how life went on along the Soviet border and, moreover, how the inhabitants shaped their lives in interaction with the policies and ideals of the state. I have drawn attention to the "hidden histories" of people who lived on the edge of the Soviet Union, histories that were increasingly obscured by the need to freeze or forget the Soviet past. Although I have aimed to show that people are as much products as producers of history, it is essential to recognize that being a product of Soviet history—to whatever degree—was not something inhabitants of Ajaria would easily admit to.

In Ajarian publications that appeared after 1991 reference to the period between the 1920s and 1980s is absent. Historical textbooks, political pamphlets, Church histories, as well as books on urban development and architecture by and large omit the seventy years of Communist rule. Soviet history is left out and ignored, reduced to a few sentences that textually bridge seven decades. One reason the Soviet past is dismissed has just been mentioned—the Soviet past shows too clearly the limits and incongruities of primordial ideas of identity. Freezing the socialist past is not, however, limited to discourses of ethnic and cultural identity. As Verdery argues, the process of "writing the communist past out of history" is part of the political project to put local history back on the "progressive track" of capitalism (1999, 112; 1996). Or, as Wedel explains, socialism is often understood as deviating from "natural" Western history, as a case of "misdevelopment" unavoidably running into a dead end (Wedel 2001, 21). The practice of the political elite and the Christian clergy of presenting the 1990s as a period of "resurrection" and "revival" indicates that they saw it as a period that would reconnect the region and its inhabitants to the "normal course of history." This normal course of history ties in with dominant ideas about the pre-Soviet past; it connects the region tightly with Christian history and promises a "return to Europe."

Because the Communist past could no longer be presented as a stage in the "development" of the region, it was left out of historical narratives. In addition, the Soviet past was also potentially destabilizing. Put simply, the Soviet past could not be presented as an unambiguous period of repression, because the memories of compliance with the regime were still too fresh. This was true for elite groups as well as for many ordinary citizens. People had adjusted to the rigidities of the Soviet regime and had developed their own ways of dealing with its structures. In other words, they had not been "outside the system" but had been tightly embedded in its structures. Leaders in postsocialist Ajaria, many of whom used to have significant positions in the Soviet state apparatus, needed to legitimize their rule by stressing their differences with Soviet rule. Residents of Sarpi had actively participated in the maintenance of the iron curtain, but after the opening of that border they felt a need to present their experience as instances of unambiguous victimhood. The Soviet past was obviously discomforting. It needed to remain frozen until it became "a foreign country" (cf. Lowenthal 1985) that could be studied and analyzed without undermining the sense of self.

Distant Neighbors and Immediate Dangers

Soviet rule did not simply repress culture or hold social identities in the grip of permafrost but provided tools to fix and channel ideas about culture in ways that continued to be influential after the collapse of the Soviet state. The discussion so far has illustrated how peoples' frames of reference changed. It has shown why Ajarians were likely to adopt Christian Georgian identities, why Laz stressed their connections to the Georgian nation, and why inhabitants of Batumi perceived their city as European.

However, this historical analysis does not explain why, *in the border region*, these ideas came to be so vigorously defended. Three factors may explain why the ideas dominant during socialism were reinforced after the collapse of the Soviet Union and the opening of the border. First, recent sociopolitical changes made the coexistence of multiple identities problematic. Second, new cross-border contacts involved confrontations with unexpected differences and unwanted resemblances that reinforced the need to set boundaries between self and other. Third, dominant ideas proved important in preserving the dreams of modernity that were challenged by the realities of postsocialist change.

Although public life in Ajaria had become well attuned to Soviet Georgian ideals, "hidden ambiguities" remained. For example, although in Ajaria Islam largely disappeared from the public sphere it remained important as a personal haven. Similarly, the Laz of Sarpi, although effectively integrated into the wider Soviet Georgian society, continued to value their ties to Laz in Turkey and looked forward to times when contact could be reestablished. After the collapse of the Soviet Union these "hidden ambiguities" initially seemed to enrich the available options of combining and constructing new forms of social and cultural identity. Indeed, the ad hoc conversions of Ajarians in the early 1990s, the numerous visits between cross-border relatives right after the border opening, as well as the initial opportunities for transnational trade all seemed to point to hybridizations of culture that transcended and overcame the rigidities of the Soviet border. But with time, instead of hybridization a hardening of cultural and social boundaries came about. The dominant ideas that had crystallized during the preceding decades were challenged by the new visibility of "hidden ambiguities," as this visibility undermined their cultivated naturalness.

As Hall writes, "The concept of identity does *not* signal that stable core of the self, unfolding from beginning to end through all the vicissitudes of history without change; the bit of the self which remains always-already 'the same,' identical to itself across time" (1996, 3). Nevertheless, cultural, religious, and ethnic discourses derive their strength and attractiveness from the belief that such stable cores do exist. The return of hidden ambiguities in the 1990s posed a threat to religious, ethnic, and national identities because it drew attention to the absence of these "cores" and brought unwanted connotations to the center of attention. This demanded clarification of what it meant to be a Muslim or a Christian, of what the differences were between Turks and Laz, and of how a category like "European" connected to Ajaria. The construction of new boundaries can consequently be seen as an effort to purify identity and to conceal those features that reveal the absence of a stable and timeless core.

Cultural identity is threatened most severely when challenges are unexpected and come from what is near (Blok 2001, 123). It is not difference per se but the social context within which people confront difference *or* resemblance that matters. With the reappearance of Islam in the public domain, the assumed differences between Ajaria and Turkey became blurred. This provoked the intelligentsia and political elites of Ajaria to intensify their claims about the Christian and Georgian roots of the region. When inhabitants of Sarpi reestablished contact with their cross-border kin, the shared Laz identity they had assumed turned out to be absent. This motivated Sarpi residents to reinforce ideas about "pure" Laz identity, contrasting them with ideas that existed across the border. The changes in the relationship between social actors made the experienced differences and resemblances immediate and problematic, activating mechanisms that triggered new social tensions.

The ambiguities also tended to threaten ideas people had about their future. Before the Soviet collapse, inhabitants of Ajaria saw themselves as more developed than their Turkish neighbors, while Batumians thought of their city as a typical European town. The breakdown of the local economy and the realization that across the border standards of living were higher was frustrating and problematic because it undermined the ideas Ajarians had of themselves in relation to Turkey. The discrepancies did not automatically mean that people abandoned their dreams. The dream about modernity and progress was too precious to be abandoned. Indeed, the dream was vital in dealing with impoverishment and economic insecurities. Moreover, the dream was used by local elites to legitimize their rule. To rectify the disparity between "dream" and "reality," the dislocations of postsocialism were often blamed on the "immediate other," notably Turkey. The renewed importance of cultural identity created its own contradictions and rigidities. After socialism people had to reposition themselves vis-à-vis religion and ethnicity, and straddle the connections between those categories. My respondents often needed to make unambiguous choices concerning where they did and did not belong. In elaborating on perceived and experienced differences they also set new social and cultural boundaries.

The ideas that were so vigorously defended—dreams about the West, the Georgian national ideal, Christian roots—had not been part of Communist ideology, but they had developed as a consequence of Soviet rule. Such ideas had become part and parcel of everyday life, of how people went about defining themselves and others. The disappearance of these "Soviet certainties" meant that people were forced to reconsider the very basis of self. When religion returned to the public sphere, when ethnic kin from across the border appeared on one's doorstep, and when ideas about progress were challenged by the realities of postsocialist change, combinations of identities became increasingly problematic. The imagined primal unity of Georgian nationality and Christianity was challenged by the renewed visibility of Islam in Ajaria. Ideas about Laz identity that had developed throughout the Soviet period were in danger of becoming "contaminated" by Turkish influences. The ideas about and hopes for a "modern" future were shattered with the actual opening of markets and the disillusionment about goods and economic opportunities. Answers to these challenges were found by suppressing or renouncing certain layers of identification. What happened in all three cases was that imperfections or incongruities in ideas of "self" and "other" were brought to the center of attention, thereby challenging previously held notions and moral maps.

Defending the Border

The nature of the Georgian-Turkish border changed dramatically during the 1990s. Oppositions between Islam and state atheism, between capitalism and socialism, and between cold war enemies disappeared from official rhetoric and political practice. Instead the governments of Georgia and Turkey started to display a favorable attitude toward each other and repeatedly expressed the need for cooperation in the new transnational economy. Changes in government rhetoric and renewed border permeability did not mean, however, that the contrasting dimensions had simply evaporated. Although the border had become easier to cross than before, it continued to regulate movement and communication in ways that could not have been anticipated beforehand. In the midst of new dangers, the inhabitants created new divides, fortified them with stereotypes, and solidified them with ethnicized versions of culture and religion. These processes had the paradoxical effect of creating a contemporary divide that in some regards was more impermeable than the Iron Curtain had been.

The fortification of identity offers an important antidote to views of hybridity and intermingling on and across state borders. It suggests that in a world that is characterized by transnational contact and the absence of grand ideological divides between states, it may be cultural boundaries that become more rigid and less permeable. Instead of seeing the situation that emerged after the Soviet Union collapsed as a "vacuum" in which new ideologies could freely compete, it is more useful to see the 1990s as a phase in which the restructuring of ideology and power allowed for specific modes of identification. Ironically, in a situation where the border regime relaxed and cold war enmities ceased to exist, the differences between people on both sides of the border did not diminish. Instead, the former cold war border became more "truly" a divide between Islam and Christianity, Georgians and Turks, and Asia and Europe. I suggest that the largest paradox of the Soviet border is exactly this: the Soviet Union did not effectively erase its borderland ambiguities, but its fall sparked incentives to fortify and essentialize the cultural boundaries it produced.

Bibliography

Abashidze, A. Kh. 1998. *Adzhariia: Istoriia, diplomatiia, mezhdunarodnoe pravo*. Moscow: RAU Universitet.

Abbott, Andrew. 2001. *Time Matters: On Theory and Method*. Chicago: University of Chicago Press.

Ach'aris mkharedmtsod muzeumi (AMM). 1900–1917. "Materialy o panislamistskom ili pantiurkitskom dvizhenii sredi naseleniia Adzharii." Russian Series, no. 50.

Adler, Nanci. 1999. "Life in the 'Big Zone': The Fate of Returnees in the Aftermath of Stalinist Repression." *Europe-Asia Studies* 51 (1): 5–20.

Agadjanian, Alexander. 2001. "Public Religion and the Quest for National Ideology: Russia's Media Discourse." *Journal for the Scientific Study of Religion* 30, no. 3: 351–66.

Akiner, Shirin. 1983. *Islamic Peoples of the Soviet Union*. London: Kegan Paul.

Akhvlediani, Kh. 1941. "Kratkii istoricheskii obzor Adzharii." Ach'aris mkharedmtsod muzeumi, Russian Series, no. 25.

Allen, W. E. D. 1929. "The March-Lands of Georgia." *Geographical Journal* 74: 135–56.

Allen, W. E. D., and P. Muratoff. 1953. *Caucasian Battlefields: A History of the Wars on the Turco-Caucasian Border, 1828–1921*. Nashville: Battery Press.

Alvarez, R. A., Jr. 1995. "The Mexican-U.S. Border: The Making of an Anthropology of Borderlands." *Annual Review of Anthropology* 24: 447–70.

Andrews, Peter A., ed. 2002. *Ethnic Groups in the Republic of Turkey*. Wiesbaden: Dr. Ludwig Reichert Verlag.

Anderson, John. 1994. "Islam in the Soviet Archives: A Research Note." *Central Asian Survey* 13, no. 3: 383–94.

Appadurai, Arjun. 1986. "Introduction: Commodities and the Politics of Value." In *The Social Life of Things: Commodities in Cultural Perspective*, edited by A. Appadurai, 1–63. Cambridge: Cambridge University Press.

Arslanian, Artin H. 1996. "Britain and the Transcaucasian Nationalities during the Russian Civil War." In *Transcaucasia, Nationalism, and Social Change: Essays in the History of Armenia, Azerbaijan, and Georgia*, edited by Ronald Suny, 295–306. Ann Arbor: University of Michigan Press.

Aves, Jonathan. 1996. *Georgia: From Chaos to Stability?* London: Royal Institute of International Affairs.

Bakradze, D. 1878. *Arkheologicheskoe puteshestvie po Gruzii i Achare.* St. Petersburg: Imperatorskaia Akademiia Nauk.

Bakradze, Rezo. 1971. *Sabch'ota sarpi.* Batumi: Sabch'ota Ach'ara.

Ball, Alan M. 1987. *Russia's Last Capitalists: The Nepmen, 1921–1929.* Berkeley: University of California Press.

Ballinger, Pamela. 2004. "'Authentic Hybrids' in the Balkan Borderlands." *Current Anthropology* 45, no. 1: 31–60.

Baramidze, Irak'li. 1996. "Muhajiroba da muhajirobastan dak'avshirebuli p'olit'ik'uri protsesebi samkhret-dasavlet sakartveloshi: Mizezebi da sotsialuri asp'ekt'ebi (XIX s. 70–80–iani ts'lebi)." In *K'ult'urologiuri da ist'oriul-etnograpiuli dziebani sakartveloshi,* edited by D. Khakhutashvili and V. Shamiladze, 107–26. Batumi: Gamomtsemloba Ach'ara.

Barth, Frederick. 1969. Introduction to *Ethnic Groups and Boundaries: The Social Organization of Culture Difference,* edited by F. Barth, 9–38. Boston: Little, Brown.

———. 1994. "Enduring and Emerging Issues in the Analysis of Ethnicity." In *The Anthropology of Ethnicity: Beyond 'Ethnic Groups and Boundaries',* edited by H. Vermeulen and C. Govers, 11–32. Amsterdam: Het Spinhuis.

Baud, Michiel, and Willem van Schendel. 1997. "Toward a Comparative History of Borderlands." *Journal of World History* 8, no. 2: 211–42.

Bellér-Hann, Ildiko. 1995. "Myth and History on the Eastern Black Sea Coast." *Central Asian Survey* 14, no. 4: 487–508.

Bellér-Hann, Ildiko, and Chris Hann. 2001. *Turkish Region: State, Market and Social Identities on the East Black Sea Coast.* Oxford: James Currey.

Bennigsen, Alexandre, and S. Enders Wimbush. 1985. *Muslims of the Soviet Empire: A Guide.* London: Hurst.

Benninghaus, Rüdiger. 2002. "Zur Herkunft und Identität der Hemşinli." In *Ethnic Groups in the Republic of Turkey,* edited by P. Andrews, 475–97. Wiesbaden: Dr. Ludwig Reichert Verlag.

Berdahl, Daphne. 1999. *Where the World Ended: Re-unification and Identity in the German Borderland.* Berkeley: University of California Press.

Bibileishvili, I., and N. Mgeladze. 2000. "Pirvelad didach'arashi." *Ach'ara* (Batumi), 24–30 August 2000.

Birina, A. V., ed. 1956. *Gruzinskaia SSR: Ekonomiko-geograficheskaia kharakteristika.* Moscow: Izdatel'stvo Akademii Nauk SSSR.

Bloch, Alexia. 2003. *Red Ties and Residential Schools: Indigenous Siberians in a Post-Soviet State.* Philadelphia: University of Pennsylvania Press.

Blok, Anton. 1995. *De Bokkerijders: Roversbenden en geheime genootschappen in de landen van Overmaas, 1730–1744.* Amsterdam: Ooievaar.

———. 2001. *Honour and Violence.* Cambridge: Polity.

Bonnett, Alastair. 2002. "Communists Like Us: Ethnicized Modernity and the Idea of 'the West' in the Soviet Union." *Ethnicities* 2, no. 4: 435–67.

Borenstein, Eliot. 1999. "Suspending Disbelief: 'Cults' and Postmodernism in Post-Soviet Russia." In *Consuming Russia: Popular Culture, Sex, and Society since Gorbachev,* edited by A. Barker, 437–62. Durham: Duke University Press.

Borneman, John. 1992. *Belonging in the Two Berlins: Kin, State, Nation.* Cambridge: Cambridge University Press.

Bornstein, Avram. 2002. *Crossing the Green Line between the West Bank and Israel.* Philadelphia: University of Pennsylvania Press.

Bourdeaux, Michael. 1995. Introduction to *The Politics of Religion in Russia and the New States of Eurasia,* edited by M. Bourdeaux, 3–12. Armonk, N. Y.: M. E. Sharpe.

Braudel, Fernand. 1976. *The Mediterranean and the Mediterranean World in the Age of Philip II.* Translated by S. Reynolds. Glasgow: Fontana Press.

Bringa, Tone. 1995. *Being Muslim the Bosnian Way: Identity and Community in a Central Bosnian Village*. Princeton: Princeton University Press.

Broers, Laurence. 2001. "Who Are the Mingrelians? Language, Identity, and Politics in Western Georgia." Paper presented at the sixth annual convention of the Association for the Study of Nationalities, April 2001, Columbia University, New York.

———. 2002. "Tolerance and Mission: Strands of Messianic Thought in Georgian Nationalism." Paper presented at the seventh annual convention of the Association for the Study of Nationalities, April 2002, Columbia University, New York.

Bugai, N. F., and A. M. Gonov. 1998. *Kavkaz: Narody v eshelonakh (20–60–e gody)*. Moscow: Insan.

Burawoy, Michael, and Pavel Krotov. 1992. "The Soviet Transitions from Socialism to Capitalism: Worker Control and Economic Bargaining in the Wood Industry." *American Sociological Review* 57, no. 1: 16–38.

Burawoy, Michael, and Katherine Verdery, eds. 1999. *Uncertain Transition: Ethnographies of Change in the Postsocialist World*. Lanham, Md.: Rowman and Littlefield.

Caldwell, Melissa. 2002. "The Taste of Nationalism: Food Politics in Postsocialist Moscow." *Ethnos* 67, no. 3: 295–319.

Carsten, Janet. 1998. "Borders, Boundaries, Tradition and State on the Malaysian Periphery." In *Border Identities: Nation and State at International Frontiers*, edited by T. Wilson and H. Donnan, 215–36. Cambridge: Cambridge University Press.

Casanova, José. 1994. *Public Religions in the Modern World*. Chicago: University of Chicago Press.

Castells, Manuel. 1997. *The Information Age: Economy, Society and Culture*, vol. 2, *The Power of Identity*. Oxford: Blackwell.

Chanturia, V. 1932. "Magometanskaia sistema shkol'nogo prosveshcheniia." Ach'aris mkharedmtsod muzeumi, Russian Series, no. 20.

Chavchavadze, I. 1955. "Osmalos sakartvelo." In I. Chavchavadze, *Tq'zulebata sruli k'redebuli at tomad*, vol. 6. Tbilisi: Sakartvelos sotsialist'uri resp'ublik'is gamomtsemloba.

Chavleishvili, Murad. 1989. "K voprosu ob avtonomii Adzharii." *Sovetskaia Adzhariia* (Batumi), 21 July 1989.

Ch'ich'inadze, Zakaria. 1915. *Kartvelebis gamakhmadianeba any kartvelt gatatreba*. Tbilisi: N.p.

Cole, John W., and Eric R. Wolf. 1974. *The Hidden Frontier: Ecology and Ethnicity in an Alpine Valley*. New York: Academic Press.

Conquest, Robert. 1970. *The Nation Killers: The Soviet Deportation of Nationalities*. London: Macmillan.

Cornell, Svante E. 2002. "Autonomy as a Source of Conflict: Caucasian Conflicts in Theoretical Perspective." *World Politics* 54: 254–76.

Cornwall, J. H. M. 1923. "The Russo-Turkish Boundary and the Territory of Nakhichevan." *Geographical Journal* 61: 445–49.

Creed, Gerald. 2002. "(Consumer) Paradise Lost: Capitalist Dynamics and Disenchantment in Rural Bulgaria." *Anthropology of East Europe Review* 20, no. 2: 119–25.

Crego, Paul. 1996. "Wende zum Gottesstaat: Religiöser Nationalismus in Georgien nach 1989." *Glaube 2 Welt* 24, no. 3: 26–29.

Darchiashvili, David. 1996. "Adzharia—perekrestok tsivilizatsia." Working Paper. Tbilisi: Caucasus Institute for Peace, Democracy, and Development.

Darchiashvili, David, and Tamara Pataraia. 2001. "Vozvrashchenie v Evropu? Nekotorye aspekty orientatsii sistemy bezopasnosti Gruzii." *Tsentral'naia Aziia i Kavkaz* 1, no. 13: 64–77.

Das, Veena, and Deborah Poole. 2004. "State and Its Margins: Comparative Ethnographies." In *Anthropology in the Margins of the State*, edited by V. Das and D. Poole, 3–33. Santa Fe, N.M.: School of American Research Press.

Davitadze, Sh., and P. Khalvashi. 1986. *Adzhariia*. Moscow: Izdatel'stvo Planeta.

Davitaia, F. F., ed. 1967. *Sovetskii Soiuz: Geograficheskoe opisanie v 22 tomakh. Gruziia.* Moscow: Mysl'.

Derluguian, Georgi M. 1995. "The Tale of Two Resorts: Abkhazia and Ajaria before and since the Soviet Collapse." Working Paper 6.2. Berkeley: University of California, International and Area Studies.

Donnan, Hastings, and Thomas M. Wilson. 1999. *Borders: Frontiers of Identity, Nation and State.* Oxford: Berg.

Donnan, Hastings, and Dieter Haller. 2000. "Liminal No More: The Relevance of Borderland Studies." *Ethnologia Europaea* 30, no. 2: 7–22.

Douglass, Willam A. 1998. "A Western Perspective on an Eastern Interpretation of Where North Meets South: Pyrenean Borderland Cultures." In *Border Identities: Nation and State at International Frontiers,* edited by T. Wilson and H. Donnan, 62–95. Cambridge: Cambridge University Press.

Dragadze, Tamara. 1988. *Rural Families in Soviet Georgia: A Case Study in Ratcha Province.* London: Routledge.

—— 1993. "The Domestication of Religion under Soviet Communism." In *Socialism: Ideals, Ideologies, and Local Practice,* edited by C. Hann, 148–56. London: Routledge.

Driessen, Henk. 1992. *On the Spanish-Moroccan Frontier: A Study in Ritual, Power and Ethnicity.* Oxford: Berg.

——. 1996. "What Am I Doing Here? The Anthropologist, the Mole, and Border Ethnography." In *Ethnologie Europas: Grenzen. Konflikte. Identitäten,* edited by W. Kokot and D. Dracklé, 287–98. Berlin: Dietrich Reimer Verlag.

——. 1998. "The 'New Immigration' and the Transformation of the European-African Frontier." In *Border Identities: Nation and State at International Frontiers,* edited by T. Wilson and H. Donnan, 96–116. Cambridge: Cambridge University Press.

Dumbadze, Nodar. 1986. "Ne boisia mama!" In *Sobranie sochinenii v dvukh tomakh,* vol. 1: 457–637. Translated from Georgian into Russian by Z. Akhvlediani. Tbilisi: Izdatel'stvo Merani.

Epstein, Mikhail. 1995. "Response: 'Post-' and Beyond." *Slavic and East European Journal* 39, no. 3: 357–66.

Fairbanks, Charles H., Jr. 1996. "Clientelism and the Roots of Post-Soviet Disorder." In *Transcaucasia, Nationalism, and Social Change: Essays in the History of Armenia, Azerbaijan, and Georgia,* edited by Ronald Suny, 341–74. Ann Arbor: University of Michigan Press.

Ferguson, James. 1999. *Expectations of Modernity: Myths and Meanings of Urban Life on the Zambian Copperbelt.* Berkeley: University of California Press.

Feurstein, Wolfgang. 1992. "Mingrelisch, Lazisch, Swanisch: Alte Sprachen und Kulturen der Kolchis vor dem baldigen Untergang." In *Caucasian Perspectives,* edited by G. Hewitt, 285–328. Munich: Lincom Europa.

Filatov, Sergei. 1998. "Tatarstan: At the Crossroads of Islam and Orthodoxy." *Religion, State & Society* 26, nos. 3–4: 265–77.

Fitzpatrick, Sheila. 1999. *Everyday Stalinism: Ordinary Life in Extraordinary Times; Soviet Russia in the 1930s.* New York: Oxford University Press.

Flynn, Donna K. 1997. "'We Are the Border': Identity, Exchange, and the State along the Benin-Nigeria Border." *American Ethnologist* 24, no. 2: 311–30.

Freedom House. 2001. *Nations in Transit, 1999–2000: Civil Society, Democracy, and Markets in East Central Europe and the Newly Independent States,* edited by A. Karatnycky, A. Motyl, and A. Piano. New Brunswick, N.J.: Transaction Publishers.

Fuller, Elizabeth. 1986. "Islam in Adzharia." *Radio Free Europe/Radio Liberty* 221/86: 1–4.

——. 1993. "Aslan Abashidze: Georgia's Next Leader?" *RFE/RL Research Report* 2, no. 44: 23–26.

Gachechiladze, Revaz. 1995. *The New Georgia: Space, Society, Politics.* London: UCL Press.

Geladze, A. 1969. "Zemo ach'arashi mahmadianobis gavrtselebis zogierti sak'itkhisatvis." *K'olekt'iuri shroma* (Khulo), 10 September 1969.

Gingrich, Andre. 1998. "Frontier Myths of Orientalism: The Muslim World in Public and Popular Cultures of Central Europe." In *Mediterranean Ethnological Summer School,* vol. 2, edited by B. Baskar and B. Brumen, 99–128. Ljubljana: Inštitut za multikulturne raziskave.

Grant, Bruce. 1995. *In the Soviet House of Culture: A Century of Perestroikas.* Princeton: Princeton University Press.

Greeley, Andrew. 1994. "A Religious Revival in Russia." *Journal for the Scientific Study of Religion* 33, no. 3: 253–72.

Gökay, Bülent. 1997. *A Clash of Empires: Turkey between Russian Bolshevism and British Imperialism, 1918–1923.* London: Tauris Academic Studies.

Gupta, Akhil, and James Ferguson. 1992. "Beyond 'Culture': Space, Identity, and the Politics of Difference." *Cultural Anthropology* 17, no. 1: 6–23.

Hale, William. 1996. "Turkey, the Black Sea and Transcaucasia." In *Transcaucasian Boundaries,* edited by J. Wright, S. Goldenberg, and R. Schofield, 54–70. London: UCL Press.

Hall, Stuart. 1998. "Who Needs 'Identity?'" In *Questions of Cultural Identity,* edited by S. Hall and P. du Gay, 1–11. London: Sage.

Handelman, Don. 1977. "The Organization of Ethnicity." *Ethnic Groups* 1: 187–200.

———. 1990. *Models and Mirrors: Towards an Anthropology of Public Events.* Cambridge: Cambridge University Press.

Hann, C. M. 1993. "Introduction: Social Anthropology and Socialism." In *Socialism: Ideals, Ideologies, and Local Practice,* edited by C. Hann, 1–26. London: Routledge.

———. 1997. "The Nation-State, Religion, and Uncivil Society: Two Perspectives from the Periphery." *Daedalus* 126, no. 2: 27–45.

———. 2000. "Problems with the (De)Privatization of Religion." *Anthropology Today* 16, no. 6: 14–20.

———. ed. 2002. *Postsocialism: Ideals, Ideologies and Practices in Eurasia.* London: Routledge.

Hann, C. M., and I. Bellér-Hann. 1992. "Samovars and Sex on Turkey's Russian Markets." *Anthropology Today* 8, no. 4: 3–6.

———. 1998. "Markets, Morality and Modernity in Northeast Turkey." In *Border Identities: Nation and State at International Frontiers,* edited by T. Wilson and H. Donnan, 237–62. Cambridge: Cambridge University Press.

Harrison, Simon. 2003. "Cultural Difference as Denied Resemblance: Reconsidering Nationalism and Ethnicity." *Comparative Studies in Society and History* 45, no. 2: 343–61.

Herzfeld, Michael. 2001. *Anthropology: Theoretical Practice in Culture and Society.* Oxford: Blackwell.

Hin, Judith. 2000. "Ajaria: The Interest of the Local Potentate in Keeping Violent Conflict at Bay." Paper presented at the fifth annual convention of the Association for the Study of Nationalities, April 2000, Columbia University, New York.

Hirsch, Francine. 2000. "Towards an Empire of Nations: Border-Making and the Formation of Soviet National Identities." *Russian Review* 59, no. 2: 201–26.

———. 2005. *Empire of Nations: Ethnographic Knowledge and the Making of the Soviet Union.* Ithaca: Cornell University Press.

Hooson, David. 1994. "Ex-Soviet Identities and the Return of Geography." In *Geography and National Identity,* edited by D. Hooson, 134–40. Oxford: Blackwell.

Humphrey, Caroline. 1991. "'Icebergs,' Barter, and the Mafia in Provincial Russia." *Anthropology Today* 7, no. 2: 8–13.

———. 1992. "The Moral Authority of the Past in Post-Socialist Mongolia." *Religion, State & Society* 20, nos. 3–4: 375–89.

———. 1995. "Creating a Culture of Disillusionment: Consumption in Moscow, a Chronicle of Changing Times." In *Worlds Apart: Modernity through the Prism of the Local*, edited by D. Miller, 43–68. London: Routledge.

——. 2002a. *The Unmaking of Soviet Life: Everyday Economies after Socialism*. Ithaca: Cornell University Press.

——. 2002b. "Does the Category 'Postsocialism' Still Make Sense?" In *Postsocialism: Ideals, Ideologies and Practices in Eurasia*, edited by C. Hann, 12–15. London: Routledge.

Humphrey, Caroline, and Ruth Mandel. 2002. "The Market in Everyday Life: Ethnographies of Postsocialism." In *Markets and Moralities: Ethnograhpies of Postsocialism*, edited by R. Mandel and C. Humphrey, 1–16. Oxford: Berg.

Iust, K. 1998 [1922]. "Sovershchenno sekretno. Tekushchii moment v Adzharii (tezisy)." Batumi, Consulate of the RSFSR, 22 November 1922. Reprinted (with a translation in Georgian) as *Ach'ara rusi diplomatis tvalit*. Tbilisi: Int'elekt'i.

Japaridze, Sh. 1973. "Turkta bat'onobis droindeli ach'aris sotsial-ek'onomiuri tskhovrebis zogierti sak'itkhi." *Samkhret-dasavlet sakartvelos mosakhlebis k'ult'uris da qopis sak'itkhebi* 1: 101–16.

Jenkins, Richard. 1997. *Rethinking Ethnicity: Arguments and Explorations*. London: Sage.

Jelavich, Barbara. 1970. "Great Britain and the Russian Acquisition of Batum, 1878–1886." *Slavonic and East European Review* 48: 44–66.

Jones, Stephen, and Robert Parsons. 1996. "Georgia and the Georgians." In *The Nationalities Question in the Post-Soviet States*, edited by G. Smith, 291–313. London: Longman.

Kazbeg, Giorgi. 1875. *Tri Mesiatsa v Turetskoi Gruzii*. Tbilisi. Reprinted in Georgian, Batumi: Gamomtsemloba ach'ara, 1995.

Kazemzadeh, Firuz. 1951. *The Struggle for Transcaucasia, 1917–1921*. New York: Philosophical Library.

Kääriäinen, Kimmo. 1999. "Religiousness in Russia after the Collapse of Communism." *Social Compass* 46, no. 1: 33–46.

Kearney, Michael. 1998. "Transnationalism in California and Mexico at the End of Empire." In *Border Identities: Nation and State at International Frontiers*, edited by T. Wilson and H. Donnan, 117–41. Cambridge: Cambridge University Press.

——. 2004. *Changing Fields of Anthropology: From Local to Global*. Lanham, Md.: Rowman and Littlefield.

Khalvashi, P. 1994. *Sheidzleba tu ara muslimani iqos kartveli?*. Batumi: Gamomtsemloba ach'ara.

Komakhidze, Teimuraz. 1999. *Ach'aris k'ult'uris ist'oria*. Batumi: Gamomtsemloba ach'ara.

Konstantinov, Yulian. 1996. "Patterns of Reinterpretation: Trader-Tourism in the Balkans (Bulgaria) as a Picaresque Metaphorical Enactment of Post-Totalitarianism." *American Ethnologist* 23, no. 4: 762–82.

Kopytoff, Igor. 1986. "The Cultural Biography of Things: Commodization as Process." In *The Social Life of Things: Commodities in Cultural Perspective*, edited by A. Appadurai, 64–91. Cambridge: Cambridge University Press.

——. 1987. "The Internal African Frontier: The Making of African Political Culture." In *The African Frontier*, edited by I. Kopytoff, 3–84. Bloomington: Indiana University Press.

Kotkin, Stephen. 1995. *Magnetic Mountain: Stalinism as a Civilization*. Berkeley: University of California Press.

Kurbanov, Rafik Osman-Ogly, and Erjan Rafik-Ogly Kurbanov. 1995. "Religion and Politics in the Caucasus." In *The Politics of Religion in Russia and the New States of Eurasia*, edited by M. Bourdeaux, 229–46. Armonk, N.Y.: M. E. Sharpe.

Kvinitadze, General G. I. 1985. *Moi vospominaniia v gody nezavisimosti Gruzii, 1917–1921*. Paris: YMCA Press.

Lampland, Martha. 2000. Afterword to *Altering States: Ethnographies of Transition in Eastern Europe and the Former Soviet Union*, edited by D. Berdahl, M. Bunzl, and M. Lampland, 209–18. Ann Arbor: University of Michigan Press.

Lane, Christel. 1981. *The Rites of Rulers: Ritual in Industrial Society—the Soviet Case*. Cambridge: Cambridge University Press.

Law, Vivien. 1998. "Language Myths and the Discourse of Nation-Building in Georgia." In *Nation-Building in the Post-Soviet Borderlands*, edited by G. Smith et al., 167–96. Cambridge: Cambridge University Press.

Ledeneva, Alena V. 1998. *Russia's Economy of Favours: Blat, Networking and Informal Exchange*. Cambridge: Cambridge University Press.

Lieven, Anatol. 2001. "Georgia: A Failing State?" *Eurasia Insight*, 30 January 2001. Online at http://www.eurasianet.org/departments/insight/articles/eav013001.shtml.

Lilienfeld, Fairy von. 1993. "Reflections on the Current State of the Georgian State and Nation." In *Seeking God: The Recovery of Religious Identity in Orthodox Russia, Ukraine, and Georgia*, edited by S. Batalden, 220–31. DeKalb: Northern Illinois University Press.

Lowenthal, David. 1985. *The Past Is a Foreign Country*. Cambridge: Cambridge University Press.

Mars, Gerald, and Yochanan Altman. 1983. "The Cultural Bases of Soviet Georgia's Second Economy." *Soviet Studies* 35, no. 4: 546–60.

——. 1987. "Alternative Mechanisms of Distribution in a Soviet Economy." In *Constructive Drinking: Perspectives from Anthropology*, edited by M. Douglas, 270–79. Cambridge: Cambridge University Press.

Martin, Terry. 1998. "The Origins of Soviet Ethnic Cleansing." *Journal of Modern History* 70: 813–61.

——. 2001. *The Affirmative Action Empire: Nations and Nationalities in the Soviet Union, 1923–1939*. Ithaca: Cornell University Press.

Martínez, O. J. 1994. *Border People: Life and Society in the U.S.-Mexico Borderlands*. Tucson: University of Arizona Press.

Mauss, Marcel. 1990. *The Gift: The Form and Reason for Exchange in Archaic Societies*. Translated by W. D. Halls. London: Routledge.

Mdivani, David. 1992. "Dva berega: Fotografiia dlia spetssluzhb." *Stolitsa* (Moscow) 3, no. 61: 13–14.

Meeker, Michael. 1971. "The Black Sea Turks: Some Aspects of Their Ethnic and Cultural Background." *International Journal of Middle Eastern Studies* 2: 318–45.

——. 2002. *A Nation of Empire: The Ottoman Legacy of Turkish Modernity*. Berkeley: University of California Press.

Megrelidze, Shamshe. 1964. *Ach'aris ts'arsulidan (muhajiroba 1878–1882 ts'lebshi)*. Tbilisi: Gamomtsemloba metsniereba.

Meiering Mikadze, Ekaterina. 1999. "L'Islam en Adjarie: Trajectoire historique et implications contemporaines." *Cahiers d'études sur la Méditerranée orientale et le monde turco-iranien* 27: 241–61.

Merkviladze, V. N. 1969. *Sozdanie i ukreplenie Sovetskoi gosudarstvennosti v Gruzii, 1921–1936*. Tbilisi: Gamomtsemloba sabch'ota sakartvelo.

Merridale, Catherine. 2001. *Night of Stone: Death and Memory in Twentieth Century Russia*. New York: Viking.

Meyer, Birgit, and Peter Geschiere. 1999. Introduction to *Globalization and Identity: Dialectics of Flow and Closure*, edited by B. Meyer and P. Geschiere, 1–16. Oxford: Blackwell.

Mgeladze, Nugzar. 1994. "Ajarians." In *Encyclopedia of World Cultures*, vol. 6, *Russia and Eurasia, China*, edited by P. Friedrich and N. Diamond, translated by Kevin Tuite, 12–15. New York: G. K. Hall.

Miller-Pogacar, Anesa. 1995. "Varieties of Post-Atheist Spirituality in Mikhail Epstein's Approach to Culturology." *Slavic and East European Journal* 39, no. 3: 344–56.

Mitchell, Timothy. 1999. "Dreamland: The Neoliberalism of Your Desires." *Middle East Report* 29, no. 1: 28–33.

Mostashari, Firouzeh. 2001. "Colonial Dilemmas: Russian Policies in the Muslim Caucasus."

In *Of Religion and Empire: Missions, Conversions, and Tolerance in Tsarist Russia*, edited by R. Geraci and M. Khodarkovsky, 229–49. Ithaca: Cornell University Press.

Motika, Raoul. 2001. "Islam in Post-Soviet Azerbaijan." *Archive de sciences sociales des religions* 115: 111–24.

Nekrich, Aleksandr M. 1978. *The Punished Peoples: The Deportation and Fate of Soviet Minorities at the End of the Second World War.* New York: W. W. Norton.

Neuburger, Mary. 2004. *The Orient Within: Muslim Minorities and the Negotiation of Nationhood in Modern Bulgaria.* Ithaca: Cornell University Press.

Nişanyan, Sevan. 1990. *Zoom In: Black Sea.* Istanbul: Boyut Publishing Group.

Nodia, Ghia. 2000. "Georgian Orthodoxy Revisited: Is Georgia Threatened by Religious Fundamentalism?" *Profile* (Tbilisi) 3.

——. 2001. "Ten Years after the Soviet Breakup: The Impact of Nationalism." *Journal of Democracy* 12, no. 4: 27–34.

Papuashvili, Tamaz. 2001. "K voprosu o printsipakh vzaimootnoshenii mezhdu gosudarstvom i pravoslavnoi tserkov'iu Gruzii." *Tsentral'naia Aziia i Kavkaz* 3, no. 15: 164–72.

Patico, Jennifer. 2003. "Consuming the West But Becoming Third World: Food Imports and the Experience of Russianness. " *Anthropology of East Europe Review* 21, no. 1: 31–36.

Paustovsky, Konstantin. 1969. *Southern Adventure: Story of a Life.* Translated from Russian by Kyril Fitz Lyon. London: Harvill Press.

Pelkmans, Mathijs. 2002. "Religion, Nation and State in Georgia: Christian Expansion in Muslim Ajaria." *Journal of Muslim Minority Affairs* 22, no. 2: 249–73.

Pereira, M. 1971. *East of Trebizond.* London: Geoffrey Bless.

Pine, Frances. 2002. "Retreat to the Household? Gendered Domains in Postsocialist Poland." In *Postsocialism: Ideals, Ideologies and Practices in Eurasia*, edited by C. Hann, 95–113. London: Routledge.

Pitt-Rivers, Julian. 1977. *The Fate of Shechem or the Politics of Sex: Essays in the Anthropology of the Mediterranean.* Cambridge: Cambridge University Press.

Platz, Stephanie. 2000. "The Shape of National Time: Daily Life, History, and Identity during Armenia's Transition to Independence, 1991–1994." In *Altering States: Ethnographies of Transition in Eastern Europe and the Former Soviet Union*, edited by D. Berdahl, M. Bunzl, and M. Lampland, 114–38. Ann Arbor: University of Michigan Press.

Pohl, J. Otto. 1999. *The Ethnic Cleansing in the USSR, 1937–1949.* Westport, Conn.: Greenwood Press.

Potto, V. A. 1912. "Tri proshlykh kampanii: V sviazi voennymi deistviiami v raione Batumskoi Oblasti." In *Batuma i ego okrestnostei*, edited by I. Veru, 115–71. Batumi: N.p.

Put'k'aradze, Merab. 2001. *Ach'ara: Ek'onomik'ur-geograpiuli dakhasiateba.* Batumi: Gamomtsemloba batumis universit'et'i.

Quataert, Donald. 1993. "The Age of Reforms, 1812–1914." In *An Economic and Social History of the Ottoman Empire*, vol. 2, *1600–1914*, edited by Halil İnalcık with Donald Quataert, 759–943. Cambridge: Cambridge University Press.

Ries, Nancy. 2002. " 'Honest Bandits' and 'Warped People': Russian Narratives about Money, Corruption, and Moral Decay." In *Ethnography in Unstable Places: Everyday Lives in Contexts of Dramatic Political Change*, edited by C. Greenhouse, E. Mertz, and K. Warren, 276–315. Durham: Duke University Press.

Rupnik, Jacques. 1996. "The Reawakening of European Nationalisms." *Social Research* 63, no. 1: 41–75.

Sahlins, Peter. 1989. *Boundaries: The Making of France and Spain in the Pyrenees.* Berkeley: University of California Press.

Sammut, Dennis. 2001. "Population Displacement in the Caucasus—An Overview." *Central Asian Survey* 20, no. 1: 55–62.

Sampson, Steven. 2002. "Beyond Transition: Rethinking Elite Configurations in the

Balkans." In *Postsocialism: Ideals, Ideologies and Practices in Eurasia*, edited by C. Hann, 297–316. London: Routledge.

Sanikidze, Giorgi. 1999. *Islami da muslimebi tanamedrove sakartveloshi*. Tbilisi: Aghmosavlet-dasavletis urtiertobata k'vlevis saertoshoriso tsent'ri [International Research Center for East–West Relations].

Saroyan, Mark. 1996. "Beyond the Nation-State: Culture and Ethnic Politics in Soviet Transcaucasia." In *Transcaucasia, Nationalism, and Social Change: Essays in the History of Armenia, Azerbaijan, and Georgia*, edited by R. Suny, 401–26. Ann Arbor: University of Michigan Press.

———. 1997. *Minorities, Mullahs, and Modernity: Reshaping Community in the Late Soviet Union*, edited by E. Walker. Research series no. 95. Berkeley: University of California, International and Area Studies Digital Collection.

Seidlitz, N. 1884. "Statischtischer Überblick über die Gouvernements des Kaukasus im Jahr 1882." *Russische Revue* 24: 435–69.

Sezneva, Olga. 2001. "Fashion for the Past: Historical Revival in a New Style Architecture in Kaliningrad, Russia." Paper presented at the sixth annual convention of the Association for the Study of Nationalities, April 2001, Columbia University, New York.

Shami, Seteney. 1999. "Circassian Encounters: The Self as Other and the Production of the Homeland in the North Caucasus." In *Globalization and Identity: Dialectics of Flow and Closure*, edited by B. Meyer and P. Geschiere, 17–46. Oxford: Blackwell.

Shatirishvili, Zaza. 2000. "Stalinist Orthodoxy and Religious Indifference." *Profile* (Tbilisi) 2.

Shlapentokh, Vladimir. 1996. "Early Feudalism—the Best Parallel for Contemporary Russia." *Europe-Asia Studies* 48, no. 3: 393–411.

Shnirelman, Victor. 1998. "National Identity and Myths of Ethnogenesis in Transcaucasia." In *Nation-Building in the Post-Soviet Borderlands*, edited by G. Smith et al., 48–66. Cambridge: Cambridge University Press.

———. 2001. *The Value of the Past: Myths, Identity and Politics in Transcaucasia*. Osaka: National Museum of Ethnology.

Slezkine, Yuri. 2000. "The USSR as a Communal Apartment, or How a Socialist State Promoted Ethnic Particularism." In *Stalinism: New Directions*, edited by S. Fitzpatrick, 313–47. London: Routledge.

Smirba, Aslan. 1999. *Tetri kalaki shav zghvaze/White Town at the Black Sea*. Batumi: Gamomtsemloba Ach'ara.

Smith, Graham. 1998. "Post-Colonialism and Borderland Identities." In *Nation-Building in the Post-Soviet Borderlands*, edited by G. Smith et al., 1–22. Cambridge: Cambridge University Press.

Stokes, Martin. 1993. "Hazelnuts and Lutes: Perceptions of Change in a Black Sea Valley." In *Culture and Economy: Changes in Turkish Villages*, edited by P. Stirling, 27–45. Huntingdon, England: Eothen Press.

Suny, Ronald G. 1993. *The Revenge of the Past: Nationalism, Revolution, and the Collapse of the Soviet Union*. Stanford: Stanford University Press.

———. 1994. *The Making of the Georgian Nation*. Bloomington: Indiana University Press.

———. 1996. "The Emergence of Political Society in Georgia." In *Transcaucasia, Nationalism, and Social Change: Essays in the History of Armenia, Azerbaijan, and Georgia*, edited by R. Suny, 109–40. Ann Arbor: University of Michigan Press.

Svašek, Maruška. 1999. "History, Identity, and Territoriality: Redefining Czech–German Relations in the Post–Cold War Era." *Focaal: Tijdschrift voor Antropologie* 33: 37–58.

Thomson, R. W. 1996. "The Origins of Caucasian Civilization: The Christian Component." In *Transcaucasia, Nationalism, and Social Change: Essays in the History of Armenia, Azerbaijan, and Georgia*, edited by Ronald Suny, 25–44. Ann Arbor: University of Michigan Press.

Tishkov, V. 1997. *Ethnicity, Nationalism, and Conflict in and after the Soviet Union; The Mind Aflame*. London: Sage.

United Nations Development Programme (UNDP), Regional Bureau for Europe and the CIS. 1998. *Human Development under Transition: Summaries of the 1997 National Human Development Reports for Europe and the CIS.* New York: UNDP.

Vanilishi, G. 1978. "Lazuris satskhovrebeli da sameurneo nagebobani (sarpis etnograpiuri maselebis mikhvedit)." *Samkhret-dasavlet sakartvelos mosakhlobis k'ult'urisa da qopis sak'itkhebi* (Batumi) 6: 119–31.

Vanilishi, M., and A. Tandilava. 1964. *Lazeti.* Tbilisi: Gamomtsemloba sabch'ota sakartvelo.

Veenis, Milena. 1999. "Consumptie in Oost-Duitsland: De zinnelijke verleiding van dingen." *K & T Tijdschrift voor Empirische Filosofie* 23, no. 1: 11–36.

Verdery, Katherine. 1996. *What Was Socialism and What Comes Next?* Princeton: Princeton University Press.

——. 1999. *The Political Lives of Dead Bodies: Reburial and Postsocialist Change.* New York: Columbia University Press.

Vitebsky, Piers. 2002. "Withdrawing from the Land: Social and Spiritual Crisis in the Indigenous Russian Arctic." In *Postsocialism: Ideals, Ideologies and Practices in Eurasia*, edited by C. Hann, 180–95. London: Routledge.

Wedel, Janine. 2001. *Collision and Collusion: The Strange Case of Western Aid to Eastern Europe.* New York: Palgrave.

Weller, Robert. 1994. *Resistance, Chaos and Control in China: Taiping Rebels, Taiwanese Ghosts and Tiananmen.* Basingstoke, England: Macmillan.

Wendl, Tobias, and Michael Rösler. 1999. "Frontiers and Borderlands: The Rise and Relevance of an Anthropological Research Genre." In *Frontiers and Borderlands: Anthropological Perspectives*, edited by M. Rösler and T. Wendl, 1–27. Frankfurt: Peter Lang.

Werth, Paul. 2000. "From 'Pagan' Muslims to 'Baptized' Communists: Religious Conversion and Ethnic Particularity in Russia's Eastern Provinces." *Comparative Studies in Society and History* 42, no. 3: 497–523.

Wolf, Eric. R. 2001. *Pathways of Power: Building an Anthropology of the Modern World.* Berkeley: University of California Press.

Zambakhidze, G., and A. Mamuladze. 1979. *Po Adzharii.* Moscow: Tsentral'noe reklamno-informatsionnoe biuro turist.

Zhgenti, S. 1956. "Turetskaia agressiia v iugo-zapadnoi Gruzii. Materialy." Ach'aris mkharedmtsod muzeumi, Russian Series, no. 82.

Žižek, Slavoj. 1990. "Eastern Europe's Republics of Gilead." *New Left Review* 183: 50–62.

Zverev, Alexei. 1996. "Ethnic Conflicts in the Caucasus, 1988–1994." In *Contested Borders in the Caucasus*, edited by B. Coppieters, 13–72. Brussels: VUB University Press.

Zürcher, Erik J. 1993. *Turkey: A Modern History.* London: I. B. Tauris.

Index

Abashidze, Aslan, 8, 68, 118, 195, 201–5, 210; religion and, 110–12, 115–16, 119
Abbott, Andrew, 14
Abkhazia, 47, 183; refugees from, 6n
administrative-territorial structure (of the USSR), 7, 9, 103–5
aghordzineba. See Revival Party
agriculture: post-Soviet changes, 6, 182–83; in Soviet Ajaria, 5–6, 114. *See also* collectivization
Ajaria: image of, 11, 109, 212; incorporation in Tsarist Empire, 98–99; naming of, 7n; overview, 5; part of Ottoman Empire, 96–97; Soviet depiction of, 5–9; Soviet incorporation of, 25. *See also* Ajarian autonomy
Ajarian autonomy, 7–8, 10, 103–5; attempts to abolish, 8, 111; attitudes toward, 167t; changed significance, 8, 195; contested nature of, 7, 104
Ajarians: category of, 10, 129; partial abolishment of category, 104–5, 122; religious connotations of, 7, 10, 56, 129, 139
alcohol consumption, 93, 191; absence of, 135; cross-border contact and, 76, 78; Islam and, 113, 124–25, 127–29, 136. *See also* hospitality
Allen, W. E. D., 96–97
Altman, Yochanan, 77, 128, 184
ancestors, 131, 167t; role in conversion, 149–50, 156, 161–63
anti-religious measures, 7, 10, 61, 102–3, 106–8. *See also* Islam
Appadurai, Arjun, 197n

architecture, 209–11, 220
Asia: as metaphor, 51, 132, 224
Atatürk, 20, 27
atheist ideology, 11, 102, 109, 121
authenticity, 4, 45, 59, 63, 69–70, 154; corruption and, 58, 67, 86, 220; innovation and, 132
autonomy. *See* Ajarian autonomy

baptism, 56, 84, 110, 146, 149, 161–63; mass, 142–43, 165
backwardness, 72, 131, 153–55, 194. *See also* civilization
Barth, Frederick, 12–13, 45–46
Batumi: description of, 5; as economic center, 6, 56, 176, 198; history of, 6, 20, 209; image of, 208–9, 219, 222; as political center, 111; population of, 9, 105; post-Soviet changes in, 182
Baud, Michiel, 85, 216
Bellér-Hann, Ildiko, 12nn, 28n, 54n, 63n, 70, 177n, 183
Berdahl, Daphne, 12n, 13, 24, 42, 86, 175, 215, 217
betrayal, 75, 78–79
bishop. *See* Christian clergy
Blok, Anton, 72–73, 86, 216, 222
Bolsheviks, 25, 59, 104, 106. *See also* Communist Party
border: as bridgehead, 32, 59; concept of, 12–14, 215–16; culture, 85; of fear and control, 23; internal, 23, 55–56; specifics of Soviet borders, 23–24, 216–18. *See also* Soviet-Turkish border

Mingrelians, 63, 65
missionary activities, 91, 95, 114, 144
Mitchell, Timothy, 7, 212
modernity, 173, 194, 211; conversion and, 143–44, 154–55; Islam and, 124, 135. *See also* civilization; Europe; transition
money: betrayal and, 37; changed significance of, 185; comparing usage of, 134; distrust of Soviet, 31; ideas about capitalism and, 79–80
morality: immorality, 194, 206; role of religious leaders, 120, 123
Moscow, appealing to, 37, 40, 103, 115
Mosques: attendance at, 113, 122–23, 143, 166; closure of, 106, 114–15; construction of, 84, 112–13, 115–16, 133, 165; empty, 124, 166; opening of, 115; pre-Soviet, 96, 114
mufti / muftiate, 116–17, 133
mullahs, 100, 131; self-styled, 109, 112
Muratoff, P., 96–97
Muslim identity: comparison with Bosnia, 121–22; difficulties related to, 125–33; Georgian hospitality and, 127–29; Georgian nationality and, 124, 129–31, 139; multiple dimensions of, 166–67. *See also* Islam
Muslim leaders (clergy): declining influence of, 122, 124–25; negative attitudes toward, 120, 131, 153; public roles of, 112–14, 120; relations with secular authorities, 115–18, 120; Soviet state and, 104–7; Tsarist state and, 98, 100–101; views on conversion by, 148, 149n. See also *imams*; *mufti/muftiate*; *mullahs*
Muslim Religious Board, 107, 116
myth: of Georgian-Christian primordiality, 95, 102; about Georgian history, 64; meanings of, 196–97; of modernization, 196–97, 211; of transition, 211

naming practices, 1n, 123; changes in, 48, 60, 80, 97; ethno-religious connotations, 50, 130
narcisism of minor difference, 72, 86
nationalism: Georgian, 11, 106–9, 120, 139; Soviet and post-Soviet, 9–11, 59, 219; Turkish, 79, 81
nationalist movement, 97–99, 102, 110, 115
nationality: celibration of, 61; discussions about, 60; politics, 9, 21, 24, 59, 64, 103–4; identification with Georgian, 9–10, 99, 101–2; religion and, 93, 110, 122, 129–31, 139–40, 162–64, 167t, 220, 223; Turkish, 69
neoliberalism, 212; neoliberal economists, 196; neoliberalist policies, 7, 212; neoliberal visions, 8, 11, 193

nostalgia, 67–68, 172, 188; selective, 174, 185; for state atheism, 121
NKVD: operations in Sarpi, 31–35, 38, 41–43; role in religious repression, 107. *See also* KGB
Nodia, Ghia, 110, 173n

oil: Batumi and, 209; the British and, 25; refineries, 5, 182; trade, 6, 209n
Orthodox Christianity. *See* Christian clergy; Christianity

passports, 82; deportations and, 34, 43, 217; early passports, 26; ethnic labels in, 14, 79, 80; state surveillance and, 107
patronage, 180–81
Piedmont principle, 24
Pitt-Rivers, Julian, 77
postsocialism: anthropology of, 11–12; concept, 8
prices (of commodities): changes in, 6, 189–93; cross-border differences of, 26–27, 176–76, 184; difficulty of establishing, 186–87; fixed, 26, 189; ideas about, 189–92; manipulation of, 190; nostalgia and, 188; "real," 189–91
priests. *See* Christian clergy
primordiality: in ideas about culture, 45, 220; myth of Georgian-Christian, 95, 150
public sphere: Christianization of, 164; depiction of, 120; religion banned from, 164, 222; return of religion into, 110, 163, 223; shaping of, 96; transformation of, 120–21
purges: in the border region, 33, 36; conversion and, 160; relation to Soviet Communism, 38–39. *See also* Soviet repression

reciprocity: in cross-border contact, 76–78; networks of, 76–77; three demands of, 77. *See also* hospitality
relatives. *See* kinship
religion: deprivatization of, 119–20; nationality and, 129–31, 137–39; public and private, 129; public dimensions, 165. *See also* Christianity; Islam; public sphere
religious difference: cross-border, 56, 70, 84–85; migration and, 98–99; talking about, 130
religious renewal, 109, 163. *See also* Islamic renewal
research: discussions about my, 44, 50, 137; languages used in, 15n; short overview of, 15
resistance and accommodation, 119
Revival Party, 8, 112, 199, 202